TRAIL-LINE
CHATTER

Life and Love with
'Last Alaskan' Bob Harte

By Nancy Becker

PUBLICATION
CONSULTANTS
We Believe In The Power Of Authors

PO Box 221974 Anchorage, Alaska 99522-1974
books@publicationconsultants.com www.publicationconsultants.com

ISBN Number: 978-1-59433-940-0
eBook ISBN Number: 978-1-59433-941-7

Library of Congress Catalog Card Number: 2020904597

Manufactured in the United States of America

This book was written in celebration of

nancydancingbird

&

the spirit of Bob Harte

Foreword

By Bill Pfisterer

Retired Ethnographer:
Shandaa In My Lifetime and *Kaiiroondak Behind the Willows*

The Hudson Bay Company opened parts of Alaska to trading and trapping in the late 1840s. Fort Yukon was founded in 1847 by Alexander Murray and the company established trade there with local people. The area was rich in furs and Gwich'in people were happy to have access to guns, knives and beads.

In 1867 Alaska was purchased by the United States from Russia and it was discovered that Fort Yukon was in US territory. The trading post was moved up the Porcupine River to a site above what is now Canyon Village. This site also proved to belong to the new owners of the country and the British Hudson Bay traders moved again to what is now known as Old Rampart. Finally the post was established at what is now called Rampart House or New Rampart. The actual US/ Canadian border runs through this townsite.

Non Indian trappers were attracted to the area because of the abundance and high quality of the fur and began to settle along the Porcupine and its tributaries. A hunting, fishing, trapping lifestyle evolved which consisted of living in remote areas in the winter, traveling to a trading post in the spring, fishing for salmon in the summer and returning to remote trapping areas in the fall with a winter's supply of fish and other foods. Spending summer in settlements was an important part of this lifestyle. It gave folks who spent months often alone in remote places an opportunity to recharge their batteries and reestablish human contact as well as get supplies ready for the next trapping season. In the late summer people moved up rivers by track lining boats before the introduction of gasoline engines.

By the end of the second world war this lifestyle had come to an end. Rampart House was closed and the village deserted. Old Native people had died or moved to town when there was no longer anyone to help care for them in the small villages along the Porcupine. The number of trappers living alone in small cabins on traplines had diminished. Now some trappers were living in larger villages and running traplines closer to town. Only a few, mostly non-Native trappers, spent their year involved in a what would be called a traditional trappers lifestyle. Bob Harte was one of those.

It takes a large area to support a successful trapline. The area encompassed by the Yukon River on the south, the Brooks Range on the north, the US/ Canadian border on the east and the Chandalar River on the west is larger than the state of New York. Bob's trapping area covered a small part of this. Yet when a fellow trapper moved in 100 miles below Bob's cabin this trapper was informed that he was crowding Bob.

Bob arrived in Fort Yukon in the late summer of 1974. It was noted that he arrived with a good looking dog and a beautiful Aleut woman. The beautiful Aleut woman left in the middle of that first winter but the dog remained. No one blamed the beautiful lady. Living on a trapline is an often lonely and hard life.

That first fall Bob was flown by bush plane into a burned over area. The fire had forced most of the game and fur animals out of the area. Bob lived in small cabin he had built before heavy snows came. The cabin was low and partially dug into the ground. During the winter a grizzly bear that had not hibernated tried to get at Bob through the cabin roof. One of Bob's dogs raised the alarm and Bob rushed outside only to be met by the bear. Only one lived to tell the story and it was not the bear. Those bears are called ice bears by local folks since their fur coats are often covered by ice like armor. This bear was starving and desperate. To make matters worse that very cold winter the pilot who was suppose to pick Bob up before Christmas had left town and had

5

only told one other trapper the approximate location of Bob's camp. Luckily Andy Fairfield, a local minister, flew out and found Bob.

The following year Bob moved to an established trapline on the Coleen River and built a new cabin. This trapline was where he spent winters for most of the rest of his life. He had several trapline trails branching off on tributaries of the Coleen. For many years he trapped with sled dogs and then switched to a snow machine in later years. Trapline trails are narrow paths through the woods and over frozen lakes. Many times they can only be traveled by foot. Bob spent many winters traveling more than 10 miles a day by snowshoes in extremely cold weather checking and setting traps. Then his evenings were spent skinning his catch and preparing for the next day. Often the only human speech he heard came in the evening when he listened to Trapline Chatter on the radio station KJNP.

Bob always came to Fort Yukon in his younger days in the summers and rented a cabin there. He usually came to town for a brief stay in the winter also. Bob was known as a hard worker. His father was a stone mason and Bob grew up accustomed to hard labor. He was very strong and determined when working on projects. He was a skilled woodworker as well as a woodsman. His furs were well skinned and stretched and commanded the best prices.

Trappers protect their traplines for it is their livelihood. Bob was no exception. I witnessed one incident when someone attempted to claim Bob's trapline. A young fellow came into the yard at the cabin where Bob was staying for the summer and said that Bob was on this trapline. Bob reviewed how he came to be rightfully on his trapline. A fight followed and Bob wrestled his accuser to the ground. Bob held him on the ground and said, "Say uncle."

The response came, "Uncle."

Bob said, "Now this is over between us. If you agree say uncle."

"Uncle" was repeated again and the fight was over.

Bob was always pleasant to be around, and ladies who knew Bob commented that, "Bob is always a gentleman." I always saw Bob as belonging to a different group of people in our generation. Native people of Alaska are skilled woodsmen. They are at home in the woods and can live comfortably no matter the weather. There is however a small, unique group of non-native men and women who are drawn to wild areas where grizzly bear tracks might well cover their footprints over unmapped trails. It is great to realize that these folks still exist in the early part of the 21st century. They are the last of the mountain men and women.

Acknowledgments

Writing a book was more difficult and more rewarding than I could have ever imagined. None of this memoir could have been possible without my editor and new friend, Brandi Jo Nyberg. Thank you, Brandi Jo, for being the guiding light that extracted my story. Also, a very special thank you to all the writers at the University of Alaska Writing Center, who helped transcribe my story and naturally open up the writing process for me.

I am eternally grateful to my mom and dad for always accepting me for who I was and for showing me goodness in parenting and in living. Thank goodness they saved all my letters!

Another big thanks goes to my sisters, Gail and Jeff. Thank you both for your encouragement, and for supplying me with photos, letters, and some information I had forgotten.

Of course, my awesome kids, Traver and Talicia, deserve a big applause and thank you, for without you, I would never have this story to tell. I love you forever!

I'd like to thank Bruce Sweet, my buddy, for directing me to the University of Alaska for help, absorbing my story, and offering advice on what I might not see.

Thank you Randy Zarnke, President of the Alaska Trappers Association. When I first called to ask if I could use an article from Alaska Trapper Magazine, you took my hand and supported my project from the beginning to publishing. Your help has been much appreciated.

Justin Maple, thanks for so willingly helping with the maps in the beginning of the project, when I had no idea where to start. Thank you to Brandi Jo for completing those maps.

For his skillful creativity in layout and design I owe a special warm thank you to Ryan Ragan. Your calm, confidence helped me feel secure for the next step.

Thanks to Mark D. Ross for his sketches, so long ago for Bob's river business, Porcupine River Voyages, and now, for the sketches offered to share and enhance this book.

Although I've never worked with a publisher before, Even Swensen (Publication Consultants) would be my choice for further books as he teamed with me bringing such honest expertise and professionalism. Much thanks and respect to you, Even.

Thank you to Sandy and Joe Mattie. You two have always been there for Bob, me, and our family in so many ways. Thank you for your friendship, and especially for being there for Bob in his last days.

Also thank you to Carl and Sandy Bakken – you are extended family. I appreciate how you jumped in to help us throughout the years, during the trapline times all the way to present day. We love you two!

Dawn Jagow, thank you for sharing and laughing with me during trying times, and for reminding me who this book is about.

A big thank you goes to the Binkley Family. All of my family, starting with Bob, have been employed by you for around the past 40 years. You have cared about us and given us so much to be thankful for. We are very grateful for your family.

Lastly, Bob Harte. Thank you for the adventures and all I have come to learn and experience because of you. And with all my heart, I thank you for our daughter, Talicia.

More thanks:
Front cover family photo – Roger Kaye
Author photo – Levi Rowland

Table of Contents

Part 1 - In the Beginning...

Part 2 - Life in ANWR

Part 3 - Different Paths

Epilogue

Glossary

Introduction

"Even more amazing than the wonders of nature are the powers of spirit."

– Hellen Keller

In the beginning, Bob and I, Nancy, were always planning to write a book about our life together on the trapline. During those years together (1980-93), I wrote detailed letters to my parents requesting they save the letters. The letters were our "journal," which would help in the writing of our book.

Well, here it is, finally! Yes, under different circumstances than we thought- I was going to write this book when I was "old" and unable to be out and about so much, and I had the title planned as Trapline Chatter (not many readers will understand the meaning of those two words, but anyone living on the trapline, or in wilderness Alaska would- I'll explain that later), but life does not always cooperate with our own specific plans, does it? I began writing this book in the fall of 2017, a few months after Bob passed into eternity. This book is about life (physical and mental experiences of an individual or individuals) and love (strong affection, warm attachment)–those are definitions from Webster's dictionary, 2008 edition. However, my definitions of life and love are different: "what God breathed into us in the beginning."

In 1979, Bob and I met in Fort Yukon, Alaska. He was trapping, I was teaching. We shared a flight to Fairbanks, and got to know each other briefly. He continued to trap, I continued to teach. One year later, we met again, spent more time together, and decided to stay together. That was the beginning of our lives and love together for the next twelve years in Arctic National Wildlife Refuge (ANWR), which became our home. We both agree – those were the best years of our adult life.

In 1993, after being together for twelve years, Bob and I divorced and went our separate ways; however, we remained family and part of each other's lives, always. I would also say our spirits are closer than they have ever been. A major portion of this book will be about our lives on the trapline, but who we were before and after those days plays a big part in this story.

In this book, I'll be sharing from those letters I wrote to family members long ago. There will also be portions taken from stories that Bob wrote during his trapline days– some when we were together and some when we were apart. Also included will be stories I have written or letters I wrote before I met Bob, after I first came to Alaska. Bob was very adamant during the last several years of his life about getting his stories out. At first, his thinking was to capture and save his unique lifestyle before the information completely vanished, like an endangered species. During his last two years Bob knew his health was failing, and he also wanted to leave our daughter Talicia with a legacy and some inheritance to help with her living situation.

During the last three years of Bob's life, he was asked to participate in Discovery Channel's The Last Alaskans series, a show about the last few families living in ANWR. Bob became recognized overnight as he shared the love of his life (his trapline, not me) with viewers, and over 17,000 fans. Our daughter Talicia, and her daughter Carmella, along with myself, were participants in The Last Alaskans also, especially in the 2018 episodes, when we spread Bob's ashes in ANWR.

So, I invite you into Bob's trapline cabin for a cup of coffee or tea, and me. Get yourself comfy by the fire, and I'll share with you about living a very unique lifestyle with the most unique human being I know.

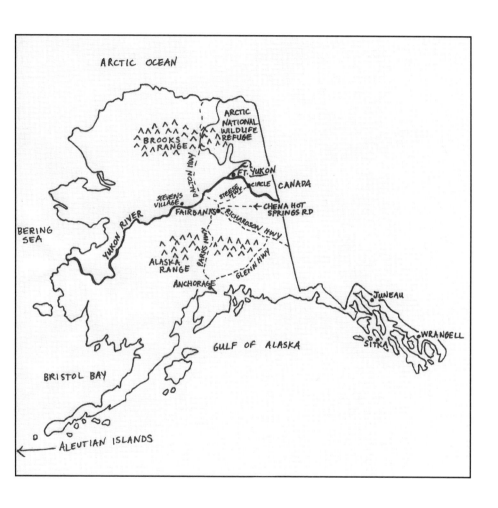

Part 1

In the Beginning...

Chapter 1: History

"It takes courage to push yourself to places that you have never been before. To test through limits, to break through barriers."

– Anais Nin

We met in Fort Yukon. He was coming to town to get supplies. He was a trapper. I was in Fort Yukon for a teaching interview. I was a teacher. It was wintertime and probably 30 below. Bob wore a parka, homemade mukluks*, heavy wool pants, and a big smile trying to hide the fact that he had no front teeth! I couldn't really see what he looked like underneath all those clothes. Just your average height and weight. However, his looks were not what attracted me to him. Bob was not the average guy, but he was doing what the average guy might want to be doing. He lived life! And his lifestyle was what he loved most over anything. I could tell that right away – Bob was passionate and committed to his home on the trapline. I remember very early on in our relationship he said he would never leave the north country. He never has; his ashes and spirit are still there.

What was it about Bob that was so inviting? The part of Bob I saw that first day we met is the same part I am so fond of today. The realness. Simpleness. The love of nature, adventure, freedom, and life. Bob was an authentic individual.

We got to know each other a little on that flight to Fairbanks together. He gave me some advice I still remember. Since I would be living in a tiny native village on the Yukon River near the Arctic circle, as a cheechako*, he said, "If you start to feel like you are going crazy, just go outside and take a long walk, outside the village in nature." I have experienced 'cabin fever' maybe once or twice, but regardless, to this day, every day, I get out and walk in nature.

I speak of him fondly as I remember the trapping days. Bob was the most unique man I ever met- he was also my friend, husband, companion, partner, father of our child, step-father to my son, 'Pop Pop' to our grandchildren, and the most difficult relationship I ever had. So, yes, Bob did appear to be your normal, average guy. Even during these past few years, as The Last Alaskans was revealing him to the world, Bob would stop in his tracks, ponder a moment and say, "How can this be? I'm just a trapper living my life." Yes, just a trapper- but very passionate about who he was. He did whatever it took to learn about the life he chose and loved to live. He was courageous, honest, simple...and a bit wild . I think Webster's definition of wild fits Bob like a mukluk: "living in a state of nature and not ordinarily tame or domesticated; very unusual, often in a way that is attractive or exciting." Other definitions entail that if a person is wild, he might be unrestrained, enthusiastic, and not held back by rules. Sounds like Bob to me. I once read a book called *Imitation of Christ*. A quote from the book stuck with me: "Imitation of Christ doesn't mean to live a life like Christ, but to live your life as authentically as Christ lived his." That is what Bob did, at least as long as he was on the Trapline.

Bob did have a family that loved him. His parents adopted Vern (Bob's older brother), and after Vern's adoption, Bob was born. The family eventually grew with the birth of two more sons (Yikes! Four lively rascals). Bob would be the first to tell you that they fought! They played hard, but their method of communication was fighting with one another, in contrast to their mom, who was gentle, kind, loving and soft. The disciplining was left to Bob's dad, mostly. Bob's father was loving, but also very commanding. He was the ruler of the home, and I can see where Bob learned a lot of his behaviors. He must have learned to not talk at meal times, because that is what Bob desired and told the kids. I was raised just the opposite, where meals were time to share. I used to tell Bob that he was a lot like his dad, but he would immediately deny it.

Though Bob was raised in a neighborhood, his family would visit grandparents in the country where Bob learned a deep love of nature in the outdoors; he spent many days exploring and adventuring, some with his grandpa, who taught him a great deal about the outdoors and his own work as a stone mason. Even at an early age, Bob would read about what he wanted to learn, then do it, which continued throughout his life. He is what you call "autodidactic."

At a young age Bob began to trap. In those early days of exploring and getting to know the natural world, Bob met one trapper who sparked his curiosity about living things and guided him to the investigation of trapping and studying animals. Bob's mom once gave me a map that Bob had drawn when he was about eleven or twelve, of the area near their home, where he explored, set traps, and had many adventures. The map included a color-coded legend showing trees, a river, a beaver lodge, trap sets, etc. I gave that map to Bob some time during the years we were separated. Since Bob has passed, I've been looking for the map, but have yet to find it. It's definitely a treasure I'd like to pass on to my grandkids. I don't believe he trapped to endanger any species or for any reason other than to learn. Of course, trapping became his lifestyle and means of income later. He loved wildlife and he came to identify with that community.

Bob's family was always an anchor for him and, though he wouldn't openly express it, his love for his family ran deep in his soul. The few times we visited Bob's family, I would get glimpses of their family life and hear stories that helped me know a bit more about Bob. There was definitely a limit on the amount of social time he could spend among other humans, whether it was family, friends, or crowds. If you were paying attention, you could observe the anxiety begin to surface and take over in Bob's actions. He would become very frustrated and the urge to leave was rapidly firing in his brain. He was somewhat like a caged wild animal.

I mentioned earlier that Bob had a bit of wild in him. I felt that in him early on, and it is part of what attracted me to him. In some ways he was untouched by society; that is rare today. I believe this is part of what others were also attracted to in Bob. He was similar to how nature is, the wilderness untouched by society– pure, simple, beautiful, honest, and rare. Bob sought out the wilderness like a young Davy Crockett or Tom Sawyer. He lived in the wilderness a good part of his life, and therefore it was in him. It was his nature.

Few people can totally understand this way of life unless they have experienced it. You have to live it to know it. You can't just read about the lifestyle– there's a huge difference. Understanding and knowing, learning about the perspective of a wild animal is very different than the perspective of a pet owner who loves the feeling of watching nature shows on TV (this is coming from somebody that has touched both points of view and is part of both; there is no judgment, only a difference in perspectives). Though I felt this wild nature early on with Bob, I didn't understand it. Different than any relationship I had had before, it drew me in, like nature does, but I could never get as close as I desired. Therefore, it was both a delight and a trial for me.

After high school graduation and experiencing college life for a period of time, Bob decided to leave everything and pursue what he loved. He loved learning about and living among wilderness. He loved the freedom to do what he wanted to do and not rely on society. He loved a simple, back-to-nature lifestyle. Alaska is the place that called to him. Around the age of twenty, Bob left the East Coast and headed to Alaska by hitch-hiking, which must have been a wild adventure on its own. I believe that is when Bob lost his front teeth. He never went into too much detail about his stories from back then, but I do know he was grateful to have lost only his front teeth. Maybe this was the beginning of the many, many more accidents and mishaps that continued for the rest of his life. Though many others might see some of these mishaps as reckless behavior, to Bob, it was just pursuing his goal and accepting whatever happened.

Our Alaska-bound East Coast cheechako hitch-hiked to Southeast Alaska where he was to begin his indoctrination to trapping for the next few years. Wrangell was the area that Bob trapped in those early years when he arrived. Wrangell is located along the inside passage, accessible by boat or plane, and is a fishing community surrounded by wilderness area.

Here is a story Bob wrote about Southeast Alaska:

Southeast Alaska

I came to Alaska hitchhiking from Mexico up to Seattle. I tried to hitchhike across Canada, but they refused to let me cross the border. This is during the Vietnam War. I went to three border stations in a row. The third station called the trooper to check me out. The trooper picked me up. He asked me what I was trying to do. I'm trying to go to Alaska, I told him. He said go to Bellingham, and I picked up a boat. The captain of a gillnetter gave me a ride up to Alaska. I drove the boat halfway up to the state. I got let off at Wrangell.

The captain wanted me to stay with him and fish the season, but I was getting seasick crossing Dixon Entrance and didn't want to pursue that. Trapping was in my blood. I wanted to go up the Stikeen River in Canada, but I spent two years in the Wrangell area. I worked in the logging mill at first to earn some money because I had less than $50 in my pocket. I slept in the park in a sleeping bag, then got a job in the local mill. I worked in the pond at the mill. I worked there for several months. I got a skiff fixed up, a wooden skiff, a 14-foot boat. I repaired the bottom and got a 10 horsepower engine. I trapped 40 miles south of Wrangell on Etolin Island, Burnett Inlet. There was an old abandoned cannery there and that was my base. I picked one shed in the best shape and fixed it up. It was a 10'x10' shack. I insulated the walls with moss and built the bunk and put in a stove. I fixed the roof and that's where I lived for two years. I was set up to trap mink, marten, and I tried to get otter and wolf.

In Wrangell, you trap the beaches. Take a skiff to the beach and make a rock cubby in the tidewater. Use fish for bait on a stick in the back of the cubby. The trap is in front. A mink could be caught and held there and would drown when the tide came in. I think I was getting $19 a hide back then. And the fishing was excellent. Red snapper were plentiful. You drop a line with two hooks on and pull up two 5 to 10-pound fish. There were plenty of fish to eat.

Hunting, I learned to drive the deer off of islands. On small islands you could land on, check out any beach, and see if there were deer tracks. Small islands a half an acre to 2 or 3 acres in size. You could drive easily. You could hear the deer jump in the water as it was swimming to another island. You just intercept them in the water.

I also hunted seals for the hides. I skinned and tanned the hides and sold them in Wrangell. There would also be fresh meat to eat and liver. That was important. The meat had a liver taste, which I didn't like. It was very strong. I also shot some ducks and I shot some geese with the 30.06.

Photo taken by Bob in his early Southeast Alaska days.

Not knowing anybody in Alaska, and not knowing much about the area, Bob at first found most of his information at the local bar. One clue led to another and Bob was able to locate an area where he could resurrect a makeshift home and try his skills at trapping. I can imagine his excitement at finally being in the wilderness in a practically untouched area to explore. He was at least somewhat prepared, as he was an avid reader and had devoured written information about Alaska. You will often hear stories about some humans, desperate to experience the wilderness of Alaska, that, sadly, end up dying, mostly because they did not comprehend the need for being prepared for survival. Bob had done his prep-work in the woods and countryside of his family-home. He was knowledgeable in survival skills, hunting, trapping, and fishing. Southeast Alaska was an appropriate place for indoctrination to the Alaskan wilderness.

Trapping in Southeast Alaska was different in many ways from the northern country in Arctic National Wildlife Refuge (ANWR), which became Bob's home. Southeast is warmer, and much wetter. The availability of fur changes with temperature, and human population in the area would affect trapping results.

Bob's trapping in Southeast was excellent training and preparation for moving to a more harsh climate. I'm sure he learned invaluable information which he would later need and be thankful for when he experienced a less forgiving wilderness. Bob's temporary location in Southeast was near a fish hatchery: Etolin Island was the first area Bob trapped in 1972-1973. In Bob's words, "When I was in Etolin Harbor, I had to go to town to get supplies every two months or so. I motored back and forth, which was very scary because it would blow like crazy four days a week. I had to watch the weather all the time. I lived in the Brig Bar in Wrangell right up from the fishing docks, and I usually drank with the fishermen and logmill workers. I'm a pool player. I'd shoot pool all night long and have my dog with me. I love my beer and I was learning how to live in the woods. It was the first time I lived alone."

In 1973-74, he explored a different area around Burnett Inlet, but after spending two winters in Southeast, Bob decided to head north, not having any final destination in mind, only ready to experience and pursue a more wilderness lifestyle like he had read about before coming to Alaska. Again, in his own words, "I hitchhiked to Eagle and asked about the trapping. Then I hitchhiked to Circle and asked about the trapping. Next, I got a canoe and canoed down river to Fort Yukon. That was deep interior and top fur country in the state of Alaska. That caught my eye."

Fort Yukon became Bob's home base as he trapped in different locations around the area. He quickly established a name for himself and met many lifelong friends. In Bob's own script, here is his story about the first winter he spent in the interior.

A portion of the hand-written letter appears as an image on the next page, followed by the transcribed letter.

It was my first interior winter
on the trapline. I had been looking
for some untrapped country where I
wouldn't interfere with other trappers.
Getting little help from the locals, I
wound up ~~picking~~ choosing some lakes in the
middle of no-where away from the
traveled rivers + villages.

A dug-in cabin got built on the
shore of a good size lake. It was
finished by late fall + I was
committed for the winter.

I was new ~~with~~ at dealing with
air charters + thought I had
everything covered. Gear wize anyway.
But on the flight out "Vern" asked
my opinion concerning his chasing
a married woman back in Boston.
Vern was my only link back to
town + only a couple of people on the
planet knew where I was setting up.
Now red flags were flying with that
question but I thought he was a big
boy + could figure it out. Just let
me out with my gear + fly away so
I can get wild + free. "OH, Vern,
stop by with my mail before

25

My First Interior Winter

It was my first interior winter on the trapline. I had been looking for some untrapped country where I wouldn't interfere with other trappers. Getting little help from the locals, I wound up choosing some lakes in the middle of nowhere away from the traveled rivers and village. A dug-in cabin got built on the shore of a good size lake. It was finished by late fall and I was committed for the winter.

I was new at dealing with air charters and thought I had everything covered. Gear-wise, anyway. But on the flight out Vern, the pilot, asked my opinion concerning his chasing a married woman back in Boston. Vern was my only link back to town, and only a couple of people on the planet knew where I was setting up. Now red flags were flying with that question, but I thought he was a big boy and could figure it out. Just let me out with my gear and fly away so I can get wild and free. "Oh Vern, stop by with my mail before Christmas. Bye-bye."

Well, I had enough food until January. There were moose tracks on the lake shore and I had shelter. I had 4 or 5 village dogs, a toboggan*, and a lot to learn. But I was game.

I was still making a lot of noise with the saw, finishing the cabin, building dog houses and putting up some firewood. When the lake froze, I took a walk around the lake on the ice. There was just enough snow on the ground to see tracks. The lake was blown clear of snow except on the edge. It was about a 3 mile walk, and I remember seeing a duck egg underwater and some muskrat bank dens with trails of bubbles. And some marten, mink, and ermine tracks. Then grizzly tracks coming out of the woods and walking the lake edge like I was. A good sized mature bear. He circled the lake and headed into the woods a couple hundred yards before my cabin and kept going.

Trapping season started and I forgot about that bear. My first interior marten was a big old male in a pole set. After 2 years in S.E. Alaska getting mink and marten, this animal blew me away. So thickly furred! I fell in love with marten trapping right then!

I worked on trails, driving dogs and getting fur. It was a deep snow winter and cold. It got down to -66° that winter. It was around Thanksgiving when the bear entered my thoughts again. I had checked the line straight back from the cabin that morning. Maybe 4 miles out. It was -35° with a breeze.

By late morning I was back and in my long-johns, reading in my bunk. Staying warm. It was quiet. Then the dogs started barking, some growling. They were tired, wanting to be in their houses. It wasn't a loose dog that was causing the ruckus. There was no trail into this lake. So no people could or would be expected. It had to be the bear.

I had a warm .06 by the door. I grabbed that and started around the cabin to the back. The cabin was dug-in with a 5' high back wall. We were about 10' apart when we both saw each other. He was on his hind legs, paws on the roof. His head looked huge with the fur all fluffed out. I put the sights between his eyes and put him down. I remember opening the bolt to put another round in but it was already there!

So we had some fresh meat and a prime hide. Not the best meat, but there was no moose.

Why was he out at -35°? He was hungry. And looking. His head was big, hide full and long. But I'd guess his weight was about 180 lbs. I don't remember more than 2 cups of fat from him. Ice balls on his back. Out of hibernation? But most significant, he was missing a small digit on one paw and had a deep gash across the pad of the other front paw. Like a knife cut. Clean and long.

After he was taken care of, I back tracked him. He walked into camp using the trapline trail we just checked that morning. There were spots of blood in his tracks, and the cabin smoke was blowing right down the trail. He disturbed all the marten sets he passed, but what caught my eye was where he intersected my trail. Within 10 feet of where he crossed it in the fall, months ago. There was no trail. Not as much as a rabbit trail.

I followed his trail for a while. Just brush country. He was coming from the N.W.; Christian Village was out that way. 18 miles. Abandoned. It looked like he got in trouble somewhere. But I'm just guessing.

I learned to keep my rifle hot. Or at least to bring the bolt in. A few minutes on the stove will take care of any moisture problems from humidity and temperature fluctuations.

Okay, about Vern, the pilot. He forgot all about me. A friend noticed I wasn't in town for Christmas. He went to Air North (a small air charter service out of Fort Yukon) and inquired. "He didn't say for us to drop mail or check on him," replied Air North. When I later heard this, I wondered, "Is that how it works?" I don't think so. I don't know if Vern pursued the Boston woman, but he did apologize for forgetting me that spring. Thank God he's flying passenger liners now and is out of the bush!

A missionary with a plane checked on me and let me resupply. That was early February. By then the dogs were eating dogs. They were chained inside. And I had a cup of beans a day. With a squirrel, if I was lucky. Snow was deep, about 3 feet, and it was cold. No trail to Ft. Yukon. I wouldn't have made it. My equipment and energy were poor by then.

I did find some better trapping country after that winter. I've been on the Coleen since '75. That first interior winter was hard, but it just whetted my appetite. I learned what it really means to be alone. How to drive dogs. How bears think. About being hungry, and trusting pilots. Being on the edge is intense and stimulating. Like a walk at -66°. I love trapping!

After that first interior winter, Bob heard about an abandoned trapline in the lower Brooks Range, and it was there that he finally found his home of more than 40 years.

Below, you'll find another story of Bob's – one about his first year on the Coleen River. This story was told by Bob, recorded, and then transcribed:

My First Year on the Coleen River

I arrived upon the Coleen approximately in August my first year. I found a good stand of timber on a peninsula, so I decided to build my cabin there, a 16 by 16-foot cabin. I was finishing the roof when the snow started to fall. It was cold work. I had half a log floor and a peeled pole ceiling. I was putting the dirt on the poles when it started to snow.

I spent the first winter there and then in the spring decided to build some log cabins, line cabins. I had found the upper abandoned cabin that winter approximately 20 miles north, so in the spring, I decided to build a line cabin midway between my main cabin and the upper cabin. That cabin was small, approximately 8 by 8 feet. But it was so poor. I used it for a couple years. Maybe that's it. Log cabins settle 2, 3, 4, 5, 6 inches after the first year or two, you must account for that when you build.

Upper Cabin

I floated to town that year. Approximately June 6, I put together four or five logs, lashed them together with snare cable, and floated them to the starting point close to my cabin. I think I had four dogs and one box of food and gear in the center of the raft and one long pole to maneuver and steer the raft. The ice had gone out and the water dropped a little bit and that's when we started. We made good time getting out of the Coleen, but halfway down close to the southern end of the Coleen I saw a grizzly bear on shore. We were about 30 yards from the bear, which was swatting a cub up a small spruce. She turned and came to the bank, put her head up, and sniffed the air trying to get our wind. She didn't know what was going by. My dogs saw the bear and started to growl and bark. They weren't sure what to do. They were scared. I was rather safe, so I growled at that bear. I wanted to get some action to see what it would do.

Bob's homemade raft with his dogs and gear. Canvas ratting canoe in the foreground.

The bear ran downriver to keep up with us. It would run down 20 yards and look at us, run down another 20 yards and look at us. Finally, it jumped in the river and swam towards the raft. That's when I got my camera out and made sure my rifle was handy. I got pictures of the bear swimming when it was 20 yards away. It was so waterlogged, just his head above water, and it turned back to shore to leave us alone. I floated another 200 yards, and that's where I planned to build the line cabin. So we had pulled the raft in and secured and checked the creek. We were walking rather carefully at that point in time, hoping the bear was going upriver and not coming down.

I did build a small cabin there, approximately 8 by 8 feet, small logs, about 5 inch logs. I used that cabin for many years until fire got it. Then we floated the rest of the way down the river towards Fort Yukon. On the Porcupine, we came across a calf moose on a cut bank. The bank was only about 6 feet above the water and the calf was on a ledge close to the water. It couldn't get up again onto the mainland. We saw the cow on top, encouraging it to come up. The calf was bawling and we heard the calf from a mile away, at least. Any bears in the area would've made a quick *meal out of that calf. We floated rather close to the calf, and the cow finally jumped down in the water, and I believe the calf followed it safely, but am not sure about that. We continued to flow towards Fort Yukon and maybe 20 miles up the Porcupine from Fort Yukon. We ran into Joe Firman in a boat. He gave us a ride, me and the dogs and my gear, back to Fort Yukon.*

The new cabin was small. It had a bunk and one small table to hold the stove. The military Yukon stove*. It was a dirt floor and it was not any warmer than a tent. It was a place to spend the night, dry up, harness, dry your gloves, and cook your food. It had a flat roof covered with dirt. I believe it took three or four days to build.

This cabin was at the south end of my line on the Coleen River. From this cabin, I had trails going west to some lakes. That was an old trail. I opened it up. Then I had a tent camp up on the lake. Another long trail west from there to another tent camp. One winter during a high population marten year, I caught 77 marten on that trail.

"Trapper Bob", early 1970s – written on back of photo by Bob's mom and sent to me.

Sometime during his time in the Southeast, or early ANWR days, Bob met and, on a dare, married his first wife, who was an Aleut woman. They were not married (and together) for very long; a few months, I believe, and Bob only spoke of her when I asked him. I know she had a young son from a previous relationship, and that they were briefly with Bob on his trapline. There are no recordings in his log book about her during the early 1970s. Only recordings of dog names and animal 'catch'– no human 'catch.'

As much as he loved the life he was living, Bob did want somebody to share it with. When he and his wife split up, Bob would get another chance!

Chapter 2: Herstory

"Tell me what it is you plan to do with your one, wild precious life?"

– Mary Oliver

As Mentioned, Bob and I met in Fort Yukon in 1979 when we were both waiting for a plane ride back to Fairbanks. Bob was heading into Fairbanks for supplies. And I, having just completed an interview to teach in the bush, was heading to Fairbanks to catch a flight back to Sitka, Alaska (in the Southeast) where I had been living. I have explained my first impressions of Bob as I remember him that cold winter day. Seeing beyond his average looks, I was impressed with his passionate spirit. But his impression of me, I can only guess at.

My appearance is quite normal, average height and weight. I don't remember exactly what I wore. It was winter, and because Sitka was a lot warmer than the interior, I had purchased a heavy down parka from Big Ray's in downtown Fairbanks before heading to the bush. It was dark green, men's medium, and had a big wolf ruff. I probably wore long johns, my bib overalls, and wool pants. Maybe Sorel boots on my feet. Our bodies were pretty much hidden under lots of clothing, but we were able to meet eye to eye during our conversation on the plane ride from Fort Yukon to Fairbanks. He had blue eyes. I had brown eyes. I had two big front teeth. He had no front teeth.

Bob probably had some spark of interest in a single woman, his age, living in interior Alaska from "outside." Alaskans use the term "outside" to mean anywhere outside of Alaska. Another term we use is the "lower 48"– obviously meaning the 48 states below Alaska (mainland USA).

In 1980, the ratio of men to women in Alaska was about 113 to 110, and the census of 2010 stated that Alaska was the highest ranked state for the most men to women. In Alaska, women have a saying, "The odds are good, but the goods are odd!"

Bob is relatively shy, so he didn't come on strongly. I liked that. He told me about his lifestyle, and I told him I would be an itinerant teacher in Fort Yukon School District, living in Stevens Village on the Yukon River. What I didn't know at the time was that Bob was married, although not living with his first wife. We parted ways in Fairbanks, he gave me a contact number to call in case I was in town again at the same time he was. Our next meeting would be more than a year later. I used to wonder a lot about how I would ever meet the one person I was meant to be with in all the world, how would I ever get around to all the places in order to meet that one person. I think about things differently now, but do find it interesting that Bob and I had our beginnings on the east coast and ended up together in the far northwest.

My parents met and fell in love in college. Dad used to tell us that he would whistle at mom and she, being two years older, would ignore that youngster. He still pursued her heart and eventually won it. Dad was Jewish. Mom was Catholic. Neither set of my grandparents were happy about those differences, so my parents eloped. Their marriage was a great partnership, as they were open minded and communicated well, sharing the responsibilities and activities of family life. They raised three very different and independent girls. As a family, we moved around a lot, experiencing different lifestyles, but my favorite times as a young child were family outings and adventures we shared together.

After a year of junior college, I applied to several universities in states that I had never been to, and Central Michigan University became my home for the next three years. Never being very interested in going to college to begin with, I went, but found other interesting subjects that kept my attention. While in college, I remember writing a curriculum paper about Alaska, thinking about how the state intrigued me. I wondered, how can I get to Alaska? I decided to write to the Chamber of Commerce. It was a good plan, but very discouraging to hear back that I should definitely not pursue Alaska without a job lined up. Was this because I was female? Years later, I wondered about that. My Alaska dreams were put on hold for a while, but I continued adventuring nonetheless.

For instance, I took off for Europe to see an old boyfriend but ended up hitchhiking around Europe and Scandinavia with a girl from South Africa. Or, like the various places I lived while attending college, my favorite being the communal farm called Ragged Rainbow. There, I lived in a barn with other like-minded folks– milking mama goats, feeding pigs, collecting chicken eggs, laughing at baby goats as they kicked up their legs discovering themselves, and gardening nude are some of the memorable moments of this simple 'back-to nature' lifestyle that I thrived on at this shared property.

Even some of my methods of transportation during college days were sources of adventure: bicycling, my 200ccXL Honda motorcycle, hitch hiking, and an old Checker Cab named "Chubby" (with pop-up seats) passed down from my older sister, Gail, to me, and eventually to my younger sister, Jeff. During summers I worked in kids' camps, and during the school year I held a variety of jobs including dishwasher, reader for the blind students, waitress, server at the student center, and pumping gas at the very first ever gas station in Michigan to hire women. We wore uniforms of blue jackets and white, fluffy hats with puffy pompom ties.

 After graduating, my first real job was at a career center in Bay City, Michigan. While working that first job, I was also taking grad classes, where I met and, three months later, married my first husband, Tim. We took off traveling cross-country, lived in Montana, worked at summer camps together, and after three years, in 1977, our son Traver was born. Three months later, Tim and I separated. I never considered separation or divorce would be something I would experience in my life time. When it happened, I was devastated and went into depression and some kind of psychotic state. I was lost for about two years, wondering about my life: What now?

Okay Nanc, time for some adventure and to a place I've always wanted to go.

I discovered that an old friend of mine from college was working in Southeast Alaska, so in March of 1979 I flew into Wrangell, Alaska (same area Bob was, just four years earlier), then into Sitka (to visit my friend). The moment I landed, I knew I was home. Alaska was more than a dream come true to me. I knew in my heart for years that Alaska was calling me, and though I didn't know why, I did know that I would be making Alaska my home, somehow.

After returning from my first trip to Alaska, I was still living in Michigan at the time, sharing custody of Traver with my husband. We were still married but not living together. I needed a good plan. Below is what I was thinking and writing to my mom and dad:

Dear Mom and Dad,

I didn't know what your next letter would bring to me regarding my thoughts about Alaska. I was anxiously awaiting. I was so happy to read this part: "and regardless, your father and I have never wanted anything more than that you be happy. I'd hate to be without it."

If that's really what you want for me, that's all that really matters. Thanks so much, and I love you very much. Being happy is all that matters to me. I am not happy now, although I know I soon will be. My Alaska trip was more earth shaking than you can ever imagine. If I do see you this summer, I'd like to share more of that, but as for now I want to go to Alaska. Who knows what for or for how long? I feel there's something to learn there, very important. I want to go back. I can always return home! So, I'm going. A job? Not yet. I interviewed when I was in Sitka. I can always sub when I get there or can always stay with one of several friends I met until I settle.

Tim and I are not yet divorced, and as far as custody of Traver, that's between us now. I told Tim I was leaving. He was upset at first, then things were okay for a while. Now he's upset again and doesn't want me to take Traver. So we'll be going through some stuff around that, and I don't know yet where it will end up.

As for long cold winters– Sitka, Alaska has a much milder winter than Michigan. It is on an island. When I was there in March it was sixty degrees. I'll answer any more questions if you would like to understand more. It's work sometimes, it's painful sometimes, exciting and scary, but all worthwhile and very alive! I know what happiness feels like, and my direction will be that which my heart leads me to... I love you both very much. Thanks for accepting me for me.

Love and respect, Nanc

In the Fall of 1979, the day after our divorce finalized, I left Michigan. After packing my little red car with our belongings, my son Traver (now two years old) and I headed for Wisconsin, where my sister Jeff lived. It was my plan all along to head for Alaska from there, but I did not reveal that to Trav's dad. That would not have gone over well. With my car parked at my sister's, and Traver with his beloved "blankie," we hopped on a train heading for Seattle with a sign in my mind: Alaska or Bust. From Seattle to Prince Rupert, we traveled by bus and train. The final leg, Prince Rupert to Sitka, Alaska was by ferry. I chose Sitka because I now had at least two new friends there from my trip in March.

This journey to Alaska proved to be quite upsetting, at times. I was used to traveling– but not with a two-year old. They say trouble comes in threes, and on this particular trip, three awful things did happen. First, Trav lost his beloved "blankie." We went through emotional hell over that one. Thankfully, after several mournful days, a sock became the replacement for "blankie."

Second, Trav got lice, and I know how he got them. On one of our bus rides up, there was this young, scruffy looking guy sitting behind the driver. I kept observing him on the bus, picking and scratching his head. I did not think about lice then, or I might not have moved up to the scruffy guy's seat after he left. There was more room behind the driver, and I could put Traver on a blanket on the floor so he could sleep. Those little buggers latched on to Trav's hair, but we got rid of them fast; I never got any. We hit the drugstore and got a bottle of shampoo from the clerk. I have to admit, I was very disgusted and a bit embarrassed with that scene but was so happy to find a remedy.

Third, when having bowel movements, Trav would howl. It hurt somehow, and the situation got so worrisome that I took him to the emergency room in Canada (which only cost $1!), only to discover his ears were infected. Needing to find a place to stay for the night, I began inquiring at the hospital. We were invited to stay with the operating room supervisor and her family, and we did. That family saved us, and quite possibly that entire trip. At that point in the journey, I was very dismayed. Bob may have lost his front teeth on his way to Alaska, but I almost lost my mind and nearly gave up with all the problems we encountered.

Thankfully, I am not a quitter. We continued onward. The last leg of our trip was on the ferry, where we slept on the deck at night and during the day experienced whales swimming, breathtaking mountain scenery, and met interesting people.

We arrived in Sitka, met my two friends, and headed for the harbor, our new home. The following portions from letters in early October, 1979 will describe our situation:

Dear Mom and Dad,

Here we are at A&B Harbor with my two friends and living on a trolling boat called Teddy. We've been out to sea the past 12 days on a fishing trip/ fun trip, as we mostly anchored at a place called Goddard Hot Springs. There were two wooden tubs filling constantly with the hot spring water and as we relaxed in the tubs, we looked out on a vast landscape of sea, mountains, and wilderness. We picked wild huckleberries and blueberries daily. By the way, since going to the hot springs, Traver's bathroom problem is resolved. Don't know what it was but I thank God or who or whatever that he is done with that agony.

It's been rain, rain, rain. And not a lot of fall colors, which I'll miss, but this is where I want to live right now and I hope I can.

Love, Nancy

For the next few months, Trav and I moved to a different boat at A&B Harbor, working for room and board on the Orca, a boat built in 1940 or so that was about 60 feet long. Wayne, the owner, was a surveyor and skin-diver, so we gleaned both harvests he made from the sea (food) and from adventures on the Orca where his surveying job took him. What a life.

There were a few subbing job I obtained in the schools, but this time was mostly an introduction to Alaska with daily living lessons in trolling, long-lining, living off the land and sea, and getting by with a simple lifestyle. We learned to harvest, clean, and eat salmon, abalone, clams, and shrimp. The boats would bring in their catch and we had huge feasts– a big potluck on the dock where we'd meet on one boat, place a clean sheet on the floor, and pile up the delicacies and feast!

Trav and I would occasionally take out Wayne's Zodiac (a rubber boat with motor) to catch our dinner of brown bombers, which are bottom fish we found near the rocks. Traver learned an amazing array of living skills on the docks, but his most famous activities were jumping in puddles and throwing rocks in the water. I can see why there are comments about having webbed feet in Southeast Alaska. It can be extremely wet.

Traver on the Orca.

41

Traver on the Zodiak boat.

During October through November, I continually searched for a compatible job that would suit my circumstances of living on the docks, having time with my son, and living simply. Though I'd been learning a lot about Alaska and experiencing a different lifestyle in southeast, I decided to move on and use my teaching degree to discover more of Alaska. December brought an opportunity for an interview for a special education itinerant teaching position in the Yukon Flats School District in Fort Yukon. That interview was eye-opening and hectic – flying to Fort Yukon (population 700) from Fairbanks, I saw nothing but wilderness. We landed on a dirt strip; no roads, no electricity, no plumbing. It was definitely culture shock, but it revved up my adventurous spirit. I stayed in a cabin with other teachers, pilots, and trappers who had come to Alaska for an Alaskan experience, so there was a camaraderie there. Then I was flown to the tiny village of Rampart (population 40 to 70) where I got weathered in due to ice fog*. I stayed among husky dog teams, mukluk and parka clad Athabascans while eating moose stew and fish strips.

Next, I jumped in the mail plane heading for Stevens Village (population 30 to 50). Upon landing, I jumped on a dogsled and was delivered (along with the mail) to a shack with a wood stove and no lights. There, I was asked if I was going to be coming to teach at Stevens Village and then leaving like everybody else. That was basically the interview, and off I went, hiking the trail to the log cabin school where I met the 11 students and principal teacher. That was it. On the way to the runway I got a quick glimpse of the cabin I would live in if I accepted the job. Then, my plane took off, headed back for Fairbanks. The entire visit was less than an hour, as I was traveling on the mail plane which needed to keep moving on! As I said, hectic.

Below is a letter I wrote to my Mother about my travels and interviews for this new job:

December of 1979

Well, where do I begin this one? So much has happened to me in the past few days. Right now, I am in Ft. Yukon, a town of 700...no roads to get into here, either. I flew to Anchorage, then Fairbanks, and then on an 'islander' to Ft. Yukon. From Fairbanks I saw 'nothing' below the plane, except wilderness. When we landed, I felt like I was in a different world...on the moon! Tomorrow I fly out in a tri-lander (I think that's a 3 passenger) to see two villages, both of about 50-60 residents, where I may be teaching if I get this job. The job is a special education itinerant position, mostly working with learning disabilities. It's a job where I would go to one village each week. Maybe four villages total. I'd stay with different teachers or native residents for those weeks, then one week in my own home, which would be in either Ft. Yukon or a village called Stevens Village.

No toilets, Mom! No plumbing! Outhouses here in Ft. Yukon. Water is delivered in big tanks, oil stoves and wood stoves in most cabins, and yes, there is electricity. There is a shower, toilet, and laundry room at the school for employees. It is "warm" here now, -5°F, and we'll get to -30° shortly... and colder. This will be a very adventurous, different, and challenging job if I get it. And I want it. I'm pretty sure I'll get it.

The arctic sun begins trimming the horizon around 9:30 and plunges down about 2:00. That is very strange... I was ready to go to bed by 3:30 today.

Tomorrow I meet the villagers. They need to "approve" me too. My salary would be around $23,000 a year. It's a nice, comfortable community here. I've met some people that I like already. Alaska is such an amazing place. I am learning so much.

Got to Stevens Village for a very quick interview. These interviews are something else. It was in a shack with no light, a wood stove... I was asked if I was going to be coming and then leaving like everybody else. Difficult to keep teachers, maybe? I was taken up the trail to the log cabin school, and in confidence was asked if I was a drunkard or a drug user. I saw the 11 students, saw the cabin I'd be living in if I decided to stay – all this in less than 15 minutes. Then off on the mail plane again and into Fairbanks, where I am now.

I'm excited about getting back to Trav in Sitka. I'll be home tomorrow by noon and then wait to hear by Saturday if I got the job. The smaller villages don't have phones, so communication is by Trapline Chatter. You call a number from your telephone to send a message to the villages. Then the messages are read over the radio at 6 or 7 a.m. and 9:30 at night. It's fun to listen to. You get all the gossip about all the villages. You know who got snowed in where, if planes are coming and going, etc. Very unusual.

Mom, will you please save this letter for me? I am going to start some sort of diary of my adventures in Alaska. I haven't had time or energy to do that yet.

My mind is very boggled at this moment. So much to think about. A few more things that stick out in my mind; when we get off at the 'airports' in the villages, which is just the end of a dirt runway, we were picked up, along with all the mail, in a 'sno-go,' which is a snowmobile.

Instead of talking about the 'lower forty-eight' up here, as they do in Sitka, now people talk about going 'outside' when they speak of places outside of Alaska. Love, Nanc

I accepted that job, released Trav to be with his dad for a while, and spent the loneliest Christmas I can remember in Fort Yukon, not knowing a soul. However, rather than being all alone, I was invited to join some community members in celebration, where I had another encounter with Bob. Here is a portion of the letter I wrote to my Mother the day after Christmas:

December 26th, 1979

It felt so good to talk to all of you yesterday. It made my day. I thought I was going to be alone for Christmas, but I was invited to 3 places, which was real nice. I ended up with a family that had 3 kids, and they had invited a few more people in. During Christmas, some trappers come out of the bush and into town (Ft. Yukon). There was a trapper there I really enjoyed talking with (Bob). I stayed the night with the correspondence teacher, Justine. She had a pilot friend over and we all had a good time. You would have loved it, Mom. The cabin was 18' by 18'. We all peed in the 'honey pot*,' so we could hear each other peeing! That was my Christmas. I missed the snowball cookies you make, Mom, and, of course, all my family, but there were plenty of goodies around, and this Becker managed to 'pig-out,' even though I wasn't with my family.

End of December from Fairbanks

Right now I am in the Roaring Twenties Motel, which is another 'home away from home' for me, as I need to stay overnight before going off to the villages...and weather depending, it could be days. I bought a $150 sleeping bag today. It's recommended we carry one when traveling, along with a survival kit, which I'm putting together. I'm also having to buy little things, like a flashlight, toilet paper, and ear plugs. It is such a different life here. Tomorrow I shop for food, then hop a plane ride to Stevens Village. Anxious to get my mail. Will write again soon, xoxoxox Love, Nanc

My new home for the next 15 months was Steven's Village on the Yukon River, where my indoctrination to living in the bush really began. The knowledge about life I received there was more than the knowledge I was able to give back with school teaching.

Flying into Stevens Village.

Flying into Steven's Village looked like the middle of nowhere- a never ending landscape of frozen lakes, rivers, and tundra. After landing on the frozen dirt runway and unloading my minimal gear, I quickly learned to get by with very little. The children taught me how to innovate, as they grew up without stores and conveniences of city life. If you don't have a teapot, make one out of an old coffee can. When it rains, and you have no rain gear, use a garbage can lid to keep the rain from drenching you. No toaster? Shake salt on the barrel stove top so the bread won't burn or stick to the stove as it 'toasts'.

The seasons in this little faraway village could be recognized through various activities. Fall time meant hunting for moose and fishing, always with the anticipation of feast or famine, and always hoping to store up for the long winter months ahead. Spring was also hunting time; ducks and geese, muskrat and bear. Winter was trapping time.

Obtaining basic necessities of firewood and water became enjoyable shared activities with the villagers, and easier done in the fall season, but still a continuous chore. I had a coleman lamp and kerosene lamp for light as I sat at my homemade table sewing my skin boots in preparation for winter. My fingers smelled like smoked moose hide. Mmmm, it is a rich pleasant smoky odor.

Picnics and potlatches* were times of fun and celebration. You could always depend on a potlatch holiday celebration to begin in the morning and continue to wee hours, sometimes lasting for days. There were continual preparations of moose-head soup, the cooked lining of moose stomach, Indian ice cream, dried fish strips, fry bread, and birds if available. Dancing and gift giving were often part of these cultural celebrations. Picnics could happen at anytime. A time to break up the monotony of winter, time to get out of the village, make a fire, and just relax with friends.

*Above: My friends, Ann and Lilly.
Right: Hanging out at a picnic.*

47

Traver hanging out with his preschool classmates.

My 2 closest friends in Steven's Village were Ann (Athabascan) and Lilly (Inupiat), who was my next door neighbor from Wiseman. We laughed when the three of us got together for a walk. Eskimo, Indian, and White, "all messed up," as Lilly would say. I learned to hunt rabbits and grouse with these two buddies. Lilly introduced me to muktuk (whale blubber) which was a unique experience for my palette. The blubber was like hard, rubbery lard but the black skin was chewy and had kind of a nutty flavor. Lilly called it Eskimo candy. I think blubber rubber is a better description. Ann introduced me to Indian ice cream which is basically a mixture of lard, sugar, and berries. I never acquired a taste for it.

I loved living in the quiet, simple village. My son Traver joined me in the fall of 1980 and he was so delighted with the strangeness and adventure of village life. He quickly learned about dog teams, fish wheels*, and hunting. When he saw fish eggs (salmon) in the fish cavity for the first time, he said, "Oh berries. Can we eat them?" Some of the new friends he made would visit us and I'd hear Traver speaking some Athabascan words. Not a skill I can claim for myself.

The Yukon Flats School District was having problems that year and I was asked to transfer to a small community called Joy, off the Elliott Highway (49.5 miles north of Fairbanks), to finish out the school year from March until May. I complied. My position as K-6 teacher with a special education aide started immediately.

During the transfer from Stevens Village to Joy, I stopped in Fairbanks to collect supplies for the remaining school year that I would spend in Joy. It was March and I wanted to celebrate my birthday. Who could I get a hold of to make this happen? I had Bob Harte's contact telephone number from over a year ago that he'd given me when we met in Fort Yukon. I called Bob! He was in town looking for work. I was looking forward to getting to know a little more about this subtly quiet, intrinsic trapper that I knew very little about.

We agreed to meet at the celebration called Trapper's Fling, which is a time to gather after an isolated, vigorous, hard-working trapping season, and is still celebrated today. Trappers came from near and far to thaw out their weary bones and participate in animated, jaw flapping storytelling which could carry on well into the wee hours. Would Bob show up? I did wonder.

Yes, our eyes met in that crazy crowd – and what a crowd! The escalating mingle of energy and voices from men and women eager to get reacquainted filled the air. When our ears were overloaded, Bob and I left for a calmer atmosphere. I can't remember where that was, but this is what I do remember. Since it was my birthday, Bob presented me with a Buddha necklace. I'm not a jewelry person, but I felt pursued in a magical way. With the closing of that clasp around my neck, we began our lives together for the next twelve years. That same evening, I remember he brushed my hair out for the first time; it was like heaven. His intimate touch and appreciation of my hair astounded me. The comments about the quality, color, and beauty were in comparison to the fur he handled constantly in the woods. I liked that too. He was very real.

Bob wanted to see me again, so he asked if we could have a dinner date. I've never been very enthused about 'eating out,' so I suggested a swim at Wedgewood Manor, where the school district puts up teachers for a night or two when they are in town from the bush. Bob showed up at the pool in cut-off jeans that were not fastened at the top. I mentioned that to him and he said something about them being torn or busted. I liked him even more then, because he didn't care about those little unimportant things. He was not particular about how he looked or what he wore. He was so cute and little-boyish in many ways. After our first date, I went out to meet Bob's dogs. At the time, he was staying with Ed and Carolyn in the Goldstream Valley outside of Fairbanks because he could stake out his entire dog team there. Bob was so very proud of all his dogs. It was obvious that he thought of them as his family. I wasn't used to all the excitement and jumping around of a dogteam; I got my baby finger caught in the collar of one dog while getting to know him...to this day I have a crooked finger from my first lesson about dog teams.

Bob with his dog team.

We had dinner with Ed and Carolyn a couple of times. Ed built small rental cabins; Carolyn worked with plants at the University. We enjoyed swapping Alaskan experiences, but Bob and I were all eyes for each other. I left all too soon to begin teaching in Joy, Alaska.

So, while Bob was hanging outside of Fairbanks, looking for some part time work in order to feed his family of dogs, I was up 50 miles on the Elliot highway teaching grades K-6. I shared a cabin with Trish, who was hired to cook and assist with teaching. We got along great and still remain friends. During the weekends, Bob would hitchhike or ride his motorcycle up to see me and we started making some plans together for the future.

Bob and I after our first date.

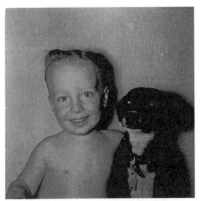

Bob with his first dog

Brothers in the tub

Sibling pose 1950s

Cowboys at Christmas

Brothers boating

Bob's teenage activity

Nancy with her first dog

Sisters in the tub

Sibling pose 1950s

Cowgirls at Christmas

Sisters canoeing

Nancy's teenage activity

Chapter 3:

Our Adventurous Beginning: On the Road, Tent Camping, and Looking for Land

Bob and I had similar backgrounds and similar interests. That's one reason why we "clicked" that wintery day when we first met in Fort Yukon. Bob was born in New Jersey and spent his childhood in neighborhoods and countrysides. I was born in New York and lived most of my childhood in neighborhoods and countrysides. Having three brothers to compete and play with didn't give Bob much experience in getting along with girls. Plus, he was shy. Living with two other sisters didn't give me much experience with boys. Bob was a Boy Scout and loved the outdoor life. I was a Girl Scout and also loved the outdoor life. Bob loved animals and trapped them. I loved animals and during college was an animal rights advocate. We both had parents that loved us. We were both drawn to nature, adventure, and a free lifestyle. Back in the 60s and 70s that was a major theme. "Do your own thing," and, "make love, not war."

So, it wasn't too surprising to find us on the road, heading back east together. We had a big adventure all planned out. Bob and I were now partners. Our plan was to travel back east, visit our families, purchase a truck and a wood stove, and pick up my son to return with us to Fairbanks. Because neither of us had wheels, except for Bob's motorcycle, we decided to hitchhike. It was a mode of transportation familiar to both of us, and we got some awesome rides.

We hitched to Haines, Alaska, where we boarded the ferry bound for Seattle, Washington, a three day trip. After landing on solid ground, the place to head next would be Colorado, where Bob's brother Russ lived. One ride we got was in a big black hearse, which drove us all day heading into Colorado. We felt like king and queen of the road. We stopped in Colorado to meet Russ, but never made the connection.

Having backpacks and sleeping bags, we would spend nights in the woods, in abandoned barns, in fields, and any place off the beaten path. Our next stop was Two Harbors, MN where my sister, Gail, lived. After a swim in the lake and partying with her friends, we picked up my car (which I had left a while ago) and headed to Michigan, where my son was with his dad. I spent a few days there, getting Traver prepared to head back with us to Alaska. Bob went off to look for a truck to purchase. We would need our own transportation now, with Traver, and the big wood stove we would be picking up from the east coast (Bob had previously done his research and wanted only this particular stove). It weighed 300 pounds, and we would be hauling it to Bob's trapline.

Bob teaching Traver how to fish.

Leaving my car behind, we took off from Michigan in a blue Chevy pickup with a Grateful Dead sticker on the rear bumper. Next stop would be Oak Ridge, New Jersey where Bob's parents were, along with his younger brother, Jimmy, and his girlfriend, Cindy. During that short visit, I got to witness Bob at "play" with his brother, Jimmy, horsing around, goofing off on bikes, and best of all, Traver had his first fishing lesson and hunt for turtles.

Bob showing off his playful, goofy side.

Like a horse after a long horseback ride, Bob was antsy to get back on the road again and head home. New Jersey was no longer his home, and home was where Bob wanted to be. So, with that 300-pound stove in the back of our pickup, Bob, Trav, and I hopped in the cab and headed northwest to Fairbanks, AK. The trip back was as fast as Bob could go. He was not much for sightseeing. Caribou, fox, moose, coyotes, and porcupines were some of the critters we spotted. We did slide through Banff and Jasper National Parks, a vast area of distant snow-capped peaks gouged by glaciers with an up close sprinkling of an array of wildflowers. The roads into Alaska back then were mostly dirt. It was a bumpy, dusty ride driving the Alaska-Canada Highway (ALCAN), a road known for cracked windshields (which we acquired four of) and flat tires due to rough roads. It is a long haul from Oak Ridge, New Jersey to Fairbanks, Alaska: 4,250 miles. Weather and road construction were always on the radar. And make sure you don't wait until the last minute to fill up on gas, or you might be hitchhiking back for some.

That was the first of my ten or so trips on the ALCAN highway. The road has changed with many improvements, but there are also a lot more tourist attractions. We spent about $500 on gas for that return road race, but as always, it was a relief to be back in The Last Frontier.

One blue Chevy truck. One motorcycle. One little boy. Half dozen dogs. And a 300-pound wood stove. No home! This was the summertime in Alaska, though. We had tents and sleeping bags. Bob, Traver, and I were all set for more adventure.

There is an unpopulated area just north of Fairbanks called Fox. Very few people live there, even today. The area is probably best known for the Fox Water Hole, a natural spring that supplies locals with fresh, clean mountain water. Bob and I always got our drinking water there, and I still do today.

Near the vicinity of Fox were a bunch of gravel pits perfect for a temporary camping spot. We set up our tents and staked out the dogs. Our closest neighbors were the resident beavers, living in and around the gravel pits. The opportunity to live outside, close to natural surroundings, is really a treasure. There is such a simple pleasure in being alive and free, so as a little four-year old boy, Traver delighted in his new "playground." Never a dull moment where there are little boys, dogs, and nature.

View of our tent camp at the gravel pit near Fox, Alaska.

This was also a time for Bob and I to look for land. We were planning to locate a spot and build a cabin which would be our home in summers when we weren't on the trapline. I had a little money saved from teaching, but since we were planning to head out to the trapline, money would now have to come from trapping. Uh, oh, I thought – I didn't know how reliable that would be, or wouldn't be.

While driving around in that old Chevy, looking for land, we did enjoy spending time with a few friends we'd met in Fort Yukon and Fairbanks. During the summertime in Fairbanks, there are many hours of daylight. Fairbankians take full advantage of that sun, since our winters creep down to only three hours of daylight in December.

Summertime in Fairbanks is June, July, and August. June was our time on the road. We would be departing for the trapline in August. That left July, and no time to find summer jobs. Along with land hunting, there was a lot of preparation that had to be done before going out on the trapline. We had no boat yet, and Bob now had additional family members to figure into the mix. I was not much help in planning this portion, as everything was so new to me... flying in the small plane with dogs? We'd be gone through Christmas, and I can't pack gifts? "Nope. Too much valuable weight wasted," said Bob. What? I can't even pack one box of Raisin Bran? "No, you don't understand." He was right. I did not understand! Necessities only: dogs, dogfood, gas, lamp oil, trapping gear, tools, batteries, some winter clothes, and minimal food. I was so shocked by what food and supplies we did not take.

There was, of course, much anticipation and excitement with all the preparation – adventure, new experiences, the Alaskan bush and all its wonder and beauty to behold. And I, of course, was in love, which made everything just fine and dandy, mostly.

Back to packing. It all sounds relatively easy – box up what you need in order to live in the woods for six months. Food, but only necessities – there would be a supply of meat and fish waiting for us to harvest.

Bob's idea of necessities:

Food – coffee, flour, sugar, rice, oats, powdered milk, baking powder, one case of Mac 'n cheese, peanut butter, one big bucket of lard (for the dogs, and us, if necessary), one can of powdered mashed potatoes, raisins, butter, one to two boxes of cream-of-wheat, and a few bags of dried legumes.

Clothes – the warmest coat you have, snow pants or wool outer pants, long johns, several wool hats, gloves, mittens, socks, the warmest boots you have, a few pairs of pants or sweats, some shirts, sweaters, scarves, and extra boot liners.

I had mukluks for Trav and myself that I had made while living in Stevens Village. It was a good thing I had already experienced an interior Alaska winter. There's a lot to learn in order to live comfortably in such a cold climate.

Trapping Gear – Bob had most of his necessary trapping supplies on the trapline already, but there were always a few things that needed replenishing, like snare wire (usually picture frame wire for snaring rabbits), scent, Buhach*, wire, and wax paper to cover traps.

Household Supplies – dish soap, kerosene (for lamps), matches, toilet paper (such a luxury in those days; we would divvy out squares when it was time to go to the outhouse), paper towels (also a luxury), hand towels, soap, maybe a new lantern, or at least the glass bulb for a kerosene lamp, and batteries. We didn't even have headlamps back then. How on earth did we manage without headlamps during the days with so much darkness?

Hobby and Entertainment Supplies – books, books, and books! And more books! Books were a necessity as far as we were concerned, for learning necessary skills, for Traver's education, for entertainment and relaxing on those long winter days and nights, and their final destination cannot be forgotten – paper for the outhouse!

Since we were also limiting our weight in this category of supplies, our choices of books were important. One of my most cherished books of all time is Where There is no Doctor. Not only were the photos and explanations in the book very entertaining, but the information, given our living circumstances, was invaluable.

Bob would take Louis Lamour and a few books on Alaska. He already had a collection of books stashed in his cache*. Traver, at age four, selected some picture books. My selection was a variety of historical Alaskan fiction and other recommended resources to acclimate fully into the interior wilderness life.

Having begun experimenting with beading and basket making while in Steven's Village, I also brought along some beading supplies and simple hand tools. I've always enjoyed making things with nature and was looking forward to opening my creativity to the already available supplies. Since Bob never had children on the trapline, we also collected a box of "kid necessities," like crayons, scissors, and glue.

It was so difficult for me to pack up that first year. I had no idea what was coming. So I simply relied on Bob. The next year I would prove better in the packing department.

Meanwhile, we were still hunting for land. After trying to get lottery land, but to no avail, we continued our search northeast of town, off one of the long dead-end roads in Alaska. If you look at a map of Alaska compared to New York, or California, or really any other state, you'll notice how few roads there are, and for such a large state!

Chena Hot Springs Road paves its way directly out of Fairbanks and ends 60 miles northeast of Fairbanks. Back in the 1980s it wasn't paved all the way. Down that road, we checked out a 2.5 acre birch and spruce lot with a sunny south slope for about $12,000. I refer directly to this purchase in a letter I wrote to my Mom and Dad the last week in August, 1981 with the postage stamp of 18 cents:

We bought two acres of land 20 miles from town. Signed papers July 31. Since then, we've been clearing the land, getting logs, and building a cache. Boy, what work! Our land is mostly birch, spruce, and willow. It's off a dirt road. No other homes in sight. When we build a cabin, we'll have a nice view. We spent lots of time clearing, and lots of time cutting spruce trees and peeling them. Now we are on round four of the logs going up (for the cache). I'm learning a lot! Bruises, aches, and pains, too. And I just put our bathroom plumbing in. I dug a five-foot deep hole for our outhouse. Oh, what fun! I'm inviting both of you up for a chinking* party here next week… Know what chinking on a cabin is? Ha! Look it up!! (My Dad always said 'Look it up' when we asked what a word meant).

Traver is learning a lot too, he knows how to tie his shoes. He collects firewood and gets the fire going when it is almost out. He waters the dogs for 25 cents because he wants money of his own. That was an interesting task to watch him learn as he got jumped on and run over by the dogs at first. Now he carries a stick with him along with his bucket of water, and he's doing real well. Since Bob and I are busy building, Traver is learning how to entertain himself as well as help out when he can.

We woke up this morning hearing grouse moving about the tent. Four of them. Tomorrow night we're having grouse for dinner.

Oh, last night a friend of Bob's (another trapper) came in from the west coast of Alaska with his new lady friend, Edna, Yupik, and her six-year-old daughter, Milly. Milly and Trav get along great. Milly had never seen trees before. She only knew trees as driftwood. She was very excited about seeing trees and asking about all sorts of things. Trav was amazed at how 'little' she knew until I mentioned she knew all about whales, fishing, and other things he didn't know about.

(This was the beginning of a long friendship with Heimo and Edna Korth's family and ours.)

Obviously, we moved our tent camp from Fox to the two acres and were then working on our cache. This fourteen by fourteen cache would be a storage place for us while we were up on the trapline. When we returned to town from the trapline, it would be our home until we got the cabin built. Our trips to Fairbanks were now limited because we were so focused on getting the cache built. When we did make a trip to Fairbanks, the day was crammed full: food shopping, showers, laundry, supplies, and water. Back then, we always took showers at the laundromat. For many folks that still live in dry cabins* in Alaska, this remains a common practice. I just recently, in 2016, discarded that practice, trading it for a real home shower and clothes washing at my daughter Talicia's, when we got plumbing hooked up there.

Our tent camp setup at our property off of Chena Hot Springs Road.

Bob working on building the cache at our new property off Chena Hot Springs Road.

When I think back to that time of the year – summertime – it was always such an exciting, rushing-around time to complete summer projects and prepare for the trapline. We were getting very close to wrapping it up in town, as my letter of August, 31 1981 states:

Dear Mom and Dad,

This will have to be short. More like bon voyage rather than a detailed chapter. Bob left today with the dogs. I'm left to get last minute stuff done--so far it's taken all day and lots more left for tomorrow. I'll be real glad to get out there. Trav's on the playground now for his final swing. He's ready to go too.

If you write in September, October, or November, use this address: PO Box 178 Ft. Yukon, AK. Maybe it will get to me. If you write closer to Christmas, my old roommate said she'd get my mail to me. Use the old Fairbanks address. Otherwise, this is the way to do a short trapline message. It's called Trapline Chatter on radio station KJNP, North Pole, Alaska. Used for trappers with no other way of communicating. We'll have a radio and will listen every Sunday evening for messages. You call (907)-488-2216 and tell them you want to send a Trapline Chatter message. You'll give your name and phone number. And they'll ask you who the message is for and where it's going. You'll say "Bob and Nancy at B.C. (Base Camp)." And then give the message. Ask them to read it 2-3 times so we won't miss it.

Or, you can also write to KJNP PO Box 0 North Pole, Alaska, 99705 with same information. Get it? Got it? Good! (Something our family always said).

You both sounded good last time we spoke. I'm feeling a little lonely for you now knowing we'll be out of touch for a while, but I'll write and hopefully it will get out before December. Now I gotta get going and finish up business. I love you both very much. Fall time is so beautiful everywhere. Enjoy it. Love Nanc.

P.S. I forgot to mention that Trav got his two kittens. Their names are Kitty and Killer. Bob named one and Trav named the other. Guess who picked which name for each kitten? Ha!

This was my last communication to my family until we were on the trapline.

Part 2

Life in ANWR

"*We can only be said to be alive, in those moments when our hearts are conscious of our treasures.*"

– Thornton Wilder

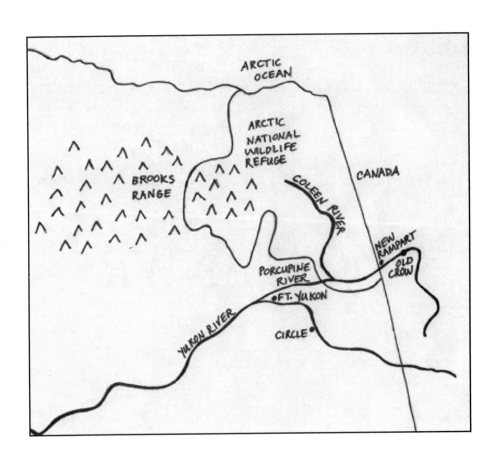

ARCTIC
OCEAN

ARCTIC
NATIONAL
WILDLIFE
REFUGE

CANADA

BROOKS
RANGE

COLEEN RIVER

NEW
RAMPART

OLD
CROW

PORCUPINE
RIVER

•FT. YUKON

YUKON RIVER

CIRCLE •

Chapter 4:

1981

The view flying into our Base Camp in ANWR.

F lying over Interior Alaska changed my perception of wilderness. With a bird's eye view of this vastness, my eyes bulged with wonder. We quickly glided over snow-tipped mountains and entered a wonderland of flat tundra terrain. There were numerous wavy braided rivers with veins of thin streams meandering through the never ending autumn colored mosaic of north country. A mottled patchwork with no rigid outlines as you would see flying over croplands. Sprawling scars trailing in and out of the spruce trees formed beginning-less and endless animal trails. I tried to capture any movement of life down there. Absolutely no sign of human life for miles and miles. And, wasn't that a moose crossing the river, that dark spot? Or maybe that's a bear up ahead by all those trees? It was hard to tell with my imagination and anticipation playing hide and seek with me. The continual 'show' presenting itself before me was mesmerizing like a campfire. I could not stop drinking it in. This inscrutable wilderness.

Sure, I had recently flown in the mail planes to small isolated villages when I taught with Yukon Flats School District, but where we were now headed was much further away from any settlement, and it was going to be my home with no other people around. No roads. No electricity. No communication. Readily accessible wilderness is an oxymoron. I'm relying on my memory here and don't have a lot of details from that first trip to our home in Arctic National Wildlife Refuge (ANWR), but I do remember knowing that this was going to be an adventure of a lifetime. I didn't know it at the time, but looking back now I can say that first trip flying to the trapline was the easiest it would ever be. Future trips would involve flying with dogs, a baby that's nursing and in diapers, and boat trips that would bring to mind the question, "What in the heck am I doing?" Those will be later stories – during this first plane ride, I thought: *my dreams are nothing compared to this...*

The feeling I had, walking up the trail to the cabin back in 1981 is the same as when walking it today, forty years later – a feeling deeper than any appearance can create, the cabin and surrounding space, the trail, trees, and creek. All the things my eyes reveal cannot touch what my heart feels.

Our Base Camp in ANWR.

The cabin itself was basically like any log cabin you might picture in your mind, but there were some unique particulars. The small windows were Plexiglas with shutters to wire up and keep out intruding critters. Hanging in the doorway was an old, partially chewed army blanket to keep out the wind, add some warmth in winter, and keep out pesky mosquitoes in warmer temperatures. The cabin walls were scattered with hanging equipment: traps, wire, small tools, surveyor tape, lanterns, rope, etc. All in all, your typical cabin in the woods. The inside of the dim cabin looked lived in, with an uneven wooden floor and a bit of a wood smoke odor. There was an old rusty barrel stove in the middle of the one room, a big old carved out log stump chair nestled on an aged braided rug by the window, and a spruce pole bed in one corner with a variety of blankets and an old army sleeping bag in disarray. Rooster patterned curtains hung in the window over the kitchen table which looked like a picnic table. I liked the table, as it had a little shelf on the underside to hold pots, pans, and other necessities. The sitting bench at the table liked me, as it tripped me every time I walked past it to build a fire in the Yukon stove, which was nestled on a smaller table in the kitchen corner. Nails positioned at varying heights held towels, coats, lanterns, rope, gloves, hats, socks, and anything else needing a place to hang. Several shelves were here and there, loaded with books, food staples, or tools.

But, the essence of our place in ANWR? If I were blind, I could feel it drawing me in. Just like the first time I met Bob. It was not his appearance, but his spirit that captivated me. Some unknown mystery. Same with Base Camp. The cabin itself, at first sight, is nothing spectacular. Base Camp, however, is far, far from the madding crowd. We are alone out here. The wilderness and all its four-legged, winged ones, water critters and rooted beings were our neighbors. That ignited my very soul. This is taking life to its profound richness, a place to uncover mysteries. The following is taken from my first letter home.

September 6th, 1981

I was in awe coming across the Interior to the Lower Brooks Range. So vast! No one for miles and miles. Then, spotting the cabin far below carpeted with surrounding trees...and a tiny speck of motion. Bob! My heart jumped.

The first day was more lack of feeling than lots of feeling. I was overwhelmed with the thought that this is my new home. Too many feelings piled up on each other, so I couldn't feel any of them at that first moment of arrival. Traver immediately started playing in the creek – just another "camp" to him. Since that first day, I'm loving it here more and more. So quiet, so beautiful. Indescribably delicious.

I've been here for about a week. We just had a five minute discussion trying to figure out what day it is, either Sunday or Monday. Kind of nice. Can't get those Monday morning blahs if I don't know what day it is, and don't even care. Time has flown by. We get up around 6:30 a.m. and to bed by 9 o'clock. Working most of the day, putting on a new roof and floor in the cabin. Lots of work and sleeping in a tent again. I'll be glad to move into the cabin. Three big meals every day. We had my favorite dinner tonight (for what is available): grayling fish eggs– fried. We fish every day for us and the dogs. We'll be glad when a caribou or moose comes by.

Today we walked about three and a half miles to a good fishing hole. I'm getting pretty good at using a spinning reel. Although we average 27 fish a day when Bob fishes, yesterday I went alone and got three. :)

There are signs of moose, caribou, bear, otter, and marten, but I haven't actually seen any of them. We're picking and cooking cranberries, too. I'm thinking about ice cream, "Tab" (pop), and a warm shower. No time for reading yet, and this is the first I've had a chance to write since I got here. Please pass this letter on to Gail and Jeff, as I won't have time to write to everyone. I think about you all. It seems so different to be so much farther away and no ability to communicate one-on-one. Oh, and our radio isn't set up yet. So we can't get any messages by way of Trapline Chatter.

It's so quiet here. That is probably what I notice most. Calm and quiet. A little wind once in a while. An occasional plane going by. A bird. And stillness.

We are on a winding little creek. A gorgeous spot. Bob says the clouds look like snow clouds. We've been having cold, sunny fall days and very cold nights.

Our two kittens are fat and happy. Traver is kept on the run chasing the poor things. He builds log cabins for them out of our firewood and tries to keep them confined. They are learning to escape and run when they see him coming. Kitty and Killer. Traver collects wood every day, waters the dogs, and helps me shovel dirt for the roof.

Well it's time to stop now until I can scrounge up another piece of paper to write on. The fire's getting low and it's hard to see. Almost dark at 8:45 p.m. No more paper to write on since all of our gear hasn't arrived yet. One more plane load coming in a week. Love, Nancy

Thinking back to that first week of transition into my new life, I don't remember the details, and I'm so thankful for the letters to supply those ingredients. But I do remember the general flavor, as that never really changed.

I was falling in love again. That feeling of bliss and abandonment to the moment. I had already fallen in love with Bob. This time, I was falling in love with my new life. It was simple, it was adventurous, and full of discovery waiting to happen. It was survival. We had to work and perform certain duties every day in order to live. We took care of ourselves and our own. We were free with no schedules, deadlines, or appointments. There were no roads, vehicles, banks, telephones, stores, or other humans. The nearest community was Fort Yukon which was an hour flight away. We were living along with nature– it is difficult to explain the feeling because it is very foreign to most people. It's not like going to a national park and camping, or even trekking off the road into the mountains for a week. Yes, you can get a taste of what it might be like, but to actually have your home among wildlife and being part of it all? The connection is captivating, precious, and fulfilling. I don't have the words to describe it. I am sorry for that. It is a treasure you'd have to find yourself. I have never loved life more deeply than those days living on the trapline.

As I am writing this book, 36 years later, my mind and emotions are traveling back to B.C. (Base Camp) and our first year together on the trapline. There are many letters that I'm re-reading in order to share our story– letters are mainly my focus and perception, as I'm relating the stories to you. I'll be telling you about what my life was like in ANWR, but it will be an easy puzzle to put together, with some imagination, to envision what Bob's life was like. You'll notice I don't get into much about the animals that Bob hunted and brought home. Much of the time, I was not present for that. I'll only describe how Traver (and later, Talicia) and I helped, or I'll simply write about how we used the animal for our necessities. I was never an avid hunter, but did consider it a necessary skill for living in the wilderness. Therefore, I do know how to hunt and care for the meat that is caught.

That first year I had no idea about how much preparation was necessary for the harsh, long winter and trapping. Bob kept me busy with so many things to learn. Skinning animals, patching tents and our canoe, repairing the cabin, and fishing. I loved all this – working with him and Trav side-by-side. There is much to be said about such a close and necessary relationship. There is kind of a natural flow to the division of labor as you work together. Efficiency, skill, strength, endurance, and interest all become part of the pattern that evolves through working together.

It didn't take me too long to realize all of the "little" things I had become used to and would miss at first. Simple things like a fresh piece of fruit, paper towels, toilet paper, a reading light, salad, paper to write on, ice cream. Part of the letter below to my mom and dad expresses, in my own words at the time, how I felt:

September, 1981

Ahhh, found two more pieces of paper in the cache. Cleaned that thing out yesterday– took all day. Today is the eleventh. The rest of our gear may be here tomorrow– yay! Something different to eat. Never thought I'd look forward to boxed macaroni and cheese, dried fruit, and cream of wheat. But I'll be really glad to taste all of them.

Well, since I last wrote, I've patched and painted the canoe, dug holes and got dirt for flowers to be planted, made several trips to the gear (one quarter mile away where the plane landed) and hauled stuff in, chinked the cabin, and all sorts of things. Our new floor is almost in and we should be moving into the cabin tomorrow. Bob's making bunk beds. Traver's all excited about having his own ladder to his bed.

One of our kitties got killed. Too confident and too close to one of the dogs.

Bob set some snares and some wolf traps. Hasn't snowed yet. Only two days of rain, so we can work all day. It's quite dark by 8:30 p.m. now. I've got to leave this letter once again— maybe finish by tomorrow. Bob's been working for an hour now, and I've been sitting by the warm fire— beginning to feel guilty (heaven forbid!). BACK TO WORK!

It's now the 12th and we figured the plane won't come today. No message on Trapline Chatter. My list of jobs today include: carry boards for the floor, dig the outhouse hole, patch the trapping tent, cook dried peas for lunch, cover chinking on outside of cabin, fish... and so on. My hands tingle during the day and I shake them a lot. I soak them every night and think of how good they'll feel when this hard work stops in a few days.

Gail, I brought that shirt you made me one year made out of dish rags... It sure is coming in handy! Oh yeah! Have to make a calendar too. We forgot to get one, so I've got to scrounge up some cardboard at least for September until our gear comes. Bob likes to keep track of weather, his catch, etc. We decided we'll start a log, too. It'll be interesting to read back on.

We just finished a breakfast of bannock with cranberries. Bob had coffee. I had lemongrass tea. We found an old can of Tang from two years ago. I give some to Trav as a treat every now and then, and we found some old army food-survival packets (or MRE's) with rations of chewing gum, which was a nice treat.

Saw some fresh tracks on a walk down the Coleen River. Bob showed us where one of his trails starts and we picked blueberries. Gotta go— plane and gear here. I love you all! –Nanc.

This transition to a foreign lifestyle could have been much more difficult for Traver and myself; however, we actually began the transition in Sitka, when we lived on the boat – a simple lifestyle. Then we spent a year in Stevens Village, where we lived in a cabin and experienced the grips of a harsh winter. But, in those circumstances we always had people around, a way to communicate with the outside world, and no real, immediate need to be in survival-mode each day. Stevens Village supplied my cabin with an oil-burning stove for heat– I didn't need to worry about firewood, although I did learn the process by helping others with the task. In Stevens Village, my water was supplied from trips to the Yukon River, filling up the 50-gallon drum in my cabin with chunks of river ice. I also learned that process, but, again, it wasn't my responsibility.

Being an itinerant teacher gave me the opportunity to get supplies, including food, if necessary. Most of the villages had at least one family store, which really amounted to a few shelves on someone's cabin wall with various canned vegetables, Pilot crackers*, and some kitchen needs, such as matches, salt, sugar, flour, etc. I also remember bacon was a favorite that villagers like to have on-hand.

Although I did not have to worry so much about heat, water, and food while living in Stevens Village, I did learn some necessary survival skills. It was with my two friends in Stevens Village, Ann and Lilly, that I learned to snare or shoot rabbits (with a '22), so we wouldn't be without meat.

Living on the trapline with Bob was definitely a step up to a life of more independence, freedom, simplicity, and adventure. It also encompassed more awareness and responsibility for survival and assets. I could feel a different way of thinking take over my mind. When you make a little mistake out in the woods, you learn quickly. If you make a big mistake, it could cost you your life.

Shelter, Water, and Food

Bob was quite confident living this trapline life in ANWR, so we trusted him. He knew what had to be done to prepare for winter and trapping. Shelter, water, and food are always necessary for survival but are simply more difficult and labor-intensive to obtain in the wilderness. I learned by watching Bob. He was not the greatest verbal communicator, and I think he might have believed Traver and I would somehow learn through osmosis. Making bannock, skinning a moose, and hooking up dogs were several things I learned by watching Bob. When there was a chimney fire in my early days of tending the Yukon stove, Bob couldn't understand how I let that happen! Guess what? From that chimney fire, I learned that I needed to pay attention to the draft and temperature I created with my fire building. It never happened again.

As for winterizing the cabin, Trav and I learned the basics of chinking with moss, which is then covered with a layer of spruce bark strips or thin pieces of wood to hold in the moss. If there were leaks in the roof, we had to do repairs with moss, plastic, and spruce poles. Depending on the animal critters that had paid a visit while we were away, there might be necessary mending on cabin windows, door, or cache.

 Another daily chore for Traver was collecting fire-starter (birch bark and small twigs), as well as collecting and stacking the firewood Bob and I would cut. Bob would cut down a dead tree, I would de-limb it, and after Bob bucked it up, we would all carry smaller pieces to the cabin. When the snow fell, our dogs would haul the bulk of it to the cabin. Fall time was beautiful, and it was so exhilarating working together outside. We all enjoyed those days.

Our meals varied little at first. No time to cook with so much attention on building our cabin, preparing for winter, and we usually had no meat yet. We would eat a lot of fish in the fall, grains, and some berries or other wild veggies, such as Eskimo potato and other root plants. Snaring rabbits didn't start until the snow fell. There were grouse around, though, and we were thankful for those delicious gifts. The closer time got to winter's grip, the more we dreamed of steak, baked ribs, or moose stew... Treks down the trail to the river wore a familiar pathway to get water. If you've never had fresh, uncontaminated water, you do not know what you're missing. It was an easy dip into the river with a five-gallon bucket and we had an unlimited supply of this treasure. Drinking water, cooking water, cleaning water, dish water, dog water, and bath water. Precious stuff not to be taken for granted– especially when winter came and the river would freeze, and not to inches thick, but feet thick. That will be another story!

Meanwhile, when I managed to find time, I continued writing letters to my family. Below is one from September of 1981.

September 20th, 1981

Well, I last wrote a week ago when our gear arrived. It was really nice seeing some different faces around here: the pilot, Joe Mattie (our recent new friend) and his wife, Sandy. Joe is a fur-buyer who flies trappers and hunters in and out of the Bush. In winter he buys and sells furs. So, Bob is also business-buddies with him. Sandy retired from her air traffic control job and is working with Joe to Develop their business, Alaska Raw Fur Company. We may join them next spring getting logs for our cabin and theirs. Anyway, our gear arrived and much to our delight; we had macaroni and cheese for dinner– and some peanut butter too!

Since that day, we've gotten lots done (as I look at the calendar I made). Our new four to five-inch thick ripped-board floor is done, and we moved in on September 13th. It's quite a nice and cozy cabin and has been fun adding little things that you sent us. Curtains from material Jeff sent, mugs and a patchwork tablecloth from mom, stones and books from Gail, and a little music box (Traver's) from Aunt Dorothy. So you see, I have lots of comforts here for me.

It's so nice to be inside and cozy. I'm learning to cook on the Yukon stove; a rectangle-shaped box, 2.5' by 1'. This is the smaller stove set up chest height in the kitchen area for cooking on, and also for getting a quick fire going in the mornings. We have starch (or carbohydrates) three times a day– what a change in my diet! My body is getting stronger and tighter. I like being able to eat fry-bread, macaroni and cheese, and rice... and lots of it. We still usually have fish at night, sometimes fillet and sometimes patties. I know I talk about food a lot, but I think about it a lot: what to scrounge up a little different-tasting three times a day.

It's pretty out today. It snowed and the wind blew all day yesterday. We woke up to a white carpeted ground and winter wonderland. Bob says the animals will start moving now and we'll have a moose or caribou by the end of the month.

Last Sunday we took a walk downriver to the old trapper's cabin. His name was Ed; he was a trapper here from 1911 to 1972 and raised three kids here too. Bob heard about Ed while in Fort Yukon and this is what drew him to his present home off the Coleen River. Bob has taken over Ed's old trapline. But our cabin is about two miles up from Ed's place.

Ed became a part of our family in many ways. We visited his cabin, borrowed his magazines, and told each other our fantasized stories about what we thought his family was like. The baby carriage left behind by his daughters was cherished by our family for years to come.

Yes, the field trips to Ed's place were much looked forward to each year, and I am sure Ed was also pleased. Ed would sometimes visit us at night when all was quiet, and not a creature was stirring– not even a mouse. All of a sudden, the door might creak open or something would clang on the window shutter... We would all look up at each other and wonder, "What? What is that?" And Bob would perkily say "It's Ed!" We'd all have a good howl before settling down again.

Ed's old cabin.

Below, another letter continues:

We got two grouse since last week, too. Very tasty. On the 18th, a sunny day, we had to float our big three hundred pound stove down to camp from where the plane left it off, maybe half a mile. This new stove will be the main heating source for the cabin which is replacing the 50 gallon barrel that Bob has used until now. It will be much more efficient. We tied logs together, loaded the stove, and Bob steered it with his little ratting canoe* and rope. I watched from the shore with fingers crossed. He made it and we rolled it into camp from the creek.

Bob floating a 300 pound stove downriver. to Base Camp.

I'm building a frame for an outhouse, which will be covered with visqueen*. I'm also pulling hairs from a moose hide to be used on our toboggans, which Bob is in the process of making now. The hide must be soaked in the creek for five days or so, hair pulled out, and the process repeated.

We lose 7 minutes of daylight every day. It seems to happen so quickly. A Fairbanks weather report just came on and said, "looks like winter is finally here." It's only September 20th!

Well, it's time to start another day. It's 9:30 a.m.– dishes and breakfast done. There's no time at night to write. I'm too tired. I'm up usually 2-3 times during the night with my shaking hands. I think I have arthritis, or whatever. When the wet weather comes, I'm in agony. You know how you learn to live with certain hassles, but I'll be glad when December comes and I can hopefully get one wrist taken care of.

Despite my hands, the three of us are doing fine. Learning more about each other day by day. I just said to Bob last night how close you get to someone FAST out here. And he said, "Well, you kind of have to."

Hey, will you please save these letters? I don't have time or energy to keep a log like this– so, after the letters are passed around or mimeographed, or whatever, just stash this for me, o.k.? Thanks.

September 29:

Snowing everyday now. Looks like winter's here. Bob thought it would be two more weeks away, but the creek's freezing up, snow is accumulating, and Fairbanks is having cold weather too.

The outhouse is done, we got a porch up, winter wood is cut, toboggan built, moose skin scraped of hair (horrible, horrible, time-consuming job).

October 1:

No moose yet, but Bob got a grouse this morning that was hanging around our cache. He put it in the cabin to see what the cat would do. I don't know if it was the cat or the grouse that was more scared. Traver thoroughly enjoyed the show.

Today we started clearing a toboggan trail through and around the backwoods for a practice run and to use for hauling our wood back. Getting excited for the first toboggan run. Can't believe Bob starts trapping in two weeks. There's so much to do everyday now, but nothing demanding. It's so nice to be able to nap or read or walk when I want to. No schedule.

Now I'm reading Hunters of the Northern Forest, and Bob's reading The Mad Trapper of Mud River, which is a true, and I guess, quite unforgettable story. That one's next for me. Traver's doing little games from a book, Shapes and Sizes, you gave him, Mom. He's really into it.

I'm also knitting Bob a pair of socks in my "spare" time. It's been around thirty degrees, on average, lately. Only a small portion of the creek is left unfrozen. So we have to go quite a-ways to fish. I got twelve today. Bob got sixty fish the other day. I don't remember if I told you, but some fish are for us, some are dried for dog food, some are cooked for dog food, and some are cut in pieces, sitting in a can to rot for bait. Lots of fox and wolf tracks around here.

As you can imagine from reading my letters, fishing was an important aspect of our life, especially during the transition period between when we arrived in ANWR and trapping season began. We relied on fish to feed ourselves and our dogs. Below is a story Bob wrote in the few years before he passed. You'll notice he mentions Talicia, our daughter, who was born later on:

Getting Fish

When I first got to the Coleen, I went fishing. Fishing was excellent. You would catch a grayling on every one to three casts. I had a dog team at the time and had to fish for them. Most days I caught 20 to 30 grayling for the team. I would heat up a five gallon bucket with cut up fish, water, and add the rice or cornmeal to give them starch and protein. I also had five gallon buckets of tallow and they got an egg sized portion every day. This kept them in good shape and they kept their weight on.

During the trapping season, they would eat all the fur animal carcasses that I had caught. Sometimes they would get a whole marten carcass. Sometimes one half a carcass, but they always got the rice and the fat. Early on, it was still possible to shoot caribou for the dog team. That changed in later years.

I remember shooting a caribou for the dogs once, when I was out trapping. I brought the carcass home, cut it up into two pound chunks. These were left outside to freeze and were for the dogs. A caribou would only last three to four days.

Fishing at freeze up was rather exciting. Sure, I switched at freeze up and ended open channel fishing. I had a big hole half mile upriver. And a big fish bowl just downriver from camp. In these fish holes would be hundreds of grayling. I would stand on the ice and pull out up to 300 grayling in a couple hours. They would be piled up and I'd have to make several trips carrying them back to the camp. I fished at one hole the first day then walked up river to the next hole the following day. After a day's rest, the hole would be full again. You could look in the river and see the fish milling about. Wall-to-wall fish. I think they came downriver and wintered in these holes, or south to the Porcupine River. I don't know.

There were also several pike in the area. I remember taking one hundred from the river close to camp every year. I never caught pike north of basecamp. I believe these fish came upriver from the Porcupine or Yukon. Some were small, some very large. I went upriver to the fishing hole with Nancy, Traver, and Talicia. There was a huge pike just offshore where we were fishing. I wanted a bag full of grayling for the dogs to eat. I didn't want that one big fish, but Traver had to get that fish. I told him if he caught that fish he would have to carry it to camp. He said that was okay. He worked on that pike, ended up catching him, killed him, and brought him to shore. The pike was almost as big as he was, and he dragged it all the way home.

Some days I had to go farther from the camp to find fish. I guess I was a mile or two from camp sometimes before I got my limit of dog food. Twenty to thirty fish was always a load to carry. They were in a burlap or plastic bag swung over my shoulder. It was a job just carrying them, but necessary. After several years, I did obtain a boat. That increased my range for fishing.

The first years with all the family out there, we did eat grayling several times a week, maybe even more than that. Nancy was a very good cook, but the kids got tired of fish. Sometimes that was the only protein we had when the caribou weren't around yet. If the moose weren't breeding yet, it was fish. Or, if we were lucky, we snared a rabbit.

The first few years, I had a small gillnet. I set that up at Base Camp. I had built a small rat canoe so I could check the gillnet easily. I remember catching the fish, pike, grayling, and even some salmon in the creek. There was no salmon run in the Coleen river. It was years before they showed up in any numbers. That happened very rarely. Once every ten years or so. Most years, I could pick 5 to 10 salmon along the river, close to camp, that was it. But some years, they would congregate in the hole and I could see them in larger numbers. I don't think I ever pulled in more than 20 salmon. You would see a dead salmon every mile or so on the riverbank. These salmon were dog salmon* in bad shape. They were used for bait. They weren't even in good enough shape for dog food.

Besides the continual need to fish and hunt, winter was not going to hold off until we were ready for it. There was a continual line up of learning experiences happening for Trav and me as Bob led us onward, rapidly approaching the trapping season.

October 10, 1981

Ahhhh... I'm just full to my heart's and belly's content. We're all fat and happy today. Bob got a caribou bull today. Traver and I saw tracks on the creek while we were looking for a sliding place. Told Bob and off he went. He had to cross the river to get it, then he returned to pick Trav and me up so we could go see it and watch him skin it. No details Mom, but it was all very interesting and a very beautiful and large animal. Bob says it weighed about 250 lbs. So we had caribou heart and liver for dinner. I was beginning to think we were going to be living on bannock, rice, and fish. Not many rabbits running around yet, but we just cut a bunch of willows in front along the bank of the creek to plant berry bushes, and some rabbits may come in now.

So, let me catch you up since Oct. 1st: October 2nd we took our first toboggan run. Bob went around about four times. Then I tried it – I was beat after one run. I'll be building up some stamina this winter. While Bob's off on the toboggan, I have a stick in my hand to keep the dogs quiet. When the dogs think I'm not looking, or I'm far enough away, they'll try to sneak in a few whines and howls. So, I turned around and lift the stick and the whining and howling turn immediately into yawns! It's quite humorous.

So, anyway October 2nd– first toboggan run. We've also gotten five grouse since then and almost one foot of snow. On October 5th the creek was completely frozen over and ice was running down the river, so we have been ice fishing through chopped ice six inches thick. Traver has gotten the most so far, but I think we're all fished out now.

Traver ice fishing.

On October 4th, I was fishing and looked up to see a red fox on the other side of the river. I stared and watched. He kept going. Ten minutes later he returned, saw me, and stared back, then kept going. He crossed back and forth a couple more times. That was the first time I thought, "What is trapping going to be like?"

On October 6th we walked down to Ed's old cabin.
October 7th Our second kitty died.
October 8th we saw moose tracks about one week old way up the creek where we took a walk. Next year we must bring ice skates!

October 9th Bob finished our new 'pew' for the cabin. A large seat for against the back wall.

And then today– a good day! I wake up every morning glad to be here. I wouldn't want to be any place else right now. I do think a lot about family and friends – more so than ever before.

I'll be glad to talk with all of you over the Christmas holidays. I'll wait for a Trapline Chatter message if you send one.

Traver's been very enjoyable since we've all settled in here. He and Bob have established a relationship now and we're all getting along and enjoying each other's company. I'm going to play a game of "fish" now with Trav, so goodnight.

October 11:

Bob's finishing my toboggan. Traver is supposed to be getting wood, but he's stalling as usual and watching Bob. We just saw a lemming outside the door. I'm making yogurt, preparing menus, enjoying the cabin to myself. Knitting socks, reading, and going through my Moosewood Cookbook. My cooking has been quite creative lately. We crave different tastes after so much bannock, fish, and rice. So this cookbook has been great for ideas. I've been creating crepes, pizza, falafels, curry dishes, yogurt dishes, all with ingredients we have. Everything is "mock" – mock pizza, mock falafel, but good. And fun for me too. Bob cooks once in a while.

The work gets divided pretty naturally. I do all the wash – I don't mind. He would do it (as well as dishes) if I didn't, but not as often. I take a few articles of clothes a day, heat water, use my homemade plunger (a funnel and an old broomstick) and plunge. Then, down to the creek, crack a hole in the 7-inch thick ice, and rinse several times. I think of myself out there in the middle of so much vastness...

There is about a foot of snow now. Trapping starts soon.

October 24th:

I just went out to see if I could help the boys. Bob just cut down a dead tree for firewood. Traver is stacking up all the branches for a fire. They don't need me, so I can get back to the writing I've been meaning to do for a few days. I've been sewing a lot. Getting ready for the cold. Ruffs on our parkas, skin books, mitten covers for Trav.

Bob's getting "antsy." He wants to get trapping but it's just not cold enough yet. Five days ago it got to five degrees but it's warming again. The river is now half frozen across. It's interesting that on the bottom of the river, there is ice too, yet, the water still flows on top. We have our own theories about that but none are certain. It just looks neat, like a bunch of clouds under us as we canoe across.

So, I left off way back on October 11th. That's when we started catching rabbits. Traver and I go out daily now to check our snares. Trav still catches an occasional fish through the ice. I gave it up. The week of the 12th, when it was quite warm, I caught 100 fish on the river. That was a busy week. We also got two more caribou. We have all the hides stretched and fleshed, ready for use at our tent camp (to sleep on) when we go.

Bob finished a small toboggan for Trav and me. I took the dogs across the creek for about a three mile run. I know I was more exhausted at the end than the dogs were. It was beautiful, though. I'm ready to get on the trails, too. There's not much left in the way of work to be done around here now. Trav and I made a snowman on a creek and dressed it up. We were going to make a fort but it got too cold. The snow won't stick together to make any shape.

Running out of paperbacks to read. If you're getting rid of any, send them our way. We could use a bunch!

90

Now for the exciting event of October 19th. We went down to where we had cached one of the caribou (couldn't bring it back yet because the river's not frozen enough for the dogs to run on) – only to find the caribou all eaten up! Only a few bones, antlers, and part of a skull left. And, BIG grizzly bear tracks leading to and from. Gave me the chills! Bob followed the tracks a mile down river where the bear crossed to the other side. So we're one caribou short, except for the hide. Then, on October 21st, Trav and I were off setting rabbit snares across the creek from our cabin and we spotted the bear tracks again. The first thing I noticed was that they were not fresh, so I didn't get the chills running up and down my back. We followed the tracks back across the creek and within 200 yards of camp where he then headed out back down over the hills towards where we had the caribou cached. We figured the tracks were from the same day he went from there to the caribou he found. I couldn't believe what that bear walked right over and through (as we followed his tracks.) All kinds of brush, small trees, stumps, and ditches, and when we got to the creek we saw where the ice broke and he fell in. The tracks were awesome. As Bob wrote in his journal that he sends home: "If you bow your legs way out and take big steps you'd be walking like that fat sucker." The hind foot was a foot or so long and the front pad was five inches across; we may see him again. We see other tracks on the creek and river every now and then, like otter. I sure would like to watch them at play sometime.

I think about what everyone will be doing on Thanksgiving and Christmas. I've started thinking about decorations and how we'll celebrate. After all, it is October and we've heard Christmas commercials on the radio already.

There probably won't be a plane in now until we get picked up. Makes it easier to write about the bear tracks this way – and other things – so by the time you'll get this, you'll know all is well. Ha! Knock on wood!

October 25th:

We may be having company tomorrow. We heard on Trapline Chatter last night that our pilot friend is delivering some school supplies to Heimo (who traps north of here). Bob thinks that John will stop by to say hello. I'm hoping so. I want my mail. Bob's hoping John will bring some beer.

So, maybe you'll get this unexpectedly. I hope so. Send it on to Gail and Jeff. It's hard not knowing what's going on in your lives. I'll be anxious to catch up with you on lots of stuff. So I'll get this ready for the mail now.
Love to all of you, from Nanc and Trav

Trav did some scribbles to send in this letter and I interpreted what he said as, "We built a cache. And this is a cabin we live in and we'll leave there in the 'fwing' (spring) time. And I'll be 5 and I'll have a b.b. gun and a jack knife."

Dogs

Because the dogs played such an integral part in our lives, I thought they deserved some space. Below are the dogs we had with us that first season together in ANWR:

Griz: the great faithful female lead* that gave us some awesome puppies

Rocky: solid "wheel" dog

Boulder: all around dependable

Boris: brother to Odin, trained later as a weight puller – a real clown

Odin: brother to Boris, trained later as a weight puller – another clown

Strider: a little bit of an outsider, a good companion, handsome fella

Bear: smaller, jet black, and a good natured lead that Trav could handle

Heimo: named after Bob's friend, Heimo

Huck: steady guy that worked well with the team, although he was new

Leo: a bit goofy and needing a lot of direction, also new to team

Thinking back to that year, I couldn't remember all the dogs names, but Bob had a list in his log book with names of dogs and the years they were with him. Bob read up on dog teams, learning and experimenting as he went along. They were a part of the lifestyle he wanted as a trapper. Bob and his dog team had a true partnership. They relied on him, and he relied on them. The list started in 1972 and the last entry says 12/27/89...End of dogs. Teams, that is. That's when the snow machines took over. But we always had a dog or two. Bob wouldn't be without man's best friend!

Not only were the dogs essential to Bob's trapping, but they played many roles as part of our family. We could not have gotten from cabin to cabin, or cabin to tent, without the dogs. They were our transportation across the rivers, tundra, and woodlands. We had food, gear, and children that needed to be hauled from place to place. The dogs were working machines that did not break down on us. We relied on them to guide us over "iffy" river ice, and to get us where we needed to go if it got a bit dark or the trail became hidden. Hauling firewood would have taken forever if not for the dogs. And they loved to work! They would help us haul water, check tracks, traps and snares lines, and train new pups.

Traver and I hauling water in the dusky hours with the dog team.

Living in the bush, with no other neighbors, the dogs provided companionship, friendship, and playmates for all of us. Everyone enjoyed the dogs' company in one way or another. Even Bob would get playful with the dogs. One day he draped a bear hide over his head and made his way through the dog yard growling and lumbering to get some reaction. And of course the dogs all loved some playful interaction.

Bob wearing a bear hide into the dog yard to tease the dogs.

Traver grew up with the dogs. He began a relationship with them when his chore was to feed and water them. Since these dogs are not house pets, they are chained to their dog houses, and although we would run them almost daily, they got very excited to have any company in the dog yard. Trav got knocked around during those earlier days, as the dogs weighed more than he did. As he grew, he became smarter and could also handle himself better. Bob named Traver "Twitch" when he was very young because Traver was a normal, curious, energetic boy stuck in a cabin during winter for a lot of the day. By evening, Bob would say "Twitch – go play with the dogs!" Traver was given a red lantern and off he'd go to the dog yard. Pitch dark and cold, at first Traver was apprehensive. After quite a while of quiet cabin time, I went out to see what was going on. Trav was snuggled with Rocky in the doghouse and said he didn't want to come back inside. That was the beginning of a close relationship between Trav and the dogs.

Traver in the dog yard – he and the dogs loved one another.

We always felt safer with the dogs in the yard. They would alert us to any abnormal activity. The dogs were excellent guards, and teachers too. Just as adults learn a great deal from very small children, the same goes with dogs. They have a lot to teach us if we pay attention.

By November, our base camp had truly become comfortable for us and felt like home. We had established roles and routines, figured out our survival needs, and were enjoying the satisfying feeling of work well done. Fall, however, was racing by and winter activities were to begin soon. There was never a dull moment that time of year, which you can see from my letters at the time:

November 1, 1981

Hi! Well, the plane did get here. A few days later than expected, but our mail went out. The pilot didn't bring our mail, however. Let's see, during the last week of October the river finally froze. It's about zero but getting colder all day today. Bob started trapping on Oct. 28. He's setting on three trails now. Last night, we celebrated Halloween, and I made some cookies.

I have my own 'team' of dogs. All the new ones! My 'lead' ⋆ is Bear. Then, Huck, Heimo, and Strider. I was nervous, or, rather, not confident, the first couple of times. Now things are going pretty good. We have less than eight hours of daylight. It's dark by 3:30.

Finished knitting a pair of mittens. Out of many mistakes, I got my own scatter-brained pattern. Trav gets a new knitted hat and mittens for Christmas. It's hard to write, not having questions to answer or ask, and not knowing what you're doing or what you want to hear about.

Traver made his own ski out of a piece of wood and found two sticks for poles. He's out there every day becoming quite the skier. I made him a nice pair of moose hide mittens trimmed with beaver. His hands will be really warm.

Well, Trav and I sort of have a routine set up now with ourselves. In the morning, he exercises with me (what a joke). Then breakfast. Usually bannock or oatmeal. Then Bob leaves for trapping. After I clean up, Trav and I run the dogs out to one of our rabbit snare lines. I'm trying to get Trav in the back of the toboggan now because he gets cold sitting all the time. We 'lost' the dogs twice last week. I usually tie them to a tree when I stop to check snares. They are just learning commands. So, my leader didn't turn on the river the right way. I had to walk up to the front of the line and they were so excited to go, they did just that! Left me behind. Yelling and screaming. And Traver riding in the toboggan yelling and screaming... for me! He got smart and rolled out. We finally caught them. They were trapped and tangled in the willows. We checked snares, and then on the way back, I tied the dogs to a tree while I was checking a snare. There are no big trees on the riverbank, in the willows where we set snares, so I tied the dogs to a small, dead tree. They pulled the tree up, took off, and dragged the tree a while (we found it later on the trail). The dogs then raced the rest of the way home. We walked. At least Traver was very warm that day.

We're seeing lots of coyote tracks near camp. That guy is getting quite curious.

We're also making ice cream with snow. Very good! Thick milk (from dry milk powder), vanilla, honey, and lots of snow. Tomorrow I'll make a quick chess set for us. Checkers and gin rummy aren't challenging enough.

One of our dogs, Griz (Bob's leader), is pregnant! She'll probably have pups in December sometime. Merry Christmas, Griz! No bear tracks lately. He must be in his den. There are still river otter tracks, though. I'm learning a lot about these animals by watching, listening to Bob, and going out on my own. I always carry a 9mm automatic. A present Bob got from his brother this summer.

My life is very fulfilling here. It's the longest period of time I can remember getting up ready and thankful for a new day – and then very tired and ready for bed at night. A good feeling. Alive! But I haven't gotten away from ALL hassles here. Running dogs can be a hassle. I get anxious and nervous sometimes, but I'm also getting better at controlling the team. Mostly, my dogs are very enjoyable.

I do think about all of you and will be so ready to get caught up on things in Fairbanks next month.

We have begun plans for the 'cabin' on our land outside Fairbanks. Just thoughts right now.

I don't know how close you are to making plans for visiting next August, but to let you in on our latest plan, we want to be back out here in the woods by mid-August. So, if you can, think in terms of first two weeks in August. That would be better for us. Going to make some fruit pudding now. Bye bye.

November 15:

Hi! We just returned from a four-day trip up river, about twenty miles north of here to the upper camp, where Bob is using another of Ed's old cabins. It was fun. We took our dog teams – it took three and a half hours to get there. We had some struggles with the dogs at first, and Traver was crying because he couldn't walk around and keep warm. But the trip back was real nice. And living in a different place for three days was good, too. We've been having clear, tranquil nights and a moon at its peak of fullness; so lovely. Haven't seen many northern lights though. I tried to take a few pictures but need a new battery for my light meter, so I may not get any.

We ate rabbits that I caught for three days, so we're anxious for game. Real meat now. Having ribs tonight. Ahhhh, it feels good to be home again. My legs are aching, but my thighs are getting hard as rocks. Traver is always asking us to feel his muscles. He's developing a few in his arms; not quite the 'hard balls' (as Traver calls them) that Bob has in his.

Before I left town, my friend Trish ordered us a bunch of wool from Greece (beautiful and low-priced). Trish just sent a Trapline Chatter message that the yarn arrived and looked like *a two-hundred pound sack of potatoes. So, now I'll have lots of yarn for projects. My poor hands.*

Hey Mom, it's getting near Christmas, and I find myself thinking about the goodies we used to eat as a family. If this letter gets to you in time to make some 'snowballs' and send them, please do! My mouth waters just thinking about them. I'm sure I'll be thinking of all of you around that time. Jeff, I brought the Ranger Rick's Holiday Book for Trav to use this year, he will love it. Thank you. I've got stockings for all of us. I'm looking forward to Christmas here.

Well, time to play my regular game of cards with Traver. Either fish or steal the bundle. He's getting quite good at both of them. Oh, as far as trapping goes, before we came out, I told Bob that I wasn't interested in actually trapping myself, and I reinforced that statement again recently. Snaring rabbits for food is as much as I'll probably get into trapping. Bob got a red fox on the way to the upper cabin last week. Beautiful animal. I'm living differently way up here, and it requires a different way of thinking too. Since living away from civilization, I've noticed my ways of thinking are changing. They have to. But I'm still me.

November 22:

Hi, just got back from another trip to the upper cabin. We had ptarmigan* for dinner while there. It was delicious! Hope to get one for Thanksgiving this coming week. Very pleasant trip we had. I bundled Trav up so well... stuffed him in a sleeping bag. He kept warm and quiet all the way home. This trip, it went down to minus twenty. And we now have less than six hours of light per day. On Saturday, we took a nice hike up a small creek bed. It was great walking up the ravine, reminded me of when we used to take Tracey (our old dog) to the park in the hills. Everyone remembers that, don't they?

Traver bundled up and ready for a trip to the upper cabin.

Well, I'm feeling pretty ready for a trip into town soon. Traver's starting to get geared for the trip back to see his dad.

The northern lights were out last night. So beautiful. Dancing, colored lights. They make my heart sing and I feel so lucky to experience them.

November 26:

Happy Thanksgiving! Thinking of you all. It's very quiet here.

November 28:

Hi, well, 2:30pm and it's dark out. Bob has gone up to the upper cabin. Trav and I stayed here in case Griz has her pups. Trav and I also took a new dog, Leo, out to train him, running with two other dogs pulling the toboggan. Maybe next week we can all go to the upper cabin. Thanksgiving was quiet and pleasant. Bob took the day off from trapping. We were all lazy. Got up at 9:00, had cinnamon rolls, then rabbit for lunch and pizza for dinner. We're out of caribou meat now. It's rabbit and ptarmigan when we get it.

Yesterday I started writing letters to other people so I'll be able to mail them when we get to town. I have about 25 letters to write. This letter could end anytime without notice... Bob thinks John might stop by within a month. If so, you'll get this letter. If not, you'll get it after I talk to you next month.

December 7:

Hi! Well, today was just like a holiday here. Wonderful! We were on our way back from the cabin up north and halfway back we heard a plane. It's John! Bob's pilot friend. He landed in front of us on the river and talked a while. Said he dropped off some of Bob's dog food, beans, and MAIL! YIPPEE! I'd been carrying your last letter with me, and one for Tim, just in case John came, but I had no addresses on the envelopes and no pen with me. John had a pencil with no lead showing, so Bob chewed it off. I do hope you get the shabbily addressed letter I sent off with John today. I'll find out in three weeks. Anyway, needless to say, we rushed home, mushed home as fast as we could get the dogs to go. We took the puppies with us this last trip. They were all upside down, warm and comfy with a caribou hide. They've grown so fast in ten days. Eyes should be opening soon. And they are finally quiet at night.

Well, as I was saying, today was like a holiday. We rushed in, got the fires going, I got water, we threw our junk inside the door and I put some soup on the stove. Besides the dog food and beans, there was a big sack of mail. Mostly magazines of Bob's and junk, but it will ALL be fun to look at. Bob's mom sent four boxes because Bob told her there'd be a plane before

Christmas sometime. We couldn't wait and dug right into all of them. The first was presents for us. Bob said, "We better save them." I said, "HA!" I saw the Legos for Traver and we opened everything. So Trav is busy now with Legos and a coloring book (he needed something different). I got a beautiful green sweater that Eleanor (Bob's mom) knit. And Bob got a shirt. Then, THE FOOD! Oh, we went crazy. She sent three loaves of fruit cake, which I don't particularly care for, but we scarfed one right down (and it was good!). And some cracker barrel cheese. Bob had suggested nuts, and we got those too. We also got a can of those butter cookies, a box of potato pancake mix, potato dumplings, snackin' cake, and figs.

Well, I ate too many cookies, some cheese, bread, and now I've spoiled myself for dinner. I'll never learn! There was also hot chocolate mix, which I had a little of, and used for flavoring our ice cream since the vanilla was gone. Oh, and some butter, which was good because I was scrounging the last of ours that we had and using it only for special occasions. So, we have had one heck of a good day! And my letter to you got out, so you'll be more up to date. I got your five letters and one from a friend I hadn't heard from in over a year. I'm excited about writing even though you won't get this until after I've talked to all of you. Some things I'm dying to talk about.

Oh, I'm sorry I never informed you more about my hands, and you mentioned my hands in all of your letters. I'm okay. I usually only wake up once a night, I get up and go pee, shake my hands a bit and that's that. I have to sleep on my back all the time though because other positions give me the problem – circulation cut off I guess. So don't worry about that. I'm fine. Next year we hope to, as I said, leave town earlier and fish on the way up for salmon. We'll dry it for winter and Bob says we can get a moose and dry it on the way up too. He's looking at pricing and thinking about a boat now. He knows a guy who can help him build it cheaply. A good one, too. It's a two-week boat trip up here and would be very profitable and fun.

Trav's asleep and Bob's sipping the Kahlua his folks sent. There wasn't any beer on the plane. Bob's happy with his bottle. None of us have been sick, until Bob's toothache last week, which led to a sore throat that I also got. Bob says we'll get to town and catch a cold within two days.

Just heard the news. It's finally going down to about 25 below. About time. It's been so mild.

Oh Mom, before I forget, I want you to know I think of you every morning – out in the outhouse – all of your advice about "regulation," well, I'm regulated! By no choice of my own, every morning early, so I can't even "sleep in." Did I tell you one of Trav's jobs is to knock down the stalagmite in our outhouse? He loves it! And I spelled that word right, 'cause I looked it up, Dad!

I enjoyed hearing from you Dad and am happy to know you are enjoying your present life, in all its certain little ways. I'm happy to hear when someone really finds peace and contentment and enjoyment. Mom, I'd be anxious to see the baskets you've been making and if you have some good ideas – I didn't get to do any of that this fall. Too busy. But I'm planning it for next fall. And I'm going to use various grasses again. But also maybe some animal teeth and porcupine quills for frills. Bob and I are collecting materials to use for jewelry and my baskets: teeth (boiling marten and fox heads to get them), porcupine quills I'm pulling, owl claws, and feathers.

By the way, Traver enjoyed the little faces you drew at the end of your letter to him, Mom, and he loved answering the questions you had; asking him about the chores he does, fishing, and the animals he sees. Dad, your last letter hit some things on the nose for me. There is little room for error in judgment here and situations can be life and death matters. It's taken a little while to realize that. But I do. And I live my life knowing it. That's why I said before, 'my thinking has changed' living here. I'm not afraid to go out in the woods alone, way out in the middle of nowhere – but I am very cautious and aware, and know I have to be. When Bob goes off to tent camp for the night, I realize even more how much I have to depend on myself. Bob is always willing to help and show me things. He does things for me that I can do, but that frustrate me – like chopping the waterhole – two feet of ice – that's a pain in the ass. So he does it. But when I'm learning something, he makes me learn it. Or tells me information in a causal way, not threatening – like one day, I went down to Ed's place to check my rabbit snares, and Bob had a wolf snare set up across the river down there. He asked me to set it for him, and very generally told me how, leaving it up to my common sense to figure it out. I thought he might get real specific because he wanted a good snare set. I set it! Just fine.

Even with the winter being quite mild so far, Bob's catch has been good. He figured with the fur he has, and the hours he has worked, he's made $18.50 an hour. Not bad! Anyway, getting back to it… anybody could live like this, if they wanted to. I'm just glad everyone doesn't want to. Then I probably couldn't – here, anyway.

Well, my son leaves me again shortly to see his Dad. I have mixed emotions. He's been talking nonstop for the last month or so, vying for all my attention. When Bob's away for the day, it's not so much. I don't know if that's just a 'normal' thing for his age, or if it's a good time for Traver to be one-on-one again with his Dad. Bob is more of an older brother to Traver. He leaves discipline to me, until he thinks I'm too lenient, then he enters the picture. I have a tendency to be too lenient, but I'm learning from all these dogs we have. Anyway, Trav's looking forward to seeing his Dad. He also wants to see cartoons, ride his bike, go to school, and see his friends. He has a bow and arrow at both cabins and is always on the lookout for grouse and ptarmigan (Alaska state bird). Hasn't gotten any weasel in his three traps, but looks daily. Oh, he's growing up! He gets quite "smart-assy" sometimes. We'll certainly miss him around here. (Crap, now I'll have to bring in the firewood!)

Trav comes up with some good ones. When I make bannock (bread), I have it 'raising' in the pan. The other day, when I had something else in the pan, maybe yogurt or ??, Trav asked if it was 'raising.' It was funny at the time trying to figure out what he was talking about.

Tonight, we were going to wash our hair, but the shampoo's not thawed yet. Did you ever have to wait for your shampoo to thaw? It froze when we were away at the upper cabin.

Hey, Bob's Mom wrote a letter and said she had called you to get our address. Well, funny thing, I felt she might be calling you, but for different reasons. Just from knowing Eleanor, I feel she would want to call and reassure you that things are okay out here. I know Eleanor has gone through a lot of worries over Bob and is so glad that I was coming out here with him. So, how was your conversation? None of your letters mentioned it, which makes me wonder.

December 11:

Well, yesterday I knew it was going to be cold. I walked down to Ed's place and on the way I had to thaw out my eyelashes three times. I wore my face mask because of the wind and cold. My breath caused all the condensation. My eyes were watering from the wind, and then the tears froze and if I blinked too slowly, my eyes would freeze shut. Other than that, the walk down was beautiful. Almost a full moon – big, bright, orange ball floating above the white icing of a river and darkness of the river banks. Plus, early sunset. So beautiful. One of the many signs I couldn't capture in a photograph.

106

Last week at the upper cabin, when Trav and I went up in the morning, there were fresh wolf tracks. We like to follow tracks and 'read' the story being told. It looks so nice when it's really cold, and all the trees are covered with snow and crystals form. It looks like layers and layers of tiny snowflakes stuck together, and if you touch them it would be crystals tinkling.

We may go back to the upper cabin tomorrow, or the next day. It will be Trav's and my last time. Bob's pulling his traps on that line and we'll pull our snares.

We're going to get a Christmas tree around the 15th and I'll start putting up some decorations, too. Now all I need is The Christmas Carol record (that we used to always listen to at Christmas time), a bowl of candy and cookies, and a bunch of giggling, laughing, arguing voices – then I'll feel "at home."

I'll tell you, the letters I've gotten sure keep me going. Just wanted to let you know. They are so much appreciated. Then, last night was an added extra-special treat that had me up in high spirits again. I got your message "from the mailbag" as they air on Trapline Chatter. It said, "Going out to Bob, Nancy and Trav at B.C. from Mom and Dad in Glastonbury, Connecticut." It was so great and unexpected (although every night I listen for a message, just in case). I had the biggest smile on my face and Bob said, "Well, you finally got it." KJNP repeats all the messages twice. It takes about 20 to 25 minutes (side note: in modern times, it takes less than a minute, usually, due to other means of communication available). And of course I had to listen to it twice! Just to hear it again! And you bet! I am very anxious to hear all your voices again. Not too long to wait now. We leave for the upper cabin tomorrow.

December 18:

We are home again from the upper cabin. And it is an outrageous 38 degrees above! Not too good for trapping because of overflow* on the river and creek. But just heard it was 36 degrees in Miami, Florida! Bob did get a beautiful cross fox today. We have about 55 marten now, 3 fox, and we totaled my rabbits at 55. Our last trip to the upper cabin was a NIPPY (this was one of my nicknames while growing up) one. Wind was really blowing, but the moon was out, the sky colors were fantastic, Traver was warm; so, my trip was enjoyable. We saw both caribou and moose tracks.

I can feel the tension building up already around our trip to town. We got our Christmas tree on the 16th. It's a little five-foot tree standing in a can on our bench. I brought several decorations, and Trav and I are making some. We'll make popcorn strings soon. Traver loves the Ranger Rick book you sent, Jeff, and we read from it every night – some good stories! I've got the 'stockings hung by the stove with care' and we're all set.

December 24:

Christmas Eve. Been thinking about you. Last night, we made cookies to hang on the tree. Tonight, we got out that little angel thing that spins around by the heat of the candles. You know, Mom, we used to have one when we were growing up. We keep asking Traver if he's been a good little boy. I think he's a little concerned about what's going to be in his stocking tomorrow morning. He's been going around today, saying, "Ho-ho-ho! Merry Christmas!"

December 25:

Merry Christmas! It's 3pm here, and Traver had a great day. We told him Santa probably couldn't come all the way up here, but he might send an elf, which of course, he did. He's been playing all day with the dart gun the elf brought, and he wore his new hat, mittens, and scarf I made. He was thrilled with his stocking. I gave him all I had. Couple pieces of gum, couple jawbreakers, couple sesame-squares, a fruit roll, some of those dyno-mints (for your breath), a pen, a balloon, and a plastic egg with four quarters in it. He's been talking about his goodies, and the elf, all day. So it's been nice here – quiet – a lazy day. Bob's getting all his fur cleaned and ready to take in. This will be my last page to you before we talk. I love you. Many thoughts for a Happy New Year from all of us. Nanc

You might imagine that transitioning into the wilderness would be very difficult, and it might be for some. But, I bet many individuals would find it more exciting than difficult.

Now – transitioning to civilization after living in the wilderness for several months can be a very surreal experience. For me it was going from:
- Very quiet to very noisy
- Living very calmly and mellow to hectic and sensory overload
- Being very aware to being on guard
- Natural sounds and smells to unnatural, 'civilized' sounds and smells

Transitioning into the wilderness, for me, was an exhilarating experience. Transitioning back into society, for me, was an eye opening experience of moving from a place with natural flow and peace, to a very scattered, busy place of chaos.

Turn on your imagination for a while. Imagine yourself in the wilderness with no traffic, way up North. Quiet. Motionless, except for what the wind blows in, or an occasional stirring in the brush of some critter. Daylight creeps above the frozen spruce tree horizon, teasing you for a mere three to four hours, then waving goodbye as it quickly recedes into the fading dull pink, then grey, then charcoal shadowed blanket of snow. You tune into the smells of nature readily, as they are refreshing cleanses for your body and soul. Clean air is more odorless than full of odor. Nostrils delighting in the hardy, earthy, spruce-laden fragrances of nature. Sometimes a whiff of high bush cranberry or musky rotten wood. Quiet, yet every sound so audible. The rustle of a few remaining dead leaves as the wind kicks in. The far off cry of a raven, or a nearby squirrel complaining about the traffic in his territory. Cozied up in your cabin every day for twenty plus hours with only kerosene or gas lamps for lighting. One to three other humans in your world, and a few dogs adding some drama. Your livelihood is controlled according to how well you meet your survival needs of shelter, food, and water.

Then, after meeting those challenges and establishing your own lifestyle in this vast wilderness, it's time to say goodbye to all of that. You board a small plane, leave your familiar surroundings and this home you've created; off you go, and your transition begins. You place your lives in someone else's hands in a vehicle that hopefully takes you where you want to go, and flown, hopefully, by a knowledgeable somebody that you know.

Then – town! After living for four months in a dim cabin, lights and colors are outrageous. Stop lights: red, green, yellow – before, I never noticed how bright they were. Walking by someone in a blue shirt can even be surprising: wow! I haven't seen blue in a long time, I thought to myself once. And, everywhere, there are people, people moving around – like robots, or ants in a scattered frenzy as their home is disrupted.

However, town can also be overwhelming in good ways, too. The excitement of reconnecting with familiar people and places is wonderful; the comradery of likeness. Not to mention – food! Grocery stores held so many tastes that I'd missed for months. I remember dreaming about going down grocery store isles and picking up carrots, lettuce, cheese, eggs, ice cream, and fruit, then waking up, drooling, counting down the days until we got to town for those tempting tidbits. Only, when the grocery store became a reality, it was too overwhelming to enjoy. The stresses of town interfered greatly with the desirable pleasures I was dreaming of. I could not stay in a grocery store, comfortably, for more than five minutes, at first. It felt like The Twilight Zone: so alien and suffocating with all of the noises, smells, and emotions. Too much sensory detail and stimulation at once.

We relied heavily on friends helping us with transportation around town. Our truck was twenty miles outside of town, with unplowed dirt roads and no electricity to plug the truck in. (A normal, everyday must in Fairbanks during the winter. Because temperatures are well below zero, your car will not start without first plugging it in for several hours.)

As I mentioned in letters to my family, my hands had been bothering me while in the woods – tingling sometimes, no circulation, etc. While in town, my mission was to see a doctor and hopefully take care of my concerns. Gratefully, I was seen by a wonderful Doctor Ha, who informed me I had carpal tunnel syndrome. Oh no! I thought. My mom had suffered from carpal tunnel, and I even still have the picture she sent me of when she had a huge cast, from fingertips to elbow. How could I manage something like that and go back to my chores on the trapline? Well, wonderful Dr. Ha explained that there would be no need to have a cast at all, and that, instead, he could perform an operation, sending me off with specific directions on how to properly care for myself, post op. I was able to have the operation and had no complications (even 36 years later).

While in town, it was also departure time for Traver to go be with his dad, Tim. Tim and I had shared custody and worked out a six month/ six month plan. Traver was resilient, and we continued this plan until he was junior high age. After six months in Alaska with Bob and Nancy, Trav was ready for some Dad time. So, off he flew with part of my heart.

Next on the 'town agenda' was calling home! That was always the most rewarding. After not talking with my family for four months, I was very much looking forward to some delicious conversation. Even though I am a wanderer at heart, I've always kept in close contact with my family, and still do. The phone conversations with my mom, dad, and two sisters, probably took up several long evenings.

Finally, the never-ending search and collection of supplies needed for the next three to four months on the trapline was necessary. The supplies needed would include anything from food (for us and dogs), craft supplies, trapping equipment, building items, fuel for lights, writing and reading material, clothes, and daily living supplies, such as batteries, toothpaste, soap, matches, etc. We always had to keep the weight total in mind, as our plane ride had a limited weight capacity. It was often quite disappointing to me because some desired items had to be left behind. Living in the wilderness, you just naturally learn how to do without, and you become quite innovative. Challenges are continual and creativity becomes a delightful part of living.

Chapter 5:

1982

Bob and I were back at the main cabin, alone and together once again. It takes a while to decompress after a short trip to town, and that particular trip to Fairbanks bubbled over with high-impact activity. Once back in the woods, I also got back to writing my family letters.

January 11, 1982:

Hi to everyone who reads this,

Well, we are back at B.C. (Base Camp). It is Monday and Bob is off on a "business trip" right away. He went to the lower cabin (down river) to open it up and get ready to move. We'll be there in two weeks. I hate to leave the comforts of this cabin. There won't be as many comforts down there. Like, only one window, no floor to speak of, a smaller space, only a barrel stove.... See? I've been spoiled! But, the good part is that the cabin and area will be new to me. I can explore, start new snare-lines, and experience new things.

Right now, I'm soaking my left hand, which is coming along fine. It was frustrating at first, doing things with the use of one hand, but my stitches come out Saturday. Then, two more weeks, and it should be good as new. The slice is right above my wrist and only one and a half inches long. Five stitches. I've had the tingles in my right hand but not in my left!

It's very quiet now with both Bob and Trav gone. I'm keeping busy and have lots to do. The first day back was awful with those after-high blues. Kind of like seeing family at Christmas time then having to depart. Yuck! I just cried and sulked a little. Then, I looked at all the good points and remembered how great it was talking with you. I look forward to your letters (if they'll ever get here) and to calling you again in the beginning of April. We expect a plane to come visit mid to late February, so you'll get this letter sometime. I want to thank you all for the letters and boxes you sent. We enjoyed it all. Sorry to say, Jeff, one of your boxes didn't arrive. Maybe the post office could put a tracer on it. We've been hearing the weather reports for the Lower-48, especially Minnesota and Chicago. Wow! Colder than us. It must be crazy there.

Speaking of crazy, Fairbanks and our trip to town was extremely crazy. I didn't stop for a second. In fact, the most I relaxed was after my hand operation, in the recovery room. I slept for one hour. Ahh, I hated to leave because I knew the rest of the day I'd be running like mad. But even though the trip was full, I really enjoyed seeing our friends (who were all very helpful with rides, places to stay, etc.), a movie, eating out, and of course, talking with all of you. I gave your name and address to our closest friends, Carl and Sandy Bakken. They live across the road and down a-ways from our land. Our truck is with them and we stayed with them most of the time.

Last night we were with Joe and Sandy Mattie. Joe is a fur-buyer and buys Bob's furs. Sandy and I have become friends, and I'm sure our friendship will continue. Sandy knows of a woman with all the know-how and supplies of spinning wool. I've just started collecting all the dogs fur and hopefully we'll learn how to spin it. There was an article in an old Alaska Magazine about two women who did that with their dogs' fur. So, a new project for me. Meanwhile, I brought out two grocery bags full of yarn ordered from Greece. I'll be busy with that and all the books that people gave us. And, the necklaces I'm making. We also have a new dice game and a chess set.

Hey, those photos I sent, Mom and Dad? Could you pass those around? And also, I have a favor to ask. While I was running around town, I didn't get all the pictures developed. There's one I want in particular. If you could look over the negatives and find one of Bob cleaning, cutting fish, and hanging it on the fish rack, I would appreciate it. The picture was taken from behind Bob, so you can't see what he's doing but you can see the fish hanging. It looks like a frame made of long branches/ small logs. Good luck! And, Mom and Dad, that money you gave me from Santa? How would you like to spend half of it for me? If you'd like, on your trip here this summer, keep your eyes open for some beads for me, glass, ceramic, odd-ones... I need some for jewelry using bear claws and teeth. So they can be from 1/8th" to 1/2" in size.

Bob drying fish on the rack.

The reason I ask this is because there's not much in the Fairbanks area. I was in Anchorage and got a few, but not much. And besides, the three hundred dollars I took down there to spend went rather quickly.

So, after eating all we wanted to for five days, Bob and I both have little guts on us now. Oh, and we finally opened the two boxes you sent – one of books and one of goodies. Good choices for both. We were going to bring some nuts out but got too rushed to find any. So, yay! We got them anyway. And I love having some licorice around. Thanks.

It's funny how you "switch gears" for your surroundings. I noticed a switch when going to town, but really noticed it after getting back here... No luxuries, and work started immediately... Eyes immediately searching the area for tracks... The senses are alert and more in-tune, not so boggled. It feels so good, now that we're getting back to "normal."

Well, I've got beans cooking, yogurt heating, pups yapping, and the six o'clock news ready to come on, so I figured this is as good a time as any to stop writing for a while.

January 17th:

Hi. Just finished another full day – and I am full. We had salmon that Trish gave us before we came back, and oh, was it good. Bob even made some cookies. Then I cut out a pattern and fit Bob for some moccasins, made a pair of earrings (porcupine quills and beads), and we played a dice game. Earlier, I checked snares, cut and hauled wood, took the pups out for a run, made bread, washed clothes, blah, blah, blah. I have been busy. Since Bob got back two days ago, my days have changed. I spend more time cooking when he's here and less time with the little putzy things I like to do. I've been making more jewelry and reading. Took my stitches out yesterday. My hand feels free again and almost normal. I was just getting used to chopping wood with one hand.

Before I forget, Mom: If you have any old leather stuff, don't throw it away. Send it my way. I was just wondering about that nice, gold leather coat you bought me long ago. What did I even do with it? Could sure use it now for some projects. And if you're ever getting rid of old bedding, blankets and quilts, we could always use extra.

Hey, it's been exciting listening to the weather from the Lower-48. Everyone must be going nuts. Bob and I were just saying how some people that go to work just wear shoes and don't even own a pair of boots, let alone Sorels or skin-boots. We got into that conversation as we talked about the things we could make and sell. This summer will be a beginning. Bob did a little taxidermy when he was younger and was thinking of getting into that again. I got him a book on it for his birthday. I also brought out the makings for a real cheesecake (not the boxed kind).

Oh boy, we've been getting all excited about the moose passing by. Three have passed right out on the river. We saw the fresh tracks, but not were not quick enough to follow. So, Bob's watching carefully as he makes his trips South. He saw more tracks down by the South cabin too. Maybe we'll have a moose! We'll be going to the cabin south of here this week, some time. I'm not getting rabbits up here and the dogs need to be fattened up. So, we're moving quickly. When I get there, I'll write and tell you all about it. I hear there is NO outhouse either.

Getting back to the moose tracks, the day Bob left I saw and followed two sets of tracks. It's fun, and really gets the adrenaline moving. I was testing their turds (no, not for taste–just freshness) and I saw where they slept and ate. It's like putting together a story in your mind. I could see where they laid down, the outline of the baby's ear and head in the snow, a few bits of fur left behind. A small melted indentation from moose breath. Bob says it's unusual for so many moose to be moving around here in January. We heard a pack of wolves further north last month, and Bob said maybe the moose are getting scared downriver; or, maybe there are just too many moose up that way.

This last week, it's been about 35 degrees below zero here. Not too bad. And sunshine again! What a treat to see and feel the sun again. It comes over the horizon for just a short bit and then goes down again. We have five hours of daylight now. I try to get out of the cabin around 9 a.m. or so and in by 3 p.m. Well, time for Trapline Chatter.

January 22:

It's home sweet home today. We just returned from a trip to the next cabin down south. A three-hour toboggan ride. New country and lots of tracks: caribou, moose, wolf, otter, fox, wolverine, ptarmigan, and marten. The trip down was very nice, but the dogs were getting tired and haven't had much meat lately, so they were slow. The three days at that old cabin *were frustrating for me. All the little things... like no shelves, no pots and pans, a dirt-floor so that everything was always dusty, no light coming in through the visqueen window, very dark inside, and hitting our heads on the ridgepole (if you don't duck!). We slept on the narrow pole bed, foot-to-head the first night. Bob slept on a caribou hide on the ground after that. Having no outhouse was the LEAST frustrating thing. I hated that place. I mean, I was spoiled up here at B.C. I told Bob I wouldn't mind moving on as soon as possible. So, the next camp down from that yucky cabin is 20 miles further south. We will set up a tent camp. We're moving our gear now. Half is down by the cabin now. Another big trip down in two more days. Then, we'll move gear again from the "yucky" cabin to where the tent camp will be. So, more exciting things in store. Well, I put out forty snares at the yucky cabin. Bob is setting snares on the trail from the cabin and also on the trail from the river. While setting snares, I found a caribou lung out in the middle of a field. I figured a bird must have dropped it. Probably a raven. I also came across sleeping places of ptarmigan, where they dive into banked snow and sleep or hide in the hollow it forms. Piles of turds are in there (amazing how much). When they take off, the prints made by their wings are so pretty in the snow. Reminded me of angel wings in the snow (only bird angels instead of human angels).*

I also investigated fox and moose turds. I'm just learning. And I saw where otters slide down small hills or banks to the river and drag along the shore. So, that part has been fun. I love tracking. On the way home today, Bob got a wolverine (sometimes called a bear skunk... good name for it). What a big, mean-looking critter. Bob also got an otter. A beautiful animal. The wolverine is thawing now. Peee-yew!

When we got back here we saw otter tracks right out front and two moose went right in back of the cabin. I mean, we could see the tracks from the door. Plus, I got four rabbits today, breaking my record of three. So, things are happening here for us.

The three pups we have will soon be outside. They're getting too big to keep inside and they're eating regular dog food now. Two are named Coleen and Stump. Coleen for the Coleen River, and Stump because the tip of his tail froze and will eventually fall off. No name yet for the third female. They're just like little babies: noisy, hungry, and always messin'. Bob growls at them to stop their noise-making and they usually quiet down.

Hey, Gail, I'm reading Clan of the Cave Bear now. Love it! Thanks for the recommendation!

Only 20° below zero today. But real windy on the river coming home. We get our running exercise in on those frigid days, jogging behind the toboggans to keep warm. My calves are complaining from the brutal workout. They really feel it. Guess for today, that's about it.

January 24:

I wouldn't be writing so soon again, but had to after I got my Trapline Chatter message "from the mailbag" last night. What a surprise! Bob was just saying, "Oh, let's not listen to that gossip tonight," but I always do if I can. I was so glad I did. Thanks "from Bruce Becker in Connecticut" (as the message stated). I had to listen to the message twice and have thought about it endless times. It was so very much appreciated. It was so good to hear that Traver is adjusting to things well. I think of him Saturday mornings, and know just what he might be doing. The rest of you, I'm not sure how you spend your time. But I do think of you all. It was a great message Dad, thanks so much.

We celebrated Bob's 31st, yesterday. Good day! Sunny, 20° below. Real nice. The cheesecake I made was not near as rich as the original recipe, so we proceeded to eat the entire thing. I can see that when I am writing, it makes me feel like you guys are with me, and I am just talking to you as if we were actually sitting together sharing about our lives. Writing to you is something I look forward to, and it is fun to share all this new stuff, wrap it up in an envelope, send it out and wonder what you will feel as you read it. I love you guys and look forward to hearing from you. Lots of love, Nanc

As I'm reading all my past letters I wrote home, almost forty years ago, I find it so intriguing listening to myself back then: my thoughts, my focus, my ideas, my ways of communicating. I don't remember spending so much time in the lower cabin, and I don't remember being so agitated by it. I just remember it as a dirty old cabin that we would use while traveling from our cabin at B.C. to our south location at the tent camp. My memories of Tent Camp are very fond. Sure, there were some struggles, but I felt so alive at Tent Camp. Memories of childbirth are quite similar: it's not the pain, the frustration, the complications that stay in your memory, but the treasure of delivery, and what a delight to behold what blossoms from the challenge!

Much to my surprise and delight, I discovered a story I wrote about tent camp (about one and a half years later, in 1983). I don't even remember writing it, but I'll include it here, followed by a story Bob wrote describing that same time period. However, Bob wrote his story very recently (around 2014-2016). I had no idea Bob wrote this story until finding it after his death. Here they are:

Nancy's Story: It's a Rough Life (From Cabin to Tent in Midwinter)

It was mid-January and time to move twenty miles south down river to tent camp. My partner, Bob, and I had spent the last five months at Base Camp on the Coleen River, at our main cabin. This was my first year out in the woods, and I was enjoying it.

I remember it took one hour to fly 100 miles northeast from Fort Yukon to B.C. Bob said it would take two days to get down to tent camp with our two dog teams. Halfway to tent camp, there was an old cabin we would be staying at for several days. Bob would set his two traplines in the hills there before we moved on down river. Since Bob was also trapping on the river during the week prior, he had hauled a lot of our gear part way down, including our ten-man canvas army tent. So, now we were ready to depart. I would miss the B.C. cabin in more ways than I knew.

"Let's Go!" The command was given to the two dog teams. It was a crisp, sunny day, and we were off on this new adventure (new for me, anyway). New territory. New animals, new awareness. Part of my gear load was a caribou-lined box carrying three, six-week old puppies. I felt grand! Then, 200 yards later, my grand feelings turned into utter despair. My dogs were off the trail turning around, getting all tangled up, the pups were jumping out of the box, and Bob was getting out of sight down the river. I had run the dogs before, but I was still "green" and disliked hitting them with a stick (which is what they are used to and what Bob says they understand).

Well, I got my stick out, but I did more yelling than hitting. I was furious that these dogs would not listen, and wondered: Where is Bob, and why isn't he helping me? After untangling the dogs, reloading the pups, and getting on the trail again, Griz, my lead dog, thought she might get away with it and started turning again. I thought, I've had it! This time I gave it to the leader and let all the team know I meant business. "Let's Go!" I commanded, and we were off again. My frustration died quickly and the sweat from my frustration cooled off. What a work out running the dog team was, sometimes. I was hoping the rest of the journey would be a pleasant, scenic ride. No such luck.

When we got to the gear that Bob had dropped off on the river for us to pick up, we found that there had been overflow. I almost cried when I saw our ten-man army tent frozen in the clutches of the river's overflow. We began chipping away the ice with an ax and managed to get the dog food and other gear to safety. But there sat our tent. After the long journey, and all the chipping at ice, which was exhausting, we still had to make it to the old cabin before dark.

Bob said, "Well, we can live in the other tent we brought. Let's leave this one."

I asked, "How big is the other tent?"

"Eight by ten feet," Bob replied.

That didn't sound as appealing to me, so I said, "I'll stay here all night chipping if I have to."

Bob's 8'x10' tent that he set up while out trapping, which I did not want to live in for an extended period.

After about 40 minutes of switching off with the ax, we got the tent (full of ax holes by this time), loaded up, and off we went again.

By the time we reached the old cabin, I was cold, hungry, and ready to settle in. It had been a pretty interesting day, I thought, and I was ready to relax. After tying up the dogs, making a place inside for the pups, getting wood and water, and preparing a bannock to fry, I could at last inspect my new temporary home. A bear had inspected it before Bob and I, and had left the window and whatever else it could find a mess. This cabin was not like our B.C. cabin at all… no table, no wood floor, no pots and pans, no chairs, only one tiny bed made with spruce limbs, and no outhouse. Was I spoiled?

During the next few days in that cabin, I answered my own question. While Bob was out setting his traplines, I was in the woods setting rabbit snares and experimenting with my snowshoes, which I never had to use at B.C. Once again, I worked up a sweat in frustration as I tripped on my own feet, fell into the snares I was setting, and continually landed on my back when trying to turn around. I didn't have the dogs there to yell at but I screamed out to the vast wilderness and silence, "I hate it here. What I am doing here?" I was spoiled.

The outside of what I deemed 'The Yuck Cabin.'

Meanwhile, back at the cabin, our ten-man tent was draped all over the place to thaw, and the pups were stirring up the dust playing 'catch me if you can.' After those few gloomy days at the old cabin, I was ready for anything new; just to get away from that dirt floor. But, what was I heading for next? The following day I found out.

The dogs gave me no more trouble during that last leg of the journey. We stopped every so often to let the pups out and to investigate various tracks on the river. In three hours, we were at our new home, on a willow bar that looked to me like any other willow bar on the river. We tied the dogs up and began unloading and clearing a spot for the tent. Maybe, I thought, once the tent was up things would look different. It didn't take too long to get the outer canvas tent up and the airtight stove* set up inside. But how long would it take to get all of the snow out of my home, I wondered? And what would we sleep on? And where does everything fit inside this green piece of material draped over my head? A cold cave is what the tent reminded me of – with mangled holes all over, from where we had chipped it out of the iced overflow. I debated whether or not to mend the holes. At least with the holes, I could peep out and see some daylight. But the inner liner was to go up the next day. So, mend the holes we did. That night was spent on spruce boughs, caribou hides, and then our sleeping bags. I was cold. Even with all my clothes on, plus a face mask. Morning came early, and I was glad to get up. The first night proved that if we didn't get up to stoke the fire at least once, we could be sure of waking with a layer of frost around the sleeping bag where our breath dispersed. There was much that needed to be done to begin making this green cave into what would be home for the next three months.

But, make a home we did. Bob made a hanging clothes rack to dry various items, and I put up a hanging basket to hold odds and ends. Our tent-camp home sometimes smelled like a brewery – Bob would make a batch of homebrew in one corner – and at times, had other, more unusual scents, like when a wolverine was hanging to dry out.

Daily survival chores took up most of the daylight hours. While Bob was out trapping (sometimes 4-5 days at a time) I had wood to cut, water to haul, dogs to cook for and feed, and even 'grocery shopping' too (on my rabbit snare lines). Since cutting wood with a swede saw* took a lot of my energy, I started with that task each morning. Then I would carry two 5-gallon buckets across the river and drop them while I took an hour journey on one snare line. Sometimes the ravens went grocery shopping earlier than I did and beat me to the rabbits I snared. On my way back I'd stop at the water hole, break through the ice with a big stick, load my buckets and head for home.

Lunchtime came next. A time to sit, relax, and enjoy the moment. When Bob was around, I'd spend more time preparing a meal. But if I was alone, I'd make something quick (instant potatoes, dried fruit, dried meat) and read a chapter or two from the book I was presently into. After lunch, I would chop the wood I had sawed earlier, set a few more snares on a different line, and start to heat water for dog food. Sometimes I would wash clothes at this time too.

My three to four hours of daylight were full at tent camp, and I enjoyed being outside a lot. The tent itself was more like a crude shelter to go in and out of because the elements of nature were forever present. We had spruce tree particles inside and out, snow inside and out, wind inside and out. We felt alive and in tune with our surroundings. After a few days at tent camp, I was getting quite good on snow shoes, since whenever I was outside I practically lived on them.

After daylight hours, the warmth and coziness of our shelter felt good. Some of the cabin luxuries were not present, however, which made things a little rougher. I can recall many days at the cabin; we'd be inside relaxing on our bed, or sitting in the chair looking out the window, and Bob would remark, "Oh, it's a rough life." Meaning, of course, that life was pretty nice, easy, and wonderful. I've never heard Bob say that at tent camp. I think it has to do with some of the missing luxuries.

Cooking dinner in cans instead of pans would drive me crazy some days. Especially spaghetti. And trying to plan a balanced, varied meal got to be a real challenge because most of our food was dried, dehydrated, or

126

powdered. There was one week, however, that a friend dropped by with a bag of fresh fruit – which we slept with to keep it from freezing until it was devoured. Spruce needles always found a way into our food. And there was a constant search for the two spoons, two forks, and two plates we brought with us.

After the dogs and we were fed, there was still plenty of time left before Trapline Chatter and bedtime. This was the time when Bob usually skinned and stretched his catch. If the catch was good, we'd be sharing one third of our tent space with hanging, stretched, and dried furs. I'll never forget the time Bob skinned a lynx inside and soon we were tossing and turning, scratching and itching – the fur was covered with fleas. Also, from time to time we shared the tent space with three pups. They were still staying close to their mother but would occasionally (generally mealtime) decide to wander in for a visit– or if it was real cold out, they'd try to sleep right on top of the tent sides, which caused a few problems. We let them in, one by one, every now and then, but the rest of the time we kept a willow stick by the bed – long enough to reach the tent door flap. I remember, one day, I left the flap door open while I went out to get some wood. I was gone longer than planned and one of the pups snuck in. I didn't even notice until I smelled burning fur. The pup was hiding behind the stove and leaning right on it. He had a yellow tint to his fur for a while after that.

While Bob worked on his furs at night, I worked on my craft: jewelry making. My materials came from animals. I boiled the heads of animals that Bob trapped (marten, wolverine, lynx, fox, and wolf) and pulled out their teeth to clean and use for my jewelry. I also used porcupine quills, duck wing bones, owl claws, bear claws, lynx claws, and feathers. I worked at night on my craft until my back hurt from bending over, or until my eyes hurt from the light. After completing these projects, there would be time for reading or playing cards. Often, we fought over who got the best reading spot, which was closer to the stove and much warmer.

Sometimes it was nice to simply sit and listen to the night sounds: wind blowing, river ice crackling, owls hooting, or wolves howling. It was reassuring for me knowing the dogs were sitting right there, close to the tent. We could hear them whining when it was 60 below, or we listened to them growling, and occasionally they would drive us nuts by chomping on a frozen munchie that they'd saved up for a cold winter's night. After the Trapline Chatter messages were over, we stoked the fire, washed, and dressed for bed (long johns, socks, hats). The lanterns went out, and we were cozy in our bags with another day of tent life gone by.

I got used to this life quickly and learned to enjoy and appreciate it. However, by the end of March, I was ready to head back up to the B.C. cabin with all of its luxuries. Yes, it's a rough life, and a wonderful one, living in a tent in the middle of winter in the wilderness of Alaska.

Bob's Tent Camp Story

For several years, I had a ten-man army tent. One year, I was three camps downriver from the main cabin with my wife, Nancy. We had the dog team and a winter litter of pups, which is an odd thing to have, but we took them with us. In fact, we ran two toboggans to bring all the gear down. The dog team was staked outside our tent and the pups were outside. Inside the tent, I was brewing beer. There was a big stove, a bed, and a table. It was comfortable. We were still sleeping on the ground. The pups would sleep on the tent door flap outside picking up some warmth. They would just lay down on top of the other. Boom, boom, boom. There'd just be a stack of pups leaning on the canvas. Every now and then, the bottom dog would get out and go to the top and it rotated that way all night long. They're rotating to get up top where it was warmer. They didn't want to be on the bottom of the pile.

One morning, we were up drinking coffee, and all of a sudden, a puppy falls into the tent door. He stood there and stared at us. We were as surprised as he was. He'd never been in the tent. He never knew what was in there. He was scared. I just went 'boo!' and he got out of that tent as fast as he could. We laughed. That was very, very funny.

128

I would be trapping marten and Nancy would be running a snare line around the gravel bar across from camp. She always brought rabbits home to the dogs. The pups would be watching and waiting for her to come, knowing they would get rabbit guts, or maybe even a piece of rabbit if she had many. They wouldn't leave the tent camp. They wouldn't go ten yards out of camp. They were young and afraid to. Those pups would fight for pieces of rabbit. The pecking order would be established. Quite a sight!

The three puppies, chewing on a rabbit at Tent Camp.

As one could imagine, my private thoughts back when I was in my early thirties (I'm 68 now) were not totally shared in my letters to my family. First of all, the thoughts were private, and some of my thoughts might have caused unnecessary worry for others that couldn't understand my living situation. I understood there was a high risk associated with the life we were living in the woods. Now, I look back now and wonder if I even asked myself some of these questions: *What if there were no rabbits to eat? What if Bob left for tent camp and never came back? What if we broke our saw – did we have a spare for cutting wood? What if I injured*

129

myself badly while Bob was off at tent camp? What if, what if, what if?
I recently asked my sister Gail if she recalled any memories of talking with
Mom and Dad about the risks of my living situation. Gail immediately
blurted out, "YES! Nancy! You had mom so worried back then. Especially
with the kids out there!"

As I mentioned, I don't remember how much I asked myself questions
like that– I only remember that I truly loved being so alive, and living so
simply and so close to nature. It was all such a delightful adventure. I'd
like to continue on that adventure and revisit a letter I wrote back then.

February 16th, 1982

*Hi, Y'all! Four days ago, John (Bob's pilot friend), and John's
buddy from Fort Yukon, stopped by. What a surprise. John
said my mail would be here in a week or so. I can't wait! That
night, after they left, I couldn't sleep at all, being so excited
about sending my mail out, and knowing I'll receive some
soon. Yesterday, for the first time, I was getting sick of winter.
The past three days have been nasty, windy, snowy, blowy, and
very chilly! After all that warm weather, it's sure making up for
it. And when the weather changes, there is overflow. There was
water out front up and down the river for a half mile each way
that we could see. Bob got "weathered in," and I had to take
a few days off work, which is okay. But, he gets restless after
a while. He left this morning to go down south, 20-25 miles
to put up another, separate 8x10 tent and break trails there. I
think he's going to be cold tonight. It's still quite windy. He'll be
back in two days. I have to rough it a little. He took the only
axe we have here, until he brings one down from the yucky
cabin. So, I have to carry in snow to melt for water, instead of
chipping away ice on the river. I've got a saw for firewood if I
need it though.*

*Only got one rabbit today, so I had the liver, the pups got the
guts, and the other two dogs got the rest. I didn't tell you that*

before I got the rabbit, the ravens got to it first, so it was a little mutilated. The ravens have been getting into lots of my rabbits. I think they watch where I go and then come by again hoping for a free meal. Smart birds. I'll tell you a little raven story now. Up at the yucky cabin, Bob had a trap out, and I checked it because it was right by my snareline. So, one day, there was this raven caught in a trap. I went over to the raven and saw that he didn't look so bad off and was giving me the old eyeball. Those ravens have HUGE eyeballs! They are big birds! Anyway, his beady eyes were watching me as I checked out the scene. The trap didn't seem to have done anything to his foot except twist it. So, I got a big stick and put it near the bird's beak, and he grabbed it. Then I got my feet on the trap to open it (too hard to do with my hands). I didn't want my hands to get too close to his beak either. So, his foot came out, but he didn't move. I thought I would give him a toss into the air and if he could fly, then, good. If he couldn't fly, I'd shoot him. So, I grabbed him up and tossed him. He rolled over and flew off. He circled in the air a couple of times, waving, "thanks" (caw! caw!). And that was that. But, now you know about the ravens getting my rabbits. I cuss at them and tell them off when I see them in the air by my snare lines. If you don't like hearing my animal stories, let me know, and I will tell them elsewhere.

I'm reading Atlas Shrugged. It's a great book. Thanks for sending it Mom and Dad. I'm also sitting here thinking about that bag of licorice up at B.C. Won't get it until the end of March, but I'm sure I'll enjoy it then.

By the way, Bob's asking Joe Mattie (fur buyer and friend who will be here within 2 weeks) to pick us up April 1, 2, or 3, so don't expect a call from me until after that time.

Also, my hand is almost back to normal, except doing push-ups is still hard. My scar itches.

We went out to practice shooting the .22 the other day. I was remembering when we were little and Dad used to shoot clay pigeons; we'd go looking for them (remember that, Gail and Jeff?).

I started growing sprouts again. I have to wrap them up in my wool pants at night and take them to bed with me to keep them warm. We wake up in the morning here and it's 20 degrees inside.

I won't be sending this letter with the next plane. Hopefully, I'll have a letter from you to respond to first. I like to pretend in my head how surprised you are to get a letter and then wonder how long it takes you to get through it. If you read it at the dinner table, or at work, or in the bathroom, or in bed.

Bob has started to build a small cache up in the trees so we can store things here for the summer and not have to drag it all down again from B.C. The tent, a pot and pan, lantern, etc.

February 20th, 5:00 am:

Can't sleep again. For a good reason... yesterday, Joe came and bought Bob's fur, visited, and dropped our mail. What a day! He came around 11:30. Left at 2:30. I finally got through my mail at 8 pm last night. Bob and I sat around, read, and ate junk. We are paying for that now. We both started rolling around at about 3:45am, so we finally decided to get up. I'm writing and Bob is reading Alaska Magazine and drinking hot chocolate. How he can start off on sweets again, I'll never know.

The first thing we devoured yesterday was a pineapple upside down cake. Then an apple, an orange, and a banana. What a treat! Fresh, delicious fruit from Joe and his wife Sandy. So, now the sprouts have company at the foot of the bed, keeping warm all night with our feet. Anyway, after eating fruit, we continued on. Not only did you guys send food, so did Bob's mom. We ate granola bars, cheese, cookies, and of course, those

*two chocolate bars you sent. That's what I'm sick on, I think –
no sweets for so long and then a ton at once. I ate one whole
chocolate bar, then later, dug into the other. Bob finally gave in
and helped on that last one. Please don't send chocolate again!
Needless to say, yesterday was certainly like Christmas all over
again. I was hungry for that mail. I was delighted to hear from
all of you and also many other friends. Thank you all so much
for the letters, boxes of books, and goodies. And I'm also glad
to hear you're enjoying the socks I made and sent to you. Don't
worry Gail, I won't tell on you. Someday, when I write you a
separate letter (I'm out of envelopes, as of today) I'll tell you
how many days I wear my clothes before changing!*

*We both love getting and going through all the books you sent.
So much appreciated. Bob dug right into the cowboy ones. He
also loved the National Geographic magazines you sent. I'll use
the yoga ones and we can leave a bunch here for next year. All
the goodies were so wonderful. And new undies! I have enough
to last a few years now! Thanks! Getting packages and mail
can't be beat.*

*You know, I received some letters from you that you wrote
back in November? Yup. So I just heard the news about Dad's
operation and I'm glad it went well, with no complications.*

February 22:

*We woke up today and it was 41 below, so Bob decided not to
go south to his other tent camp. He worked some more on the
cache and I did my regular stuff. I'm packing a bag of food
Bob will take when he leaves tomorrow. Since we only brought
one pan and one pot, we keep them here. I make bannock and
one dish meals and freeze them for Bob to take. He thaws and
cooks them in a can. But the little snacks everyone sent will be
great to pack for him; crackers, cheese, granola, peanuts.*

By the way, I think I told you, I'm out of envelopes, so I hope you will send out the other three letters enclosed. I could give them to John, the pilot, but I'm more assured of them reaching their destination this way. Thanks.

Bob with the cache he built at tent camp

Mom, you asked about the pups. Griz is the mom. Coleen, Stump, and Twitch are her pups. Coleen looks like Griz and was named for the Coleen River. Stump is stocky and the end of his tail froze off, he's the one with the little pink nose. It has three black dots on it, so it looks like a polka-dot nose. Twitch is very active and noisy. Bob named her after Traver. He called Traver Twitch because he was constantly moving about or talking. By the way, if you hear any more news of Traver, please pass it on to me. I have yet to receive a letter from Tim.

I'm anxiously awaiting to hear the itinerary for your trip to Alaska. Please send it as soon as you know. Mom, did you ever call Eleanor? Neither of you mentioned it, so I gather not. She sent Bob a birthday box. He likes getting his bottle of Kalua she sends. And this time she included a box of dog biscuits! I laughed at that one. So even the dogs got to pig out with us. She stuffs the box with napkins, instead of newspaper, so now we have some extra toilet paper! She made a stolen (like fruit bread), which is Bob's favorite. We froze it, but Bob wanted some for breakfast, so I brought it in to thaw after breakfast. Then I went out to check my snares. When I returned, the stolen was half gone. We have little pot bellies from eating so much starch. We are hungry for moose!

Oh, we ordered our house logs for Fairbanks. We talked with Joe when he was here with us. Bob and Joe are going to get logs together. Joe did a lot of checking around, and he decided to buy logs because that way you are sure of getting them on time. So we decided to do the same since Bob really wants to start this spring. It costs $3.95 a foot per log. We may not be able to get the boat we wanted, but we can start building for sure. And Joe offered Bob a two to three-week job helping him, so Bob will be able to earn a little on the side too. Also, if my jewelry sells well, and with the fox, wolverine, and otter to sell yet, we still may be able to get the boat too.

Thanks for the compliment on my necklaces. I'm enjoying making them; I've done many varieties now, also using claws and fox teeth too.

Mom, you asked about the pink-nosed pup. Bob says it's just pigment. The dogs with pink-colored noses will change to a grey color later, and then, this time next year, it will be pink again. Why? I don't know. Some dogs have pink mouths. Some have black.

I know it's hard for you to imagine what my life is all about here. I hope the pictures help. But, remember when I first came North and was teaching in Stevens Village? All the different ways to live. You will never know what this is for me, only what I tell you. But that's okay. You'll know how I feel about it even if you can't understand it. I think you'll appreciate Alaska more after visiting. We'll see. I have to stop myself from anticipating your visit. It will come soon enough. And this will be my first complete summer in Alaska. I'm looking forward to it.

Cabin in winter

So, Really – What's It Like Out There?

When I mentioned that it was hard for me to explain what this experience and part of my life truly meant to me, I was being honest. Very few individuals today have known and experienced this type of lifestyle. Therefore, it is not something people can easily talk about, write about, or state facts about. That is, unless a person has experienced it, and then, their own experience and feelings about it will be different than mine.

For example, Bob and I experienced shared activities during our days. However, he would talk about taking an animal's life, skinning, and eating it differently than I would. He would also talk about traveling through this vast, beautiful country differently than I, even though we both agree on the same adjectives of description. His thoughts and my thoughts throughout the day would be very different, and, some related. The preciousness of time alone and the solitude is a guaranteed treasure, if one is able to be open to that time and allow it to penetrate and remake your being. Why is that kind and amount of solitude so special? Because you get to know yourself. You get to experience how life works when you let it happen to you and "go with the flow." Nature will teach you if you observe and are aware. Observing and experiencing this is quite possible out in the woods, and much easier, far away from everyone and everything you are familiar with in society. The distractions from living life would only be self-made.

How can I explain the connection with life itself out there, in the wilderness? I might have met a wild animal around the river bend and guessed that I am probably the first human this animal has laid eyes on. What must that be like? For both of us! Or just walking in some of the places I went daily on my snare lines, I would most likely be the only person ever to leave a track in that spot. Or, I think about our family hike up to the rock outcrop above the river we called the throne. On the trail approaching the throne, there were the remains of a rock cache, made and used so long ago by inhabitants who called this place home. At the throne, there were scattered chipped off pieces of stone (which Bob called cherts) and parts of arrowheads left behind by somebody working at survival skills a bit different than ours. Sitting on the throne, looking over miles and miles of God's country, I think about how their lives must have been. What am I doing here? I wondered.

All I can really say is I love it, and that's only the tip of the iceberg for an explanation of how I feel. As you know, Bob also loved it.

It was a new, lovely world for me. I had not been raised in the woods. Nor was this like the camping my family did in the Adirondacks of New York State. This was a fascinating adventure for me full of daily lessons and challenges. I had to learn to do without many things, or figure out a new way to do something. No tool? Improvise or make one. No pot? Use a can. No fork? Use a stick. No spice? Invent a new one. No patience? Pray and laugh at yourself.

Out in the woods, I was always learning. Not just learning about the simplicity of life with nature, but about my own my human complexities. Bob and I relied on each other for certain things in order to survive. Much of the time, we were on our own and had only ourselves to rely on. It was important for us to be alert and paying attention at all times. I remember going to bed at night so content, and usually exhausted both physically and mentally. Then, waking in the morning, oh-so-looking forward to another day of meaningful accomplishments. Another day of feeling good.

Getting back to my story, and tent camp, we were approaching the end of trapping season and the gradual creeping in of springtime. Our thoughts were closing in on returning to B.C. and then back to town.

February 27, 1982

Well, we're getting 9-10 hours of daylight now. It's so nice. My freckles are starting to pop out. A good sign of spring.

March 10:

Hello everyone! Last night I got my Trapline Chatter message. "From Mom and Dad in Connecticut. Happy Birthday, Spook!" Ha! Bob and I got a laugh out of that one. (One of my nicknames growing up was Spook).

March 14:

Happy Birthday to me! I'm just being lazy today. No work. So far, this month of March has been a tough one for me. Bob says it's the hardest month, and gets harder the closer we get to leaving. It's spring fever – wanting a change, wanting to see people, and being tired of "all this." Bob's the same way. We'll both be ready for town, and I'm counting the days.

Our friends up north of here that I mentioned before, Heimo (a trapper from Minnesota) and his new wife Edna (from a small Yupik village on St. Lawrence Island), stopped by a few days ago on their way to town with our friend John, the pilot. It was good to see them again, hear some stories, and anticipate town again. Heimo left us a big hunk of moose meat, which we will dig into today. Thank goodness. I told you, Bob and I have *little pot bellies from eating so much bannock lately. But, Bob also got a lynx. They are my favorite animal, so gorgeous. Huge fluffy feet, stubby tails, and tufts of fur on the tips of their ears – $200 to $300 a piece. I cooked one up, boiled it. It tastes just like turkey drumstick. The meat is white and kind of looks like white turkey meat or light pork when it's around a big bone. I've made some lynx soup and other rice and veggie dishes with it. Delicious! But this moose is even better!*

It's been in the teens here lately during the day. Sunny and windy. Nights are about 15 degrees below zero. I got frustrated with snaring. Not getting anything, so I pulled my lines and have been lazy for a few days. Tomorrow I'll start picking up and keeping busy for two weeks. That's when we'll head back up to B.C. and get picked up. More and more, Bob and I are talking about building our log home, getting the truck fixed, building a greenhouse and a boat, planning a hunting trip. We are ready for the next phase of our lives: town.

Bob just got back from his tent camp further south and hit some good areas. He brought back 15 marten. So it looks good in that area for next year as well.

I'm getting more and more excited about you folks coming in August. It's on my calendar. You'll miss the Tanana Valley Fair in Fairbanks by one week, but that's good, because I'll have to be at a booth that whole week with my jewelry (if everything works out okay).

Bob came back from the south and said, "You gotta read this, Amityville Horror." I was hesitant because I get nightmares from those kind of books and movies, but he kept saying it was very interesting and would get me thinking about good, and the devil. So I read it in several hours and had some spooky dreams that night. It WAS a scary book. Now I've just begun reading Dune, which I've heard about for a long time. So, thanks to everyone for the books.

Well, our days are getting longer. Light now before 5:30 and still light after 6:30 pm. Daylight increases by 7 minutes a day. That's a lot.

March 21:

Happy spring! It was up to fifty degrees here yesterday. Sunny and warm. Too warm, in fact. It makes everything really sloppy here, and I can't walk in my snowshoes except in the early morning because it all "snowballs" up on the bottom of the snowshoes. Bob left this morning to go down for the last time to his own tent camp farther south. He'll be back in two days; then we leave for B.C. We're both ready to get out of the tent camp. We'll have six days up there at B.C. – getting ready for town, taking it easy, and making lists.

My mind is back to concentrating on food again, now that we're down to lynx meat, lentils, peas, and flour. I keep thinking about all the goodies I'm going to gobble when I get to town.

Pussy willows are now appearing. Bears will be appearing soon, too. There are also a couple of owls living around here. Bob has been out calling them everyday for about a week now. They get pretty close, but I haven't seen them yet. Great grey owls. A wolf walked on my snare line last night ,leaving the evidence with his tracks.

The pups are starting to follow me everywhere. I have to growl at them to send them home. It will be interesting to take them back to Base Camp. Before, I always carried them in a box in the toboggan. They're pretty big now, though.

March 25th:

We're home (at Base Camp)! Got in today. A very windy, cold ride. But we walked into this cabin and it felt like a castle (I guess). Anyway, very luxurious. I took a nice long nap AFTER I gobbled up the whole bag of licorice. Found some Hawaiian Punch, cream cheese, and batter I made and left here – ate that too! Gosh, I feel sick. But it sure feels nice sitting at a table by a window! Home-sweet-home!

Looks like many animals passed through here: moose, wolf, fox. Our caribou racks were chewed on and left sprawled all over the yard. Some mice were in here snooping. Now six days to relax, and then town.

We're melting chunks of ice now to have water. It's been too warm and things are messy. Overflow just leaves a shallow puddle on top of the frozen river or creek, too difficult to scoop, so chopping and hauling chunks of ice is preferable to wet feet. Bob got another lynx down river so we have plenty of meat for this week.

March 30th:

One day left before town. These past few days have been restful, peaceable, and easy... A real vacation. We're going to miss the peace, quiet, and easy-goingness for sure. The days are long. We get up when we want to. Usually around 7-8 a.m., and then I generally set up a few snares. I got one rabbit and one squirrel. Don't know how the squirrel managed to get caught in the snare. Oh, I forgot to tell you: that last lynx Bob got, well, guess what? It had one of my rabbit snares on its foot. I lassoed a lynx!

Anyway, I've been reading, making more jewelry, slowly packing things, and getting ready for town. We've been eating lynx all sorts of ways. Since we have a meat grinder here, I can grind it into hamburger and use it in a variety of recipes. That taco seasoning packet you sent has come in handy, Mom.

We're making all kinds of lists. Getting ready for this new phase in our lives. I'm anxious to hear all of my family's latest. So, we'll be talking to you shortly. – Love, Nancy

The year of 1982 was going to be my first entire summer spent in Alaska. Traver was with his dad, but would be re-uniting with us sometime during the summer. That was a difficult time for me, as I wondered constantly if Traver would want to stay with his dad instead of coming back up to Alaska. Shared custody was a heart wrenching experience for me. Traver's dad was still not sold on Traver spending winters with us on the trapline.

Our cache would be our home space until we completed our log house. A bit tiny of a living space for three, but we were outside for the greater part of each day. Then, there was always the question of money. Should we try to get some part time work on the side for on-going expenses? Or was having family time more important? We planned on establishing what would be our in-town home for the next ten years. The projects were endless:

1. House building
2. Starting a garden plot
3. Clearing land
4. Boat-building (possibly)

In addition to these formidable tasks, we would also be meeting our neighbors and developing relationships with new friends. The summer in Fairbanks was also a very important time for me to contact my family members and reconnect with old friends.

Remember, even though we were 'in town' at the time, our land was fifteen miles outside of town, off dirt roads where we had no electricity at the time and no cell phones. My main source of communication was still through letters, even though I'd be able to call my family every so often at a friend's house or at a payphone. As you'll see from my letter below, we began work immediately.

April 4th, 1982:

Well, I'm so glad we talked about all we did. It would be nice to keep in regular communication now. That is, as regular as I am on letter-writing. Bob called his folks and brothers. He's trying to get one of them to go (by boat) back to Base Camp this fall. An excellent trip for someone... hunting, fishing, adventure, sight-seeing... A guided tour! We started insulating the inside of the cache today. Tomorrow is a full day in town, taking care of business. Okay, I'm tired and off to bed. We'll talk again soon but I'm looking forward to getting your letters.

April 16:

Just wanted to let you know the operation went well. My doctor let me see the incision and he explained the carpal-tunnel syndrome with the artery involved. It looked fascinating. Also wanted to let you know the money situation will be okay. The logs are paid for, the operation is done, and will be paid for in another week. We still have a little left, and I'm making jewelry. Also, a possible job opportunity is coming up.

April 19th:

Bob is out using his lumber mill to make boards out of our trees – his toy. He is conscientious and looks for ways to save money.

I've been so upset and moody about the Traver situation lately. I am always wondering if he will want to come back to Alaska after being with his dad. The unknowing wreaks havoc with me. Bob asked if I was throwing a tantrum. It's hard to talk about it. I feel all churned up inside and want to throw-up. Tim understands the most, as he has also had to live without Traver. So, we are going to work things out as good as we can for all of us, grateful that there has been no major bad feelings.

I'm so thankful for people like you two who are there to help. Much appreciated. I'm so glad you're my mom and dad.

Bob's getting excited thinking of spring hunting. He wants to get some bear and beaver. A lot of the bear meat would be for the dogs, and we could make money on the hides. I called the guy about the job I was interested in, told him a few great things about myself. He had seen so many applications that he didn't recall mine. Oh well, I'm trying. The only other jobs I saw were for a part-time waitress, help in a thrift store, or being an exercise lady at a spa. Forget the first two, but exercise lady? I could probably foresee that… Or not. Anyway, the money I'd get almost isn't worth the gas money getting back and forth to town.

April 28:

Hi! Finally getting my mail from Fort Yukon; a big pile dating back to early February. My birthday package and treats would have been so sweet out in the woods. I'm still sucking on the chocolate kisses, though, and giving them to friends.

Bob just had to have a root canal and fillings. He said, "Nancy, you have good teeth. Throw them away." (He meant the candy). I didn't, and I'm still enjoying them. By the way, his dentist is trading him dental work for a wolf pelt. And when Bob goes in tomorrow, he's taking some of my necklaces (what's left). We already sent $450 worth of necklaces to his brother in Colorado who's going to try to sell them. Last night my friend came over to do some Christmas shopping and bought some more jewelry – another $155. Not bad! At this rate, I may not even sell at the fair. I'm learning new tips all the time: how to keep the quills and teeth from cracking, etc. I'm making my price tags out of birch-bark circles. Looks good. Free and quick, for now anyway. Bob, some friends, and I have been talking about the idea of a "handmade" shop someday to sell our wares in the summer to tourists. Lots of ideas for the future, but right now we're concentrating on building. Bob is at the drawing board. A wooden spool (for a table), graph paper, ruler, pencil, and "How-To" books. Bob's learning a lot. Trial and error. Talking with friends, moaning and groaning, running around, trying to find a phone to get questions answered. All of our friends and friends-of-friends are offering mental and physical work. It's been great. Just last night, Joe and Sandy Mattie brought over some beer and a guy from Jersey, near where Bob grew up. He's a carpenter and he came to Alaska to trap this last year. So, they talked until after 11 p.m., trading information.

I finished our mailbox and we should have an address today. So, in my next letter there will be a permanent address for me. That will be a big change in my life.

I spoke with Traver again last night and it did wonders for me. Looks like Trav will get here in June and plans for the fall are up in the air. I've been out meeting our neighbors (all very different with varied backgrounds) and scouting out friends for Trav. We have no next-door neighbors, which we're glad for. But land is going fast.

We received your itinerary for Alaska, Dad. It looks good. I'm looking forward to your visit, hearing of your experiences, and feelings about the state of Alaska.

I've also applied for a job with Outdoor Education and joined a women's softball team. This will be a very busy summer.

Bob and I had a big discussion about money, goals, lifestyles, and our plans. We decided to go as far as we could on the house, having no bills. We met a guy who's going to build his own river boat, so we're maybe going to build one along with him. Bob would really like to go up to B.C. this fall by boat. If not, we have a deal with Joe. He may possibly want Bob to trap some live marten for him so he can try breeding them. Bob said 'okay' and we get a nice break on airfare.

Oh yeah, the other thing that could happen is… you guys could come out to Base Camp, if you wanted a trip to the bush! Just thought I'd mention that possibility. It's a chance most tourists don't get, and you could see my "other" home. I have no idea if you're interested or not, but Bob will leave early August with the dogs. I'll be going out later in August with Traver. Joe will be flying me. We could arrange it for the end of your trip. Joe is an excellent (very cautious) pilot and has a Cessna 206. I believe that can hold six people. It is a two-hour flight to B.C. You could fly over Fort Yukon, possibly even stop there (that's one hour). Then, one more hour to B.C. Joe would probably fly back the same day after unloading and B.S.-ing a while with Bob. Or, we could do an overnight. Let me know what you think about that! Just a suggestion.

Oh, and here's another suggestion, Mom. Our outhouse is almost done here. It has empty plain walls on the outside. I was thinking it would be nice to have one of your original creations on it. I'll trade you: a painting for a necklace!
Okay. Love you both, Nanc

P.S. 4:30 p.m. two inches of new snow. Yuck.

May 22nd:

Hi Mom and Dad, this is your daughter, Nancy, in Alaska. Remember me? It feels like a long time since we communicated. I wonder what you're up to? I spoke with Traver and Tim. Both sounded good. Though Trav had a cold, it didn't stop his gibber-jabbering. I was relieved to know for sure that Trav is coming up.

Lots happening here. We got most of the foundation dug. We had to hand-dig one corner a little each day because of the permafrost. Bob's getting the footings ready, and meanwhile fourteen of our logs arrived, so we started peeling today. I have yet to work on the garden space, build flower boxes, or coat the outhouse and cache with wood-life (that's a protective coating). Bob will also be peeling logs at our friend's for work and money. We're busy, busy, busy.

Last night a friend, Bill from Maine, arrived with some lobsters. We got together with Joe and Sandy Mattie, and boy, did we pig out! What a treat! This guy Bill was telling us how he's building log cabins to rent over in Maine. He bought the same sized logs as we did. We paid $3.75 per foot. He paid .40 cents a foot. Outrageous!

Tomorrow a bunch of our friends meet for a baseball game and a potluck picnic. We did it last week and had a ball. (Hah!) Get it? Mostly trapper friends.

I bought a tub for us to take to the woods. One of those galvanized things. New, the tubs cost around $64. This was found at a yard sale for $15 – such a deal! Also picked up a bike for Trav with a banana seat for $11.

I'm getting excited about Traver's arrival now and decided not to take a job unless he could accompany me. We got up late today and dressed just in time to greet two Jehovah's Witnesses. How they found us way out here, I'll never know… God, I guess.

June 5th:

It's been raining for a week straight on and off, which makes the mosquitoes outrageous. Traver's not here yet, but got the footings done. I'm peeling a log or two a day. We're hauling in cinder blocks for the next step. Then, at night we started collecting big rocks along the roadside for our rock foundation. Bob's reading The Stone Worker's Bible to prepare the stonework on the foundation. He also has some experience with stone work from watching and helping his grandfather. Bob just left for Joe Mattie's to peel logs. He peels there (for pay) and I peel here (for free).

Nancy peeling log after log.

Lots of moose tracks everywhere. One was a tiny calf track not two inches long. There are fox and black bear tracks, too. Did I tell you, Bob and I woke up to a growl the other day and all the dogs were barking? Bob jumped up and out he went with his gun. Only saw the bushes rustling, but we both heard the growl and thought it was a bear.

The mosquitoes are awful! Peeling logs is also awful. I have blisters on my callouses! It's rainy, but gets sunny off and on and is in the 60s. It's so green and beautiful. Lots of wildflowers popping up and berry leaves are appearing everywhere. So alive and so much to do. Also a good time to transplant some of the local plants to our yard, like poppies (they don't transport well), bluebells, and lilies.

This summer I also want to try making a birch bark basket. That means collecting some bark and spruce tree roots. Doesn't look like we'll be getting a garden this year.

We're collecting plenty of books to take to B.C. The library has a bunch of free paperbacks on the racks, so we get a few every time we're in there. Good deal.

Bob really enjoys hearing what you write in letters. We share our family letters but his brothers never write and his folks rarely do. So, I know when you mention a special 'hello' or direct words to him, he is always pleased, though he doesn't really show it. I know because he wants me to read those letters to him and not just report it. Dad, in your last letter, you mentioned how you respected Bob for taking on such a big project. I'm not much help except to encourage his ideas. He's already talking about how the next one will be easier. I looked at the pile of logs outside and rolled my eyes!

And Mom, when you mention birds, Bob knows a lot about birds too. He is very observant of nature but doesn't talk about it a lot. He points out things to me, though. There are cranes, ravens, ducks, songbirds, and an occasional owl, as well as small hawks around here.

I dug up some spruce roots today to work with. Also went around trying to send my jewelry to shops. No luck there. I found out that most places double the price to make a profit. I'd have to really lower my prices. I'll wait until next year to get started and check fairs and other events. I've learned a lot, mostly what a hassle it can be. Most of the shop owners weren't around, so I had to track them down. A lot of time and energy. Bob's brother in Colorado only sold three of what we sent him, but they're not in a shop like we thought. So, blah, blah, blah. I do love crafts though, so I'm still thinking of ideas, and it's birch bark time. Next month is berry picking time. August is grass baskets. October is fish prints…

Oh yeah, I talked with Joe about flying out. He okayed all of us going. Joe gives us a deal from Fairbanks to B.C. and back. Bob and Joe are arranging trade-off for work and flights. Otherwise, a regular flight just from Fort Yukon on an air service to B.C. is over $230 an hour. Ridiculous. So, Joe it is! Now all we need is the weather to cooperate! Love, Nancy

Waiting for the return of Traver always brought on a bit of anxiety for me. I seemed to torture myself with doubting thoughts that Trav might not want to be with us, away from his dad. By mid-June Traver had arrived and we were living in the cache, rather than the tent, but still quite primitively. No plumbing, electricity, or phone; most of our living took place outside. Our log home was in the process of being built, we did all of our cooking for us and the dogs outside, and the tarp-covered "camp site" was the most used area on a daily basis. When Bob had the guys over helping with building, I usually cooked for them, and Trav would hang out with the big boys. We had to plan trips to town for supplies or other activities, as it took gas money and a lot of travel time with that gas-hog of a truck.

Bob completing some of the rock work for our home on Chena Hot Springs Road.

July 8th:

Well, where do I start? Although it seems like ages since I last wrote, it must have been about three weeks – that's about how long Trav has been here. He was a little quiet and shy when he first arrived... That lasted about a day. Now it feels like he's been here forever. Quick adjustment. I was so worried he'd want to go back to his dad's. Fooled me. He got right into everything here. The dogs brought out the playfulness and companionship Trav loves. He also proudly displayed his responsibilities in completing chores with genuine enthusiasm. And, he asks and talks about going into the woods. I'm so happy. It feels so good being a mom again and Trav is a terrific kid, as you know. He gets frustrated quickly, like his mom, and wants everything he does to "be right" like his dad, says Tim. He has certainly grown up physically and mentally. He does his chores every day. Wood, water, dogs, and now he empties garbage into the compost pile. We give him a quarter a week if he does all his work. Oh yes, he makes his bed too. He got used to mosquitoes quickly. We each have our own personal supply of 'bug dope' to carry around. I think the mosquitoes are starting to die off, though. The little black bugs (No-See-Ums) will be the next round.

Wildflowers are forever changing, too. Poppies came and went, then came again. Cottongrass is here, which I love! Each long skinny stem carries a white fuzzy character that resembles something out of a Dr. Seuss book blowing freely in the wind. And fireweed is up and coming. All the wild rose flowers came and went, but rosehips will develop now. Such a lovely variety all over our property. We also have raspberries, which are still green.

Let's see, we got the last round of cinder blocks up and tomorrow we pour cement in the 26 holes with rebar. Next week the truck gets fixed with a new clutch. Then the crane comes to move all the logs that I peeled – two a day – up to the rock foundation. That's all we have time and money for.

Bob says 'hello.' He just read over the part in your letter where you complimented him. He said, "Hang it on the wall just so you know what you've got." I laughed and Trav gave a "Huh?" in the background.

July 18:

Well our letters crossed in the mail. Trav was delighted to receive your card. Last week he was saying the three things he can't wait for were going out to the woods, the fair, and Bruce and Mary coming over (Bruce and Mary are my parents' names). This week, since hearing from his dad, he listed two more things: Can't wait to go to my dad's, and can't wait for tomorrow, so I can see if I get a squirrel. He set a rat trap to get a squirrel. He wants to start early, I guess, getting squirrels to sell to Joe.

Tomorrow, both Bob and Joe go to work for a roofer ($15/ hr). We are in need of all the money we can get right now. I'm mixing mortar and Bob's starting the first layer of rock.

I'm now reading Born on Snowshoes, about three sisters living in the Arctic, trapping with their folks, then, trapping with just their mom, then trapping alone. Bob's reading it a second time. When reading books such as these, I find it very encouraging. It gives me a comforting connection knowing that others have lived as I am living, but, many, many years ago. Two other books that fascinate me, written by Bill Pfisterer, are Shandaa (In My Lifetime) and Kaiiroondak (Behind the Willows). Both are memoir type books about old timers and life in the woods long ago.

If Trav comes to the woods with us, I contacted my friend Justine who said she'd be glad to have Traver on her traveling itinerary. She's a correspondence teacher for the Yukon Flats School District. So that would at least mean a plane coming every month, plus a visitor, and some "things" to keep Traver busy on cold nights! Love, Nancy

At this point, we were not sure if Trav would be joining us on the trapline or not, although I was planning for it, just in case. On top of that, there was so much else to think about: finishing building projects, lists of what we needed for winter in ANWR, cramming in the last of summer activities, getting ready for my parents' visit, and saying goodbye to friends. Before we knew it, my parents would be in Fairbanks, and then it would be time to return to the trapline.

August 7th, 1982:

Well, this is it! Last letter until we meet again. Can you believe it? I'm in town now, as our softball tournament starts today and it's Bob's last day of shopping before he leaves for ANWR. Too much going on these days. Berry-pickin', rock-work, jewelry for fair, softball, getting ready for the woods, etc., etc. As Bob always says teasingly, "It's a rough life." Our "easy life" starts when we get into the woods.

I got my jewelry tagged for the fair ($700 worth). Not bad!

We're going swimming later today. The weather is in the mid-seventies and sunny. Have to enjoy it while we can, as fall is coming on fast. No more lovely greens in the hills. The greens are getting more dull with a smattering of gold here and there. We won't get the rock work done, but enough is enough. We're sick of cement. And enough is done to shove dirt in on the sides of the foundation, now.

Trav is busy with his bb gun and insect net. He's out in the woods a lot, hunting and exploring. He makes his way to our friends, the Bakken's, over the road and through the woods (a good half-mile away). He also loves going to the library in town. He's great, really. Bob gets on me to discipline Traver more. I still feel the guilt of being a "divorced family" sometimes, but Traver

153

sure adjusts and learns quickly. He talks of his dad almost daily, but not with regrets, just with acceptance. And he enjoys both of his different lifestyles. He's now definitely coming out with us and we'll have a correspondence teacher in, probably once a month. He's anxious to trap, hunt, fish, and run dogs. So is Bob. So am I. And we're all certainly looking forward to your visit.

Traver with my jewelry display at the Tanana Valley State Fair in Fairbanks.

Mom and Dad Visit Us

My parents did make it out to our trapline and met Bob for the first time. I was so pleased they made the effort and took that time for us. The flight plans with Joe Mattie worked out for the day as planned – this was a big adventure for both my mom and dad! Both of my parents are into the outdoors, but in different ways. My mom loves her gardens, insect and pond life, wildflowers, and birds around the house or in the woods. My Dad is an Eagle Scout, pilot, and more of the camping, hunting, fishing, and boating type.

It was a beautiful, crisp autumn day, and Trav and I were on the first flight out to our trapline. We were flying high on our emotions to see Bob, the dogs, and our B.C. home again. Add to that, my mom and dad joining us when Joe brought them with the second flight loaded with gear.

"There they are!" Bob was the first to hear the approaching plane. Mom and Dad out here; I cannot believe it, I thought. The dogs didn't know what the ruckus was all about, but they wanted in on all the excitement. Plane buzzing, dogs barking and jumping around, a little boy with arms, legs, and mouth in constant chaotic motion, butterflies in my gut about to erupt, and Bob smiling big time. I was wondering what might be going on in my mom and dad's minds.

Joe landed on the gravel bar of the river – perfect landing as usual. Bob had shuttled Trav and I across the creek, in our ratting canoe, to get to the river where they landed. We had just seen each other hours before, but it was a relief that we were all together again. My parents, no doubt, were over-stimulated with all the unknowns, but they were all eyes, ears, and ready to digest.

Bob now had to shuttle each of us, one at a time back across the creek to where the cabin was. This may have worried my mom, but she never showed it outwardly.

Bob shuttling my mom in the ratting canoe.

That day, Bob was a perfect tour guide, like the proud owner of a successful family business enthusiastically explaining how B.C. was built and run. I soaked in the benefits of being the help-mate, and on the sly was carefully observing the interactions between Bob and my folks.

Of course, Mom and Dad were curious about my new life in the woods with Bob, and a lot of their questions were answered on that trip. As a parent myself, I am also very sure they had some concerns, although, I don't recall them ever asking us why we wanted to live this way, as Bob's dad had asked. I think Mom and Dad observed how much we loved our lifestyle, and that was all good and accepted.

The four of us, together at Base Camp in ANWR.

My dad so badly wanted to catch a big fish, like we had written to him about so often. He tried and we encouraged his efforts, but the water was high, moving quickly, and very murky, so all his casts returned unweighted by any fish at all. My parents came and left, of course. I recently (October 2017) asked my Dad, who passed on from Alzheimer's illness in December of 2018, if he recalled anything about that trip in 1982. He only replied that he remembered wanting to see the wilderness, and that the plane ride was awesome.

Of course, once my parents left, I was back to writing my letters. Below is a letter from soon after they returned home.

September 4th, 1982

Dear Mom and Dad,

Hi, guess who? It's hard to believe you were here with us a week ago. Now, you're so far away; but at least you can relate more to what I write about. I thought of you a lot this past week, memories already, like when Joe had you up in the plane and buzzed us as he swept low to the river and then zoomed up. Yikes! I bet that freaked Mom out and delighted Dad. I'm sure glad you made it out to Alaska and here with us. Bob enjoyed meeting you. Thanks so much for being here with us for a while. It took some time for me to unwind. So much has happened since the week you left. The cabin is all set up again, livable, and comfy. Trav has his new bed; he got right back into everything and is more independent this year.

Hey Dad, I made three casts for pike and got one. Then, I caught no more, but Trav pulled in another. We're getting lots of grayling too. We saw a mother bear and cub tracks up where the moose leftovers were. Yesterday, Bob saw wolf tracks down by Ed's old cabin. We made moose steak sandwiches and climbed to the top of the throne, which is down around the bend of the river. The throne is Bob's favorite place to sit, drink coffee, and scope out the surrounding area; I'm sure he felt like a king on his throne up there. Bob pointed out rock shavings (called cherts) that the archaeologists showed him near some of the rock caches you guys saw.

It rained for 2 days after you left, but it's been nice and sunny ever since. Bob's been fixing toboggans, drying fish, and he completed the outhouse. I'm digging mounds for berry bushes, cutting wood, berry picking, fishing, and planning meals.

Out here, the colors are now a beautiful combination of yellow and orange. Definitely fall already. Lovely splashings of nature's

158

bounty, plus the different smells of berries and dying leaves. The coolness in the evenings, the chill in the early mornings.

Quite a few planes are flying overhead – hunting season. Planes make me think of you two flying out here. Do you realize what you did and where you were? I must give you credit, really! Many people talk about doing that, but you DID IT! Every time I think of Mom in that ratting canoe!... I wonder what things I'll be doing when I'm near 60 years old! (As I am writing this book at age 68, I'm sitting on my couch in the cabin that Bob built back in the early 1980s, ready to take my kayak out for a spin!)

We walked down to Ed's old cabin and found some writing paper. Hip, hip, hooray! Most of our supplies for winter still haven't arrived – my writing paper included.

Oops! Gotta go, the plane is here, unexpected! Miss you lots and love you. We are all fine. Love, Nanc

Bob sitting on the throne, his favorite spot and overlook.

Planes were always a reminder of civilization for us – a connection with the rest of the world. Planes were a source of elation or frustration, depending on what the expectations were. A plane with food supplies and letters was always one of my great expectations. If the plane never showed, or didn't bring what I was waiting for, well, that would bring on frustration. A plane stopping by for an unknown reason? Hmmm, my curious mind always began spinning.

September 14, 1982:

So, our pilot friend, John, stopped by... a surprise. Good thing he stopped by (for several reasons). Our friends up river, Heimo and Edna, who just had a baby, both needed to get to town. Edna had to have an emergency operation. John was unable to take Heimo's family out, but got word for another plane to be sent out for them.

Meanwhile, we got a Trapline message that Justine (Traver's teacher) won't be able to fly for three months! She was going to bring a bunch of our food supplies, so after the message, we didn't know if we'd have any flour, let alone school supplies! And all of our other goodies! I was in a low mood.

But, since a plane came out for Heimo and Edna, they brought up all but one box of our stuff. We are eating good. I can plan a meal other than moose meat and cereal. Anyway, it's taken a while, but I finally feel very much at home. Comfortable, and ready for winter. There is a lot to do! Trav's school stuff did arrive, and we start lessons tomorrow. I'm looking forward to it. The program is called Calvert's School Program (widely used in the bush).

So, this letter may be taken in by Bob, as he has a terrific toothache (just like last year) and doesn't think it will go away. So, if another plane comes, he goes. Heimo and Edna will probably be coming back soon.

Bob's sitting at the table, writing in his journal book that you sent us a while ago. It will be his log book and he is taking very good care of it.

It's raining out. Trav is playing with that $5 hand-full of plastic, which is a motorcycle he got at the store. He is also reading two comic books over, and over again.

I'm doing several things: writing, soaking dried fruit, raising bannock, and cleaning intestines. I'm going to try to make sausage. I also need to go back out to where the plane landed– we left some items, and I need to grab the potatoes. I also want to start cutting grass for baskets, and, and, and...

Bob was sure glad to see the stack of cowboy books in the box, and I was sure glad to see that Heath candy bar. I don't even eat candy bars in town, but out here? Oh boy! Eating so much fresh fruit in town this summer spoiled us. Now we're back to cranberries (which aren't very sweet, but come in handy to throw into a lot of things). We also brought in more of a variety of dehydrated fruit to add to Bob's mainstay of raisins.
Love, Nancy

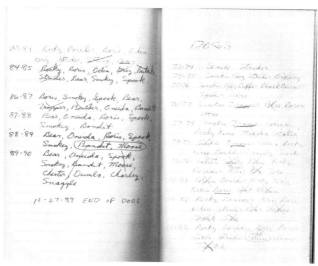

A sample page from Bob's logbook – this one lists dogs and the years Bob had them.

Bush Pilots by Bob Harte

You need to depend on pilots in Alaska, sooner or later. Pilots fluctuate on ability, experience, and reliability. Some I've had are excellent, all the way. Like the time I chartered a flight weeks or months earlier. The pilot arrived:

Pilot: Sorry I'm late.
Me (Bob): What? Late?
Pilot: Yeah, it's 12:07. I said I'd be here at noon.

But then, the charter I had from my main cabin to another cabin up river, on floats. The pilot was new-ish to bush flying. And his glasses were thick. It was a short, 20-minute flight. The plane was loaded so much that I had to lay prone on top of the load. I know better today, but back then...

He pulled into the river (can he read a river, I wondered?) and was checking the plane instruments, etc. Two minutes later we were on a riffle going downriver fast. I woke him up and told him he better pull over. He did, into the rocks. Then he pulled out and accelerated. One quarter-mile went by, then a turn, missing a gravel bar (just under water). I was worried by then. Did he notice the gravel bar just beneath us in the shallow water? If he hit the gravel and we flipped, I'd be under water, under my gear!

He pulled over on another bar, checked the floats, and found a lot of water. The float was punctured. We unloaded and he flew to get it fixed. He was back the same day, and I finally got north.

Then there's John, my first pilot who flew me out to B.C. during the first five years or so. A 180 with ten dogs thrown in, loose. I was the top-dog. Big freight dogs, mostly malamutes. John carried a 357 and said, "Any fighting, and I shoot!" I told him, "Okay, no trouble."

The dogs were so close, they wouldn't even look at each other. Never had trouble.

John would occasionally fly over to see if I was okay. I'd just wave from my cabin. The landing spot for floats was half-mile down the river. I sometimes couldn't hear a plane landing. Once, he flew by, I waved, and got back inside cooking rice for the dogs. They knew they'd be fed soon. I'm talking to them from inside. Then, there was a knocking on the door! Scared the hell out of me! First time someone ever knocked at this door (still, to this day, the only time someone has knocked in almost 40 years!). It's John. He walked half-mile up to check on me. Not an easy trail. From then on, he would choke the engine over the cabin if landing. You have to have bush pilots! It's your skin. Your life. Charter outfits hire pilots. Some pilots only know paved runways. Some pilots never drove a boat and don't know rivers. Good luck with that!

After the excitement of flying into ANWR, and settling in for the season, although each day is different, there is routine. Some clips from the letters below emphasize that routine, which usually had much to do with what critters were around:

September 17th, 1982:

Trav and I both got a pike. The secret is my homemade lure. We ate duck last night with real potatoes.

Trav is catching shrews around the cabin, I'm patching tents, chinking the cabin with moss and mending clothes. Bob is getting trapping gear ready. We just heard it's snowing a little north of here.

I started cutting grass to make baskets. We're drying moose meat. We cut long thin strips and hang them to dry over the Yukon stove. Bob munches on dry meat all day long. We also continue drying fish for the winter.

September 19th:

Got a bear. Ate bear liver and heart last night. Deee-licious. We are doing okay this year. Bears sure are awesome critters. Especially up close, out of a cage, and in the wild. I like looking at their stories in the tracks they leave. The meat tastes different depending on what they've been eating and what kind of shape they're in. I'm not as fond of bear meat as I am of moose and caribou. But I'm certainly thankful for all of it.

The water is beginning to freeze in the little ponds now. It was a nice day today, though, I got some washing and cleaning done. I told Trav it was a "domestic day."

Trav had an exciting event, as he spotted an owl in the woods today. There are mostly great grays out here. We love hearing them hoot at night and we appreciate their appetite for shrews and voles. I say, "Take them all!"

September 27th:

Today it snowed. A fluffy, white coating on fall debris, shushing everything to stillness and quiet. Trav was so excited when he got up and saw it. He dressed quickly and was out rolling, tumbling, running, laughing, and then back in five minutes because he wanted his snowsuit on. And off he went again. Even though it's currently 'school time' for the day, all he has done so far is to get two sets of clothes sopping wet. There have been moose and bear passing by along the river, and we kept missing them. So, we've been clearing the willows and old logs and dead branches around the cabin for a better view.

Today, when I went fishing downriver, I saw five otters. At first, I saw three, and followed them downriver a while before coming back. I thought they'd gotten into my fish, but no, there they were, all diving, rolling, and making chirping and snorting sounds when they came up out of the water. I kept following them and realized there were five. They were sniffing and slinking around the beach for a while before scampering to the bank. Such playful, curious little critters.

Bob and I started talking about writing a book the other day. Bob says he could tell me lots of ideas and stories, but that he wasn't a writer.

October 4th:

A few days ago, Bob brought back a partially eaten beaver that a fox was checking out. Bob will use the beaver for bait. And I can use the teeth for my craft creations. He left the carcass on the bank with the canoe. So, yesterday, we went fishing and saw that cross fox come by looking for the beaver. Oh, he was cute. He saw us and pranced around, trying to figure out how to best get away. Bob said "Let's go watch him swim!" When we got to the bank, that fox was jumping around looking at us, and then he decided to double back by the creek so he didn't have to get wet. Maybe he'll be back today.

We started getting a different kind of fish that feed on the bottom called burbot. In one of our books, we read that the Natives eat the liver and eggs from burbot. Well, the eggs are hardy and good. The liver is quite large for the size of the fish and tastes okay. The fish itself is mild and a bit like chicken. The creek has frozen, so we are ice-fishing now, getting about eight a day. Trav and I tried ice-skating, which ended in tears and sore ankles. Then, Bob started "bowling" with ice-blocks, so Traver and I joined in on that – we all wound up having a fun time together.

The weather got cold fast, but there is no snow sticking to the ground yet. We have our big stove going now and tonight I get a REAL tub bath. Can't wait. Trav had one last week, though, only in a puddle because we couldn't get enough water heated fast enough. Oh, what a treat I'm looking forward to. Love, Nancy

My Pregnancy

Because I didn't write about my pregnancy in the letters, I don't remember when I found out I was pregnant. However, it must have been about this time, calculating that Talicia was to be born at the end of June. I was probably not too surprised, because I was not on birth control. Bob and I had discussed the subject of having children. I definitely wanted to have one more. Bob said that the decision was up to me, I do remember that. He was neither very for or against having children. So, I did decide, and when I realized I was pregnant, I was delighted. Bob, as usual for him, didn't have much to say, but I believe he began thinking quite often about it, when he was alone. He was a thinker, not a speaker.

As for sharing this big event with my family – no way! I did not want anyone worrying about me any more than they already were. So, we just kept it a secret between Bob, Trav, and myself. Since I knew we would be in town for the birthing time, I didn't concern myself with the possibility of delivering a baby in the wilderness. It was actually good timing. All the normal daily activities in fall time would be during my early pregnancy months, and wintertime was too far in the distance to think about. I probably never did. This was also my second pregnancy, and I was very active until my 8th month with Traver (jogging and playing racquetball). I look back on those days now and think, "Not too smart, Nancy." Maybe that was the reason for Traver's early birth. However, back then, in ANWR, I figured I would remain active throughout my pregnancy without a problem.

October 14th, 1982:

Since I last wrote, much has happened (in our world anyway). The weather brought lots of snow, and Bob is now running dogs. Trav and I just put out some rabbit snares, but all the good spots by the willows are unreachable since the river isn't frozen over yet. While setting up the snares, Trav and I saw caribou cow and calf tracks, as well as marten, otter, lynx and fox tracks.

A couple of days ago, Trav fell in the river up to his thighs. I imagine it was very cold. He was more shocked than anything. We got him changed readily and he is a bit more cautious now. However, we can still fish on the river every so often, when the slush and ice aren't so bad.

Today, Trav and I went downriver and he spotted some tracks and said "Porcupine!" I think he was remembering last week when we followed porcupine tracks that ended at the river. "I don't think so, but I'm not sure, so let's follow the tracks and find out," I suggested. Off we went into the woods. It's like following a map, looking for a treasure. One clue at a time, track by track, and in a little while we saw the tracks lead to a little cubby near that rock cache. We looked in and there was a burbot! What a surprise. Then, off to the side were marten tracks. So, that little marten had stashed his treasure and off he went. I wonder if we scared him off? When we got back to the river, we saw marten tracks all up and down the river to the mouth of the creek. We could see that he was sniffing out the spot where we had been fishing the day before. He was "fishing" himself and had dragged that burbot a long way to where he stashed it in the cubby. I wondered if I should take it. A burbot... yum! So, I did. I later asked Bob if that marten would go back for his dinner, and Bob said yes. I felt guilty and took back a big grayling, fresher than his burbot, and left it for him. I hope he thought it was a fair-trade!

Summertime in Alaska goes by quickly, especially with all the daylight. But fall time disappears in the blink of an eye – and I love fall. There are still many daylight hours, temperatures are manageable, an abundance to eat, and fun outdoor activities on the water or in the woods. Then the long winter sneaks up and bites you in the ass. But at least there are holidays; for me, holidays have always been fun times. School projects and stories for Trav were holiday oriented, and he was thriving on the mingling of school learning with wilderness living. Halloween, Thanksgiving, and Christmas were always big in my family. I naturally lunged into these holidays with enthusiasm. Bob, not so much, but he would join in and contribute when he saw the fun we were having. Whenever possible, Bob would try to provide some sort of bird for holiday dinners. I tried to plan special meals and hand make gifts and decorations for Christmas. Advent calendars, pin the tail on the moose, and creating Halloween costumes and treats offered many hours of family activity.

I spent a fair amount of time thinking and planning for our holidays, and I always wrote to my family about our holiday activities in ANWR. In turn, I was always excited to think, and later hear, about my family's holiday celebrations.

October, 1982

It was below zero today. Although we forgot the thermometer, the radio is pretty accurate, and Bob came in with his mustache all frosted. We get frost crystals in our nose when we breathe in. To melt them, you can squeeze your nostrils together (gently) and the warmth will melt the crystals of ice... for a while.

We heard Christmas advertisements twice already since October 10th. Already! But, I'm actually getting started on a few gifts myself. I'm making Traver some mukluks out of moose and caribou hides. They should be quite warm. Later, I'll attempt some sort of trapper's hat out of the scrawny or damaged marten skins we have left from previous years.

October 24th: Sunday. And even out here, Sunday's are a little bit different than Monday through Saturday. Mondays through Saturdays we always listen to Paul Harvey and "The Rest of the Story." He's not on Sundays, nor is there much of any other news. So, Bob's out breaking a trail with the dogs. Trav is out playing with the pups. I just finished chopping wood and I'm waiting for beans to boil before I take Trav across the river to set snares. The river hasn't totally frozen yet, but we cross in certain safe spots. We've only gotten five rabbits over here, but we'll get a lot more in the willows across the river.

Last night there was a message to Heimo and Edna upriver that their Blaze-O fuel and mail would be up within a week. And, our friends Carl and Sandy Bakken, sent a message that our mail in Fort Yukon was forwarded back to Fairbanks. Unreliable mail service, but with the plane coming this way, there's hope for some letters being dropped off.

Bob leaves tomorrow to start setting up his tent camp for overnights on his long traplines. He just started putting traps out and got his first marten today. Trav got his first rabbit this week, too.

It's getting dark around 4:30 p.m. now and is quite cold. Trav and I wore face masks today to check our snares. Good thing I got his mukluks done. They're working just fine. Bob and the dogs fell through the ice in the river trying to cross last week. He chances it every year.

November 2nd:

Election day. We didn't vote. Bob left for camp a few days ago but came back the same day because he ran into huge grizzly bear tracks. He decided to come home for a couple of days in case the grizzly was headed his way. We never did see anymore tracks or signs, so Bob left again today. Sure is quiet tonight, except for the wind howling like crazy.

We had a good time on Halloween. Trav and I dressed up and trick-or-treated with each other. Mom, we brought out those Halloween disguises that you gave to Trav. And we all enjoyed messing around with those. Trav has been into drawing lately, a lot of Halloween stuff: witches, witches, and witches. Then Bob drew a skeleton, which Traver copied and sent to you. Bob drew a pirate next and Trav copied that. Mice, spiders, and anything else someone may draw, Trav will copy. He does quite well, really.

Trav, dressed up for Halloween with a scraggly frozen fox.

November 11th:

I've given up on a plane coming. Maybe you won't get this letter until after we talk in January! We're all ready for Thanksgiving. Bob got us two ptarmigan. He just nicked the second ptarmigan, and it flew a little way into the willows. He went after it and since it was white and on snow, he didn't see it until it moved. When the ptarmigan moved (about four feet away) Bob reacted and swoosh! He was interrupted by a hawk owl moving in ahead of him. The hawk owl jumped on the ptarmigan and began pecking at it. Bob said it was really something to witness, but he didn't let that owl take our Thanksgiving dinner. So we are looking forward to ptarmigan, barley pilaf with hollandaise sauce, and pumpkin pie with dream whip. Treats I have saved up.

November 26th:

And we ate it all! Delicious. But I couldn't help thinking a little bit about turkey skin, sweet potatoes, and fresh salad. Trav and I made some turkeys out of spruce cones and then of course, the turkeys made by tracing your hands on paper and coloring it. He loved that.

We recently started eating lynx. As I told you, I think it tastes like turkey and has been a nice change. Traver has gotten two of his own rabbits now – we're pretty proud of that. The only thing is, he knows when we get a fresh (not frozen) rabbit, we usually eat the liver. And, oh boy, you should see what we go through at dinner time with the liver. What a scene. First, all the faces and moans and groans. Then, the breaking of little pieces and stuffing it in with mouthful of other food to hide the taste. And then, hoping for no gags and spitting up. This all takes about forty-five minutes for half a teaspoon of liver! Reminds me of when us kids had to taste gross foods our parents thought we should try. Remember that old napkin trick of pretending to wipe your mouth but actually depositing the yucky food in the napkin? Trav figured out a trick of his own. I found a big hunk of liver underneath the table one morning.

I was so glad to get your Trapline Chatter message a few days ago. I was hoping for one. It is awful not getting any mail for three months. I know it's worse for you, but we are fine. I think Bob and Trav are developing colds right now, but besides that, no illnesses.

Right now, Bob is down at the South cabin for a couple of days. He's pretty much done up this way, and is anxious to be in new territory. He's doing quite well trapping so far. Over thirty marten, three fox, and two lynx. There's a pack of wolves roaming the river this past week. They are smart, but maybe he'll get one.

I'll be thinking of you all this Christmas holiday, knowing you are all together. I even told Bob if a plane came by I'd be tempted to hop on it and continue to the East coast, which got us into a discussion about Christmas holidays in the future. I said I was going to go home one of these years, soon, he said, "If the money is there." I replied, "That would be forever and never if we depended on trapping," and I told him it is more important to me than getting the house done. Of course, he doesn't see it that way, and I won't get into it anymore. However, I believe that was our first real disagreement. Anyway, keep me informed of the Becker Christmas plans, and if a get together is happening again, I'll start working on Bob early. Meanwhile, please send me some pictures of your Christmas together. Less than five hours of daylight now. I rush to get all the chores done. Although, it's not too cold; the weather has only been 30 below a couple of times.

December 5th:

Well, when it rains it pours. A plane last week and now this week. We weren't expecting it to stop, but it did, and Trav and I ran out with our letters. We also got a message last night from Sandy Bakken saying our mail would be coming up Tuesday. Then a message from the substitute correspondence teacher *from Fort Yukon saying he'd be out to see Traver about school – weather permitting (always weather permitting!). I was so excited last night, I couldn't sleep.*

Traver is a bit anxious about seeing his "teacher." He has learned to write his numbers, 1-5 so far, and he loves copying letters. He talks more about seeing his dad now, but not any great desires about it. Trav even said he wanted to go to tent camp with us after Christmas. I was surprised, but feel some of that is just talk. And I know Traver will be anxious to be with his dad again, as soon as we leave here in another month.

Bob's back with three more foxes from his business trip down south. He's sticking around for the plane on Tuesday, then leaves again on Wednesday. We rush to get everything done outside between 9:30am and 1:30pm when there's enough light to see. Long evenings inside, but in three weeks, the days start getting longer. Yippee! No need to send this letter to Gail and Jeff. I'll write them tonight.
Love, Nanc

Mid-December:

Yesterday was quite a full day for all of us. The plane came. Trav's correspondence teacher came, as did our mail. No packages except one the Mattie's put together for us, which was great. It's so good to hear from everyone. Trav got a little extra attention, and the pilot gave us news about our friends in town. We ate bannock and lynx a la king, and spearmint tea, too. The teacher brought us two apples, two oranges, and a bunch of celery, which we devoured rather quickly. The other student the teacher was scheduled to see that day was Heimo and Edna's daughter, Melinda, age eight. Given eight dollars on his school district budget for lunch that day, the teacher split the lunch money on groceries for us. In Fort Yukon, he bought one-half rotten bunch of celery (it was delicious), two mushy apples (they were still good), and two very tasty but very old oranges. The Matties (dear Sandy) also sent us a box of goodies: four oranges, four bottles of carbonated juice, one pound of cheese, three nutrition bars, some stationary, a Christmas story book, an advent calendar for Trav, bag of sesame carob coated treats, and a seven pound turkey! Now I won't have to think about Christmas dinner; I'm so glad we won't have to eat rabbit or lynx. Though, I am thankful for every single one of those we get. I also saved three potatoes for Christmas, if they don't die on me in the next three weeks, along with a handful of raisins and a teaspoon of cinnamon for cinnamon rolls on Christmas morning.

We're running low on supplies. Don't worry though, there's plenty to eat, but we just get tired of the same old grains, legumes, etc. I start thinking about going up and down the grocery aisles. Bob says, "It's never as good when you get to town, and you're always disappointed if you think like that." I know that from experience, but sometimes I just can't help it.

I've been decorating the cabin for 3 days and making a scrapbook for Trav to take to his dad's. I goofed up the other day, taking a picture of Trav sawing down our Christmas tree. Had to use a flash, of course, because there is not enough light to take a picture. Anyway, I dropped the flash down my sweater to keep it warm and forgot about it. Trav and I got back to the cabin, with the tree, but minus the flash...bummer. Now I won't be able to take any more pictures, unless I figure out something.

We made wrapping paper the other night and Trav wrapped up his squirrel skin for his dad, which I'm sure Tim will be "delighted" to get. I laugh when I think about him opening that one. Hope he handles it well. Trav is very proud of the gift. Everyday, Traver is talking about weasel tracks he sees, and tells us a great, big, long, carried out, made-up story about those tracks. I hope he finds a new audience soon, because it's very interesting the first couple of times, but then we get a bit "weaseled" out.

December 22nd:

Every time Bob gets back from a trip farther south, Traver is excited to see him and have him back, but those two are not physically close. Traver stays a distance away and talks Bob's ears off asking about what he got, how the dogs are, and what we did here at the cabin. Poor Bob is pooped and cold from the ride in the wind and just wants to sit and relax. Last time he looked at Traver and said, "Don't you even say hi first?" So, this time, Traver has it planned out. The exchange ought to be interesting to watch. Bob is straightforward with Traver, shares his knowledge freely, and loves to tease Traver. Trav loves it all but sometimes ends up crying and laughing at the same time from an overdose on teasing. They get along like two brothers. But Trav always knows who is boss. Although he still loves to say, "I dare you," to Bob.

We just found out Heimo had to go to town again when he discovered he had beaver fever*, an illness you get from the beaver poop in the water. I asked Bob, "What about us?" He said, "No worry, no beaver around here."

We've all been healthy, except for Bob's toothache. How much our health means to us, right? Especially as the years go by.

December 29:

We had a nice quiet Christmas. Trav was so excited. We read a book on Santa Mouse, then Trav got a small note and gift from Santa Mouse. I think that was probably the most exciting thing for him. He wants me to be sure to bring out some cheese next year for Santa Mouse.

The turkey we had for Christmas was delicious. It lasted a few days, with soup and all. Now, we're back to rabbit. We decided that when we get back to town, oranges and fresh salad are at the top of our list.

It's warm here. Unbelievably, 26 above zero. I'm enjoying the weather, but too much of this temperature is not good for the fur. Bob's writing an article to send to Trapper Magazine about marten sets. He knows his stuff when it comes to trapping.

<u>Chapter 6:</u>

1983

I don't remember where we spent New Year's that year. It was never a day that was much celebrated in my life. We were in the middle of more transition, as we all flew to town, and Traver's big departure for his dad's was immediate. We would not see Trav again until summer. Bob and I planned to pick up more supplies and quickly head back out to the woods, as it was easier than spending more time in town chaos. However, things don't always turn out as planned– especially when at the whim of interior Alaska winter weather, as you'll read about in my letters below.

January 6, 1983

We're going nuts. Got Trav off on the plane for his dad's. Salem, Oregon will be rocking with excitement tonight when Trav arrives. It's 55 below zero here in Fairbanks. Can't even rent a car. We're walking, bussing, and shopping. One big headache!

January 8:

Still in town. We're staying at Joe and Sandy Matties'. What a busy place, with Joe bringing in trappers and Sandy with her sewing business. Joe didn't want to fly us out today due to weather, so a whole day to do absolutely nothing.

Joe also just got an emergency call. Some guy in the bush broke his shoulder and the State Troopers won't send help out to get him unless he's on his deathbed. So, Joe went out to get him. He was out the door and then discovered he had a flat tire. Luckily, another friend was here to help, so now Joe, Bob, and the other friend have gone to town. Bob is flying out to the bush to help Joe with the broken shoulder guy.

January 13th:

Look at that date, and we're still in town! The weather is still too nasty to fly. We were all set to go this morning and found out that somebody had unplugged Joe's plane, so that ended our plan. We'll try again tomorrow. But this time, Bob goes alone. I was supposed to be flown to town by the school district January 17-20 for a parent conference, so I thought I might as well just stay until then. I'm looking forward to the conference, as it is for teachers in the bush, as well as parents teaching their kids in the bush. There will be about 70 parents or more, from all over Alaska. I can't wait!

Finally, the weather cooperated and Bob was able to fly out to the trapline with Joe. After attending the conference, I too headed back to ANWR. But rather than staying at Base Camp, we were instead at tent camp. With Traver back at his dad's and Bob out trapping, I had some lonely days at tent camp.

January 27, 1983

Hi from tent camp! It took me a long time to finally get here. Flew in on the 23rd, Bob's birthday. I made him a cake and brought it out. He's already gone: in fact, he left on his birthday for an overnight, and today he left again for another overnight. It's pretty lonely for me, after being around lots of people in town, and also adjusting to Traver being gone.

Coming back out, we flew right over tent camp. Bob was on the ice waving. None of us in the plane knew exactly where tent camp was, but we found it quickly when passing it by. It's been an adjustment after the motel stay, restaurants, and people... to a tent, dry food, and nobody. My headaches disappeared almost instantly. I was having them in town almost every day. It's nice to hear the wind blowing again, the ice on the river cracking, the owls hooting, and the dogs moving around, occasionally chomping on a piece of frozen poop. I'm sleeping much better and feel so much more alive. It's light by 8:30am now and not dark until 3:30pm.

I have two snare lines out. The river has lots of overflow, making it easy for hauling water. Otherwise, it's chipping ice or melting snow for water.

Since I have no window in the tent, I hung up a photo of a window with a nice scene. When I got back, the place was a mess. Bob had stacked all the boxes of food and supplies inside the tent which took up one third of the space. There was some snow inside the opening of the tent and piles of clothes along with other junk. It looks like home again now, though. Bob's going to make a backrest for the floor when he gets back. My back hurts a lot from bending over so much.

Since I flew right to tent camp, some important supplies didn't make it here from B.C. when Bob brought our supplies down. For instance, no pan to cook in... what? So, we are cooking out of cans. No sprouts. And no porcupine skin with quills for making my jewelry. Oh well, c'est la vie.

February 6:

Bob is off downriver for 5 days. I feel badly for him. Since Bob's been back, he's only got two fox, two marten, and one lynx. Not good. He's kind of bummed. Last week he saw a lot of lynx sign and got so excited, like a kid, it's all he talked about for days. But he sets for the lynx and they vanish or fox appear. Fox don't usually go to a lynx set (they are more cautious). Bob puts out feathers or pink flagging tape to attract lynx since their sense of smell isn't so great. So, our trapping lately hasn't been so good. Even rabbits. We get enough for ourselves, but the dogs could use more meat.

Since Bob left, I started writing about tent life, boiled and cleaned all the heads we have to get the teeth for jewelry (also good soup for dogs), and cleaned a bunch of lynx claws which I'm going to try out in my jewelry, too. I'm also cooking and freezing extra food for Bob when he goes on his four to five day trips.

First Marten Kill

Bob had gone downriver trapping for five days, and I said I would check his short trapline in the back of tent camp while he was gone. This was going to be a new adventure for me. Bob had explained marten sets to me, and I'd watched him set them in the past. No Problem! I thought. Up until then, the only trapline I'd taken charge of were my rabbit snares. I really had no interest in trapping anything more, but perhaps my mind would be changed.

Stuffing my parka pockets with items I might possibly need (string, knife, bait, and snares) I snowshoed toward the trail. There was a new excitement in this activity for me, which reminded me of when I first learned to snare rabbits. Going out into the woods on a treasure hunt, what would I find?

Although there were only a half dozen traps on pole sets that I was looking for, it felt as if much time passed before I reached the first set. The trap itself was actually attached to the top part of a small spruce tree, which was sawed off to create a stand for this ramp pole to lean on. Bob wired the trap to the ramp pole, then hung a piece of bait at the end of the pole. The marten has to climb the pole to reach the bait, running into the trap on the way, hopefully getting caught. Below is a diagram of a pole set Bob designed, which was published in Alaska Trapper magazine in 1991 – it should help create a visual for what a pole set is.

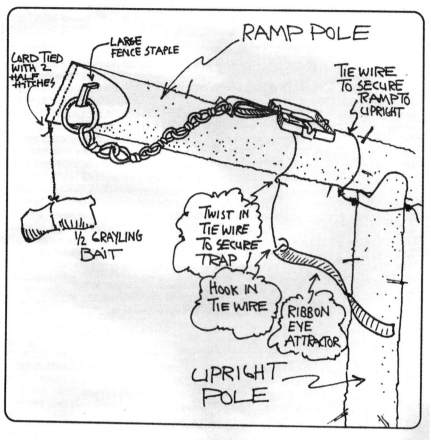

The drawing is labeled with:

CORD TIED WITH 2 HALF HITCHES

LARGE FENCE STAPLE

RAMP POLE

TIE WIRE TO SECURE RAMP TO UPRIGHT

½ GRAYLING BAIT

TWIST IN TIE WIRE TO SECURE TRAP

HOOK IN TIE WIRE

RIBBON EYE ATTRACTOR

UPRIGHT POLE

Alaska Trapper January 1991 page 17

The first set was empty and undisturbed. As I continued on my way, I observed a few marten tracks, although not many rabbits running around for them to eat. Then, I saw the dangling pink ribbon (used to attract attention) of the second set and a marten hanging from the pole on the chain. Good work, Bob, I thought. After freeing the frozen marten and resetting the trap, I was feeling more confident that there might be more ahead.

Sure enough, the third pole set came into my view. Only, it was dislodged. The pole had been knocked to the ground and there next to it stood a marten staring me down, waiting, and darn it, I forgot to pack my camera. As I approached cautiously, a thought entered my mind: oh no, I have to kill it. I hated that thought of what I knew must be done. I started to regret the adventure. Collecting a frozen, dead marten is a bit different than having to deal with a live one. A bit of panic set in. Even a little fear. Though Bob described to me what to do in this situation, I never thought I would actually have to. What if I do it wrong? I wondered.

As I got closer, the marten backed away as far as the trap would allow. We both stared out of curiosity. That was the first live and moving marten I had ever seen, and most likely, I was the first human being it had ever seen.

My curiosity got the better of me, and I wanted to see how the animal would react to a piece of bait, so I threw some. I was hoping this gorgeous critter would react like a dog. What a mistake. The marten jumped so fast, bared its teeth, and started making hissing and growling noises that freaked me out a little.

As mentioned, Bob had told me how to do a marten in, had I found one alive, but after I saw its vicious and extremely quick reaction to the bait, I wanted to be a little more cautious. I stepped out with my snowshoe, in hopes of stepping on the marten to pin it down so I could grab it. The marten, once again, quickly jumped, this time up on my snowshoe, making warning noises, and began tearing into my snowshoe. This time, I was the one that backed away. Off with the snowshoes and time for business, I decided. I grabbed a stick in one hand, a snowshoe in the other, and approached the marten with a confident feeling (maybe even baring my teeth). I was going to get him this time. With the stick, I rapped on its head, but the marten just jumped all over and rebelled loudly with its threatening hisses and growls.

I knew I should have whacked him harder, but he was on the end of his chain now, still making angry noises and warning signs. I hit the marten again with the stick and stepped on it with the snowshoe. Dropping the stick, I sank to the ground to press my snowshoe into the marten's neck. Boy, was he tough – legs all going at once, head turning and twisting, and still those awful noises. The position I had him in was not good, but I was too afraid to move to another. No way was I going to lift the snowshoe from his neck, or my knee from his chest.

182

I thought of the first rabbit I had to kill three years ago and felt the tears warming my eyes: how I hate killing these animals. Please die soon! My arms were getting tired after a while, but even the slightest lift of pressure off the snowshoe brought fierce thrashing from the little animal. Then my knee felt warm, and I thought the marten must be releasing his urine, so it had to be near the end. I could still see his fur rising and lowering with each breath. I wanted to make it end sooner.

I made a move to grab his chest and at that, the snowshoe strap fell on the marten's head and he grabbed it in his teeth and began ripping into it with revived energy. However, now I could close in on his ribcage and stop his heart as Bob had originally instructed me to do. Still, time crept by slowly before I saw his paw raise and lower, his mouth close, and the fight for life over.

My first marten kill is something I will never forget. I learned a lot, although I pity the poor marten who was my guinea pig for that lesson.

From that experience, I then felt ready to set my own marten lines and became more interested in trapping other animals. No, it's not an enjoyable experience to have to kill an animal. The chase, the thinking, the challenge, and the reward of good trapping is what makes the experience desirable. It is so difficult for me to explain my feelings about trapping. I can talk about it and understand the authentic engagement of the entire process when I am with other trappers. I understand the challenge, excitement, and accomplishment of a good trapper.

However, not being raised that way, as a trapper or somebody living in the wilderness, I also have feelings of misgivings about trapping. These feelings come from different experiences I have shared with animals and information I have read about others' sharing their experiences. I developed a relationship with animals which is more along the lines of coexisting and I do not like taking a life unnecessarily. The biophilia concept. I can understand hunting for meat when needed. But, trapping is a different situation. At least for me, unnecessary. I don't want to tell others what to do or not to do, but for me, I choose to not trap.

A Heart Felt Challenge

by Bob Harte
Fairbanks, Alaska

Over the years I've found that checking marten traps can sometimes get routine, uneventful and unchallenging. So introducing challenges can be a stimulating diversion and sometimes eventful.

I remember a routine marten-line check at my Pass Creek cabin years ago that developed into an event I'll never forget.

I was running dogs on the trail snaking through the flats of the Coleen River valley. It was a straight shot out and back

taking three hours or so to run. I had about thirty five pole sets working on this trail.

Well my catch always increases towards the end of the line, not surprisingly. And there in the last set was a nice lively female. The dogs passed the set and stopped and I got off the toboggan. The boredom left, spirits rose and a potential challenge was staring me in the face.

Now opinions on the techniques used to dispatch these beautiful animals differ. I prefer to "pinch the heart. " An old technique I consider Humanest. I have used

If I needed to, I could, and would be a good trapper. I am glad to have learned that skill. I am also grateful that because I lived with a trapper, I was entrenched with learning about animals, myself, and life.

After that challenge of killing a marten, I felt very sad, first of all, in taking the animals life. That was my first feeling. But, I was married to a trapper who saw things totally different. I also understood his feelings. I would like to have been able to feel more like Bob did at times about the animals. He loved the animals and in a more natural way. Bob was proud of me for dealing with that marten. He truly enjoyed listening to my story, which made it more acceptable for myself at that moment in time. I never did get more involved with trapping.

184

The lynx I found in a trap on the same day as my first marten kill.

That same day, after my marten experience, Bob arrived back home. I was checking my rabbit snare line, where Bob had one set for lynx, because a lynx was eating some of my rabbits. Well, that lynx was sitting there waiting in a trap. He must have heard my approach, as he was very still when I arrived. The lynx and I were face to face. I'd always wanted to see one of these cats – alive. It was a beauty! Small head, tufted ears pulled back when it saw me. Big eyes, crouching stance, and trying to hide. Although I had the 22 with me and could have killed the lynx; I called Bob and took a picture instead. Killing one animal a day was enough for me. Don't get me wrong – I hate even killing rabbits, but I understand the cycle of life and how we are all affected. All of life is not pleasant. Animals killing animals is not pleasant.

February 16, 1983

Joe just sent a Trapline Chatter message. He'll be here in two days! So I'll get this letter off. Bob just got back today. I gave him a nice welcome. Made pizza (of sorts) and handed him a bag of cookies. The day he left, it was dark and damp, so I spent quite a while figuring out how to make some cookies with the fry pan and a plate. They turned out pretty good. So, I figure I can somehow create a birthday cake for myself.

Bob also brought home some muskrat. He said, "They're tastier than rabbit." We'll see. Later on that day, I told Bob I loved him. He said, "I love you too, that's why I brought you some muskrat." I had to laugh. Muskrats, to me, are rather ugly. Guess I have a bit of an opinion formed about rats. Even sitting in the frying pan, they make me wrinkle up my nose, but they do taste good! We ate two last night. And our friends up river (Heimo and Edna) had the pilot John drop off some ribs and a hunk of moose meat for us. What a treat! We also have some lynx. So we're all set.

It got cold two days ago. 25 below. I woke up with frost around the sleeping bag where I was breathing and a very, very cold nose.

I have begun hunting rabbits lately. I was not getting many in snares, but I'd see them every so often, so I started taking the 22. They are a challenge – looking for white rabbit on white snow. And of course, their other method of camouflage is to remain still when in danger. However, I'm getting to know their ways and have become quite successful.

I'm reading an excellent book called Sacajawea, a female Shoshone Indian guide. Also known as "Bird Woman." I love this book.

So you're all caught up with my tent life here. Dad, you ought to come back to hunt and fish in the fall! And Mom, you ought to come to tent camp! Bob and I often talk about our families out here. Love you lots. Nanc.

February 27:

Boo hoo. No mail came when Joe stopped by, but I did get your Trapline Chatter message. Things were hectic here for a while after Joe left. There was a chance that Bob could work in town building for $10/hour. If the job was offered, Bob was going to take it, and we would go to town. So, things were up in the air for a few days. Our heads started to gear-up for town, just in case. It really threw us off. Well, the message came back negative a few days later: no job, so back to trapping, which has been lousy. This has been the worst year ever for Bob. He's not at all happy about it and keeps talking, thinking, and planning of how we can make some money when we get to town. He wants very badly to get the house finished this summer. We've ordered more logs and are quite sure we have a guy to help with the work.

Bob's on his last 5-day trip downriver. He's been coming back empty handed since that first trip, way back a month ago. We've decided our time is being wasted at tent camp, and we'll pack up and go back to B.C. Up there we can cut firewood and logs for an addition to the cabin. It'll also be nice and relaxing there, with a table and chair to sit at, windows, and all the luxuries of cabin life again. We're looking forward to it, and I can start back on jewelry making again.

As I've already mentioned, during the winter of 1982/1983, I was pregnant. However, I did not want to worry my family, so I did not tell them of my pregnancy. Eventually, they were bound to find out, and I knew this. As we got closer and closer to leaving the woods for the season, I felt more comfortable with them knowing, so I decided to let them in on my big secret.

End of February, 1983

I was anxious to hear from you about your conversation with Traver and Tim. I kept wondering if Trav "spilled the beans." Did he let you in on my big secret? If not, I will let you in on it now. If all goes well, Bob and I will have a baby this June. It was hard not to mention it already, because it's a big thing in our lives. The baby has been kicking like crazy for the past month. Bob is tickled, and I've enjoyed watching his reactions. He can't believe how my "figure" has changed. I didn't want to tell you in January, in case you'd worry, but we'll be out soon, so if you get this letter in March, that will be a good time.

I went to the Dr. when I was in town and heard the heartbeat. Bob's going with me next time to hear it. He was going to wait and tell his folks in April, but he told everyone he saw, and spoke to, immediately. And that Traver! I said we were going to keep it a secret for a while, so what does he do? When we called Tim, about the first thing he said was, "Guess what? Mommy has a baby in her tummy." I'm sure Tim was shocked, but he laughed when I got on the phone and said, "What have you got in your tummy?" And he congratulated us. So, that was just fine.

Of course Bob's mom was just thrilled – her first grandchild. She wrote and said she was already starting to knit and we'd have the best dressed baby at B.C.! They also asked when we'd be getting married. We hope this summer or spring. So, that's my big news. I'm glad it is finally out. And you have time to let it soak in before we talk.
Love, Nanc

Early March:

It's been lonely since Bob left this last time. He usually leaves a dog or 2 behind. This time, he had to take them all because he's hauling back another toboggan for me to use on the way back up to B.C. So, I'm alone, and it's different. Nobody to greet in the morning. Nobody to cook for. Nobody to listen to. Only the howling wind that makes everything (trapping, snaring, hauling wood and water, etc,) so much more difficult. It's right around zero and longer days. Light before 7 a.m. and light until 5 p.m.

March 8:

Well, here we are at Base Camp. Bob calls it the "Hilton" after tent camp life. Really, it is so good to be here, and feels like a huge luxury. I was even happy to trip over that darn leg on our bench by the table. The bench leg sticks out just enough to trip me on the way to make a fire in the stove…which it did… But I smiled, so happy to even HAVE a bench!

The trip back up was rough. We had to go through lots of overflow and that always freaks me out. Bob sinks in, the dogs get wet. I keep thinking we'll all go under, but Bob tells me he's never seen overflow that's deeper than 1.5 feet, so that's only as deep as we'll go. The poor dogs. We had to break trail through the woods to get past overflow and the toboggans were loaded with our gear. Hard work. It was cold, too.

After the first day, we got to the yuck cabin and spent the night. This time, I was glad that cabin was there! It was about a three or so hour trip. The next day to B.C. was over three hours and I just couldn't keep up, carrying the additional "baby weight," and the pregnancy makes me more tired. It was also more difficult to move around. So, instead of me driving my team of dogs with my toboggan, we ended up hauling my toboggan to make it easier on me. The only interesting thing we saw on that trip was a fox on the river that we must have scared. He ran away and then two minutes later turned around and ran the other way. We wondered what that was about.

Hauling two toboggans so I wouldn't have to drive one on the way back to B.C.

The dogs are glad to be back, too. They know their work is almost over for the year. Time to relax! We're busy though. Had to cut a few trees around the cabin that were falling and dangerous. Bob started cutting the logs for the addition. Tomorrow I start peeling. I have made three new necklaces but can't use porcupine quills now; the porcupine hide is nowhere to be seen. Something must have dragged it off – maybe a dog when it was loose. I noticed several other items that were laying around are also missing. Those darned dogs! They borrow but never return a thing.

We're going over house plans, as well as talking about building a boat and getting into freighting trips someday to make more money.

I finished the book, Sacajawea – excellent story, and being in the wilderness I could identify with it and have a real admiration for that woman.

I got out thirty-nine snares but no rabbits yet. As soon as I put those snares out, the rabbits left. They are catching on to me!

So many reminders of Trav around here... it makes me miss him even more. Can you believe he will be six next month? I can't wait to talk to him.

March 20:

Tomorrow is officially spring. Yippee! Feeling pretty nice here: sunny and about 10 above. Time to end this vacation out here. Bob starts getting antsy after a while with nothing to do. No trapping. I have been making jewelry and enjoying the quiet change of season. Looking outside to see what's going on in the "hood"....What's moving around here and there, and why.

We're both out of reading material now. Bob needs to make a trip to the Yuck Cabin to pick up the rest of our gear we left there, including books. He's been scrounging around at Ed's Cabin getting old magazines to read. There are Post and Reader's Digest going back to the 1930s. Some of the ads shout out, "Sugar!... a sure way to lose weight. Only 18 calories per teaspoon. A good way to curb your appetite." And, "More doctors smoke Camels than any other cigarette." Wow! We've come a long way.

My birthday was nice. I got your Trapline Chatter message, and Jeff's too. Thanks. Bob had forgotten my birthday until he heard the message. I made a molasses cake and frosted it with some cream cheese I had saved.
Love, Nanc

Nancy, pregnant with Talicia, in the spring of 1983.

Springtime brought us back to Fairbanks for another busy, busy season, starting with the road getting ploughed, shoveling our driveway, preparing a foundation for the arrival of logs, peeling logs, and finishing rockwork.

Because I was in my seventh month of pregnancy, I slowed down a bit and didn't peel many logs or shovel too much because I knew the feeling of hemorrhoids coming on. I got used to more of the lazy, pregnant life. I'd work on jewelry in the morning, chop some wood, take a walk, make lunch, shovel a bit, cook dog food and dinner, walk again, and go to bed – an easy life.

I'd visited the doctor, who said the baby's head was down, weighed about four pounds, and maybe my due date was off a bit. I was quite large. Bob listened to the heartbeat, and I don't think he quite knew what to think, but it seemed to make the baby much more real for him.

By the end of April, the snow was almost gone. We piled a big heap in the back of the cache, covered it in Visqueen, ta da – our refrigerator for a few more weeks.

My jewelry was selling well in several shops. Not only did I feel good contributing to our income, but I enjoyed making the jewelry as well. By mid-May, Bob and his friend, Bill, were midway through building the plywood river boat (costing about $1,000 dollars), which was 24 feet long by 5 feet wide. On top of all this, our neighbor rototilled a garden spot for us, and we prepared to plant.

After arriving in town, we also saw a lawyer regarding Bob's divorce, which was never finalized before, so that we could make some marriage plans for ourselves soon. (I didn't know Bob's first marriage only lasted four to five months until just recently when another trapper shared that information. It just made me wonder more about Bob and put more of his story together for me.) Our marriage license and blood work were finally picked up, but no wedding date set. Bob wanted to get a bear to barbeque for the wedding celebration, so we were waiting a while. And I had no dress yet. And no rings! I decided not to push for a wedding date before the baby was born; the baby's due date was June 28th.

Talicia is born

I was planting peas in the garden, feeling hot, swatting mosquitoes, and grunting with the extra baby weight I was lugging around. So tired. I decided to quit for the night and head for the cache (our home until the cabin was built). My idea was that we would have a home delivery of our own, and I'd been thinking about what we needed. My first delivery (Traver) had been early, so I decided if this baby came early, we'd get to the hospital. Good plan, Nancy.

After I headed for the cache, Bob and I immediately crashed, both of us so exhausted from all the summer work. We hadn't been asleep too long, and gush! I found myself wet. I knew my water had broken, and I immediately woke Bob. He didn't believe me, so I said, "Look!"

Now what? We wondered together. This was a month earlier than we expected, and Bob was clueless – and nervous. "Let's go!" He said, ready to enact our plan for if the baby came early. I don't remember too much about that drive, except that it was way too long. I was a little concerned about the early arrival, and I didn't want to deliver in the truck. Bob was nervous and trying not to show it.

Talicia Skye Harte was born on May 30th, 1983 with premature lung development and had to be in an incubator for a few days. I only remember worrying that she might die, and I was a bit unnerved myself. But of course, she pulled through, and soon we took our feisty little one home with us to begin our lives together. It took Bob awhile to get used to holding a little Harte. He was only used to puppy dogs, and he made sure that each of the dogs was introduced as he proudly showed off little "T" in the dog yard.

Bob holding newly born Talicia.

194

So, so much was happening that summer of '83. The new house, the new baby, the new boat, the garden, Bob's divorce, and then marriage plans. Whew! I'd have to say there were some turbulent emotions arising in all that activity. Too much going on. We had to sit ourselves down and discuss where we were at. We had accomplished quite a bit, but were also spread thin with finances and emotions.

I wanted my energy to go to the kids and family time. Bob was more focused on working on the house, the boat, and making money, somehow. As a new parent, Bob was inexperienced and didn't offer much help with the care of Talicia, but he did enjoy holding her. I think we were both overwhelmed with responsibilities. We were just plowing through it all and had no time or energy to celebrate Father's Day. Bob was not real big on holidays, anyway. And there really wasn't money to celebrate with. Instead, Father's Day was verbally acknowledged, Talicia and I signed and delivered a card with special applauding for the new father. Later on, I would remind Bob and myself how lucky we were to have this new baby on board, a brother to help her, and a new home to raise them in.

Since Talicia surprised us by arriving a bit early, Bob and I put off our wedding. Originally planned for the first week of June, we postponed it until the second week of June. All of our new neighbors and trapping friends were invited, but none of our immediate families were able to make it, which probably worked out for the best, as our date had to change.

It was a lovely almost-summer day, sun dappling our home site through the trees. Wild flowers naturally decorated the ceremonial spot. Sandy Mattie had lent me a dress to wear. I wore my old sandals, a new ribbon in my hair, and the dress was blue, all fit for a proper American wedding: something old, something new, something borrowed, something blue. Bob wore a jacket, a blue dress shirt, bowtie, and a top hat. And, of course, jeans and work boots. He was nervous.

The ceremony was very casual. I marched in from the cache, up the dirt path, and Bob greeted me with his smile (the one that tries to hide his missing front teeth – lips closed) like a mischievous little boy. Carl and Sandy Bakken were our best man and bridesmaid. Heimo and Edna's

Bob and Nancy exchanging rings at their wedding.

daughter, Millie, was our flower girl. My bouquet was a lovely array of wildflowers.

The Pastor that married us was somebody that came recommended by our neighbor, since we did not attend any church back then. He visited us a day or two before the wedding, and we shared our ideas about the ceremony. I remember he asked point blank, "Do you believe in God?" Good question. Bob answered, "Yes." I think I squirmed a little, and though I don't remember now what I said, it was probably 'I think so.' On our wedding day, when the pastor asked me, "Do you take this man to be your husband," etc., I answered more confidently with a prompt, "Yes, I do".

"I now pronounce you Mr. and Mrs. Bob and Nancy Harte. You may now kiss!" We were good at following some directions.
After exchanging vows, we dug into a delightful homemade wedding cake, diligently crafted by Sandy Mattie. Then – we partied! Of course, wherever Bob is, there is beer. So, naturally, beer and cake! The after

Bob and Nancy at their wedding in June of 1983.

party was actually a potluck, and we had a great time sharing the bounty. Fish and moose meat were grilling on the fire pit. There was potato salad, garden salad, dry fish strips, chili, chips, cornbread, crackers, fry bread, cheese and reindeer sausage, cut veggies and dip, deviled eggs, a variety of fruit, and brownies piled up on paper plates. My favorite food for our neighborhood picnics were the peanut butter and jelly sandwiches on white bread cut in halves and brought by our neighbor, John, who always showed up at picnics with the same item, plus his two little boys at his side.

After the wedding, the coming weeks would be filled with boat completion, final log placement on the house, and Traver's arrival, bringing more adjusting to our family life once again. There were also daily chores around camp, gardening, getting to town for supplies and a few activities like swimming or ball games, and hopefully visiting with some friends, before the all too soon departure for the woods. I don't think I would even allow myself to think about that preparation. I wanted to enjoy my family and not think about that huge chore.

June 23rd, 1983, 11:00pm:

90 degrees and hotter tomorrow. Looks like a day for the pits. Gravel pits, that is, to cool off. Bob's in bed, and Talicia is also sleeping. She'll be up soon for the last feeding (every four hours now). She's very alert and aware – and changing so quickly. She loves to sit in our laps and watch us talk to her. She can scoot really well too, and has rug burns on her knees. I think she looks more like Bob. His legs, his butt, his eyes. She's so much fun. Reminds me of playing house or dolls when I was little. I told Bob that. He has quite a sense of humor; he looked at me and said, "Well, how about playing some doctor for a while with me?"

The last of the logs arrive tomorrow. A crane comes next week, and things are moving along with the house. Enclosed are some pictures of Talicia and the completed boat (minus seats and beer holders). You like? Bob's pretty pleased with the boat. He and Bill are planning to launch it next weekend.

My softball team is in number one spot. They want me to play and Trav to be bat boy when he arrives. I think I'll only be able to sub because Bob uses the truck all the time. However, I claimed it for Wednesday and Friday to take Trav to swim lessons.

We scored some awesome stuff at a yard sale too which really helps on a minimal budget:

Snow shovel ($2), canvas backpack ($1.50), 5 lbs. Alfalfa sprouts ($1), new sorel boots ($8.50, worth $40), knife ($1), heavy baby sleeper ($1), ax blade ($1), wool shirt ($1), cast iron pan ($1), leather mitts ($2), face mask ($.50), two baby snowsuits ($8), glycerin and scent for trapping ($.50). That was FUN!

Moose are going through our yard a lot. My neighbor down the road had to chase out a cow and calf to get here.

It's 11:15pm, and get this...here come our logs! Ha! That's Alaska for you!

Did I tell you about our new refrigerator? I dug a hole one foot deep. Keeps all our stuff as cold or colder than a "real" refrigerator with the permafrost. What a treat! Trav will love it. Cold liquid on a hot day.

Bob and Nancy with the finished boat Bob and Bill built.

Progress: peeled logs going up to build our home on Chena Hot Springs Road.

July 7:

Trav got here last week. He was really "into" Talicia for the first few days and more confident handling her than Bob had been at first. Trav's already made friends with the neighborhood boys, taken swim lessons, used his bike, and been bat boy at one game. He is inseparable from our new pup, Bear. It's so wonderful to have him back.

Bob's planning to leave by boat mid-August with his friend, Bill, and Traver. That is soon! Bob's friend, Bill, is planning to stay at Bob's upper cabin this winter. Bill is into a more modern lifestyle and is getting a snow-go, generator, and a two-way radio. He and Bob are working things out now, so it looks like we may have use of a radio, and be able to call out in case of emergencies.

Talicia is growing and changing by leaps and bounds. Bob takes her out to see the dogs often, and she is getting real used to them already. They're always excited to see her.

Talicia, summer of 1983. *Traver gently holding his new baby sister.*

Bob showing Talicia off in the dog yard.

On the 4th of July a bunch of us went to a gravel pit for a swim picnic. It was great fun but we came back with 'swimmers itch.' That's snail larvae in our skin. Yuck! My friend Katie says it will go away in about a week.

Bob's mom sent a picture of Bob as a baby. We got a kick out of that. She also sent a lock of his hair and the first trapping map Bob drew when he was about 12 years old. The map was even color coded and with a legend. So, he started early. Once a trapper, always a trapper.

Living in our cache isn't so bad with all of us. Bob is used to Talicia's crying, and she only gets up once or twice a night now. Trav sleeps right through it all.

Tomorrow is town day. Besides swim lessons, the library, errands, food shopping, and softball practice, we'll have a hot shower and ice cream!

Also exciting: our logs are going up! Our first home!

Pronunciation of Talicia: I say Ta-lee-she-a
Bob says Ta-lee-sha...or just "Junior"
Tala= North American Indian for wolf
Alicia= Truth
Talicia's middle name, Skye= Traditional North American Indian naming of child after the first thing the mother saw while giving birth (the first thing I saw while giving birth was sky)
Bob had only picked out a name for a boy, which was Lynk.

Hmm, wonder where that came from?

Bob and Bill are painting the boat now with marine paint and also building Bill a smaller 14' boat. They are discussing a B&B Boat Building business for next summer. Always new ideas! Reminds me of when you (Bruce) and Mom (Mary) were thinking about a possible plumbing business and calling it B&M Plumbing. Ha!

Bill's wife, also named Nancy, and I are canning tomatoes and peaches that we got a great deal on from the grocery store. Trav and Talicia are with me, and Trav usually watches T.V. while he can (a treat). Talicia might start bawling, and she can be loud. So, Traver will say, "Mom, feed her!" If I can't stop at that moment and say that I'm busy, he says, "Okay, I'll take her." And he sits and rocks her. Such a good boy.

The whole family, summer of 1983.

Our overflowing summer was coming to an end, and it was time to prepare for that hectic departure to the woods. Traver would soon be departing for up north with Bob and Bill in the boat. I was glad all the hectic building would be stopping for a while, but I was not too thrilled about the separation of our family and the seemingly unpredictable plans being made for the boys. With fall approaching, change naturally occurs. I can't remember what I thought about taking Talicia to the trapline at three months old. Since Traver had been out with us, that made it easier. It was all the baby requirements I needed to think about, and Bob was no help in those matters. Cloth diapers were a must, as were a handheld baby food grinder, a fold up chair to hook on the table for feeding Talicia, and a Johnny Jump up. And lots of warm clothing.

Early August, 1983:

Oh how time is flying by. I'll be glad for summer to be over, when we can get back to the woods and relax. I'll also be happy not to have to cook for all the workers anymore. It was quite challenging with the space and facilities here.

Summer has been hard on Bob's and my relationship. Lots of pressures, but we did get a lot done.

Bob has a few odd jobs lined up before he leaves. Yikes, that is coming up soon. We still need to buy supplies and gear. I'm very thankful there will be a radio out there this year. I'll feel a bit more secure, especially with the kids.

Trav's been great this summer. I read to him when I nurse Talicia and he gives her vitamin drops. In the store, he wheels her around, and if people comment about her, he beams and pats her head. He really enjoys holding her too.

For the past week, Bob, Bill, and Trav have been packed and ready to go. However, problems keep popping up, so it's "we're going" one minute and "we're not going" the next. It's driving me nuts, but I'm getting used to it. Trav has said goodbye to friends at least six times.

Trav recently lost two teeth. About a week after his first tooth fell out he lost the next one chewing on a cob of corn. He said, "What's happened to my loose tooth?" And ran to look in the mirror. I saw it hanging on his corn cob and he said, "Now I look kind of like Bob!" (That was a very good one.)

I learned so much this summer, and I hope Bob did too. There were also lots of mistakes made. I don't know that much about money dealings and budgeting, but I've never been left penniless, or in the hole, as we are now. But it's only money, and there are more important things to think about.

Mid-August:

The boys! Bob, Bill, and Trav finally departed for the trapline in Bob's boat. They got up past Fort Yukon in the boat and part way onto the Porcupine River. They waited three days for the water level to go up and then had to return. I got a call today that Bob and Trav are still in Fort Yukon and was surprised. Bill and Joe flew up to the Coleen River, and the water was too low for Joe to land. That's never happened to Bob – I know he must be so totally upset. However, Trav is doing great. He caught a 36-inch pike and is thrilled.

So now Bill is back in town (Fairbanks), and I'm going to call him in a while to find out what Bob plans to do. That was another $600 trip down the drain. On the lighter side, I was quite successful today talking with the school district about correspondent studies. I collected reading and math programs, books and guides. I'm really excited about helping Traver to read. I'm sure he'll love it.

Tomorrow I'll pick the beans and broccoli from my garden. Still getting lettuce, a few onions, carrots, and peas. The spinach burned up. The garden might freeze one of these nights. Leaves are changing color and it's darker earlier.

I have since spoke with Bill: Bob and Trav made it up to camp. They had to charter a plane from Fort Yukon. Two flights, and now Bill is arranging a flight for me and him to go soon. I have a feeling our April plans for traveling back East will be delayed for a year or two...

Bob and I thought differently regarding money and the handling of it. Bob was a spender. I was a saver. I liked to shop around and compare prices. If Bob saw something he liked, and had the money right then, he would buy it, whereas I always tried to save for the future. Bob did not. Family visits, for me, were #1 on a scale of 1-10, whereas Bob's rating would be about a #7. I wanted the kids' dividends* to be saved for the kids' education. Bob wanted to spend their dividends on the house building. Differences – like a circle shape and a square shape trying to fit in a triangle shape. On top of our differences, our communication skills were not improving. When the money we were saving for our trip to see family got swallowed up by bush flights, I was very disappointed. I was frustrated. I was mad. I thought there could have been a different way to handle Bob's situation, but I also knew Bob would do what Bob wanted to do.

End of August, 1983:

Change of plans again. Bill is not going out now, but plans to instead come in October. Carl Bakken (our neighbor and new friend) is flying Talicia and me in. It's Sunday, and we plan to leave Wednesday. We'll be flying in a Super Cub – I'll have to leave a lot of things I wanted to take because that plane holds very little. But Carl is giving us a good deal, and I couldn't pass it up. He wants to hunt while he's up there, so we only have to pay one way.

Some areas in Fairbanks got snow this morning, and it was down to 26 degrees. Talicia is wonderful, I'm sure she misses Trav and her Dad. She just started sucking her fingers this past week. Sometimes they go in her mouth, sometimes two or three at a time, or a thumb, a fist, and usually a few in her nostrils at the same time. She's a cutie.

P.S. Sept 7: I'm still here in town. Up and down, up and down. Plans changed again. Had to repack for a different plane. Leaving tomorrow or Friday.

Sept. 13:

Lost track of the days. Ahhhhhhh, it's so good to be here at B.C. again! My days are full and wonderful! Bob just said we should start a log book again. Well, the log bit will just have to be these letters to you (please save them for our future book)!

Anyway, we finally made it here after so many hassles. The pilot, Charlie, was a friend of Carl Bakken's. He showed me the maps and how to find my way out if necessary (good thing to know). It was a fun trip. But, if you could have seen me driving to the airport earlier: a crying baby, a meowing cat, an opened box in the back of the truck with things rolling out, including a bag of skunk scent. AND, it was raining. Oh, I was so glad to leave the ground and get in the air.

When I arrived, I didn't see Trav but soon found him out fishing – then running to me. Being with Bob makes Traver show and practice the grownup part of himself. He seems so much older. We were all so excited to be together again. The cabin looked pretty good, especially considering there had been a flood with water up about two feet inside. Things are getting back in shape slowly but surely.

Trav is Mr. Hotshot with his fishing pole now. He can rig it, fix it, as well as catch and take off his own fish. He looks like a pro the way he casts and reels – just like Bob. Talicia has been sleeping a lot. After she found her fingers to suck on, we noticed it was identical to the way Trav sucks his fingers. We teased Traver about teaching her that.

Since the dog houses floated around in all the floodwater, and mostly got destroyed, Bob built new ones. He also put new canvas on the ratting canoe. On Sunday, he decided to start hunting. Monday, he walked downriver. Tuesday, after stalling on one more cup of coffee, he decided to go upriver... just in time! Thank goodness for that extra cup of coffee because there was a moose waiting! We're now eating liver and heart. Tomorrow, I boil the tongue and also try a shot at liver sausage. Mmmm!

Bob is quite pleased with his hunt, and today Trav spotted a moose right in front of our cabin across the creek. I could have gotten it easily, but it looked quite young, a year or so, and we really don't need another right now.

And guess what else! This is our fourth day of school and Traver can read a story out of his book. He is so proud, and I am glad I got to be part of that. He keeps saying, "I can't believe all those words I can read!" We talked about question marks today, and now when he reads where there is a question mark he is very emphatic about the end of the sentence. Bob and I get a kick out of that. Reading comes with some work, which Trav puts in... math comes easier.

September 18:

Sunday – a day off from school work. Guess what we had for lunch? Tongue! Just like when we were kids, only it's moose and not cow. Bob doesn't much care for cow tongue, so he was slow in getting me the moose's tongue. We ate it on rye bannock as a sandwich. Tonight is pot roast. Oh, and I did make that liver sausage...came out a little livery, but good. I used moose intestine for casings. Although I made some mistakes, next time will be better.

Bob's making another chair, Trav is reading a comic, Talicia is sleeping, and the dogs are eating. Talicia is getting into a routine now. She loves her Johnny Jump Up. We give her a bath in the plastic tubby Eleanor sent. She loves that too. We're all enjoying her, Bob more than ever.

Then there's the diaper washing, which is a big part of my daily

208

Talicia in her Johnny Jump Up at the B.C. cabin.

routine. There are umpteen steps involved in this chore that take a lot of time and energy. I'll share that with you at a later time.

We walked the mile down to Ed's old cabin, like we do every year to check out what's been destroyed, taken, or rearranged. Along the way, we picked some blueberries. Alaskan blueberries are such a treat. Very small, but so full of flavor – much tastier than the low bush cranberries, which are more abundant and easier to store.

Our first snow flurries came yesterday. We're not sure if Bill still plans to come out or not. I did bring up our April travel plans to Bob and he said, "We'll still plan to go, but we won't be able to do some other things." I guess he really wants to go to, probably to show off his little girl to his family.

Since none of our family attended our wedding, or had yet been introduced to Talicia, Bob and I had been discussing a trip 'outside' to see our families during the upcoming spring of 1984. As I mentioned, I was always up for visiting my family and it was a top priority. Bob was a daddy now, and I think that motivated him to make an effort for traveling across the country. His mom was so ready to meet little T. Every now and then I would bring up 'our trip' to Bob, to make sure we were on the same page. I didn't want to write family saying we were coming and then not come.

September 25, 1983

Winter is here! We got caught unprepared. The creek froze over in one day and it dropped to minus two. This is a whole month earlier than normal. Yuck, what a short fall season. Trav is out ice fishing already. Earlier, one of the dogs got loose and ate a bunch of our moose meat. He ran off with ribs. Bummer – we've only had one meal of ribs so far. Bob is going to build a better place for meat storage. That mutt ate all but two of the sausages I made, too. Well, I guess they must've been tasty.

October 2:

Well, after all that cold winter weather we now have spring weather. Crazy! It's in the mid-thirties, very sloppy, and the river that was almost frozen over is now flowing again. Even the creek is unsafe to walk on.

A fox has been hanging around and found a chunk of ribs that was hidden by our loose dog. The fox dragged it into the creek ice where we found it. Finders keepers! Bob found the rest of the ribs out back. Birds were feasting on it.

Fishing is good once again, and Trav has learned to make his own feather lures. School is also going well for Traver, and Bob teaches science once in a while. Trav loves to take Talicia out every day. We put her in a box, all bundled up, and Trav pulls her with an attached rope. He enjoys it and says, "Boy, that's work," after it's over.

Trav and I built a great snow igloo, which I must admit is pretty neat. It's so rare that the snow here is actually packable, and with enough moisture to stick together so an actual structure can be formed. We put candles in our igloo and can have mock picnics inside.

Traver pulling Talicia around in the snow.

October 30:

We've given up on Bill coming out...

For other news, Talicia had her first solid food today: Mother's milk and rice. She really went for it, but not much actually stayed in her mouth. She still sucks on all her fingers, but her thumb has become a favorite. Trav enjoys her so much. When he reads to her, she really seems to respond to him, which makes it great for both of them. School's going well for Trav; he can read, spell, write a little, add, and subtract. He's come a long way, although he likes to test me.

We still have our cat, Mouser, with us. He goes on walks with us, and follows Trav and I when we set snares. He goes everywhere except the dog yard. Smart cat.

Trav, Talicia, and I are planning to fly back to town in early December with Trav's Fort Yukon correspondence teacher. Trav's plane leaves December 16th to go to his dad's. Then Talicia and I will fly back here for Christmas with Bob. I'll stay here at Base Camp with Talicia instead of going to Tent Camp this year. After some consideration, I don't think I'd be real excited about Tent Camp with Talicia and diapers, etc. So Bob will be coming to B.C. every eight to ten days, trapping up and down on the river, but mostly down at Tent Camp, rejoining us here in early March for that last month. Trav won't be here, and I'll have a bit more time for myself then, but I'll have to keep busy. It can get lonely with nobody else around to talk with. I haven't had too much time for myself lately though; I haven't even read a book yet and need to get some knitting done for Christmas. So, the time will be good for those things. Bob is gungho on trapping this year, he's all set up and ready to go. Sign looks good; wolf, fox, marten, and lynx tracks. Otter too. He's going for a big year this trapping season, which opens Nov 1st. Bob won't go to town in December with us this year.

He's also busy making some furniture, one and a half chairs so far. He uses spruce wood for the frame and moose hide strips (called babiche) for the seat and back which are woven. Very sturdy and nice.

End of November:

Happy Thanksgiving! Thinking of you all. We got your Trapline Chatter greeting, thanks! We also got two boxes you sent, one sent two months ago. The reading material was much appreciated. For dinner we made steak with the can of corn Bob found upriver that some campers left behind. I used dry fruit for some yeasted fruit pastry too, it was yummy. It was a good, lazy Thanksgiving. Trav loved the comics you sent him, Mom. His comment was, "Good ol' Mary, she knows I love comics." The wrapping paper came in handy, and the napkins you sent too. I'll save the napkins for Christmas unless Bob runs out of TP while we're in town. One more week and we'll be leaving.

I can't help but think about our April trip. Bob's folks will be in Florida until the end of May. Bob wants to spend most of the vacation there. He's talking about going to Connecticut to see you guys for a few days.

(Sidenote: Since my folks were in Connecticut, we were planning to visit them first. Next stop would be Florida to see Bob's folks. Then, Bob would return to Fairbanks, while Talicia and I would travel to Oregon and visit Traver for a while before we also returned to Fairbanks.)

Talicia is changing fast. Just today she started saying 'Dadadada' all day long. She doesn't want to eat solids unless she holds the spoon, and, oh lordy, what a mess that is. She just adores Traver, and is all eyes for him. Bob accidentally let Talicia slip off of him to the floor the other day, and that's the first time I saw him hold her close. But he's very affectionate in his own way; he always plays with her feet when she sits or lays next to him. She loves that. When he gets home from a day or two away, he always rushes to her bed to talk to her. Anything new she does is entertainment for all of us.

The days are feeling long here, but there is only light from 9:30am-2:30pm. The temperature is mild, 0 or 10 above or below – that's where I like it best.

Bob wants me to check out snow-gos when I get to town. I may buy and bring one when I come back in December. He'll be making trips down south while I stay with Talicia at B.C. this year, so a snow-go would help. Trapping is okay, not quite as good as Bob hoped, but I think he's always overly optimistic (no complaint there, though). We've already gotten as many marten as we had last season. No fox, though, and last year we had lots of those. He got one wolf and is after some lynx now, but there aren't many of those around. Anyway, January through February I'll have lots of time to make jewelry, work with fur, read, write, and of course there's all the interaction with Talicia.

This year in the woods, I've been noticing my age. Bob got me doing leg lifts for my wrinkly belly. Just little things like that to remind me, "I ain't no spring chicken no more!"

How Bob loved to hold Talicia – in his lap,
with her feet in his hands.

December 1:

Traver, Talicia, and I are leaving tomorrow if all goes well. It's been warm here: 20 above. Almost too warm. I heard Fairbanks was having high 30s! If it's still this warm, we'll stay in the cache while in town.

Bob says hi. And Trav wrote "hello" to you on paper. Love to you all from all of us.

Trav, Talicia, and I flew to Fairbanks. Talicia and I waved goodbye, once again, to Traver as he boarded the plane to rejoin with his dad in Oregon. The weather in Fairbanks was rather mild, so Talicia and I stayed in our cache, running town errands with friends, until our departure time to rejoin Bob at B.C. later that month.

December 23:

Talicia and I are back at Base Camp, and it's good to be home. I'm beginning to wind down and catch up on sleep. So is Talicia. As soon as we landed, and heard the dogs barking and Bob talking, T (I began calling Talicia 'T' in my letters) perked up and seemed to know where we were. We came back in a 180 plane and the pilot was great. Bob was anxious, very anxious to see us back, and says we'll never do it that way again. And, (no kidding) I agreed!

It only got to minus 34 while we were gone. Still a very mild winter. Bob got a wolverine, lynx, and a few marten. He's still doing better than any trapper I've heard about so far. So that we could get caught up on all the news, Bob stayed one whole day, then left today. We also cut a small tree for Christmas, which I decorated, and I'm starting to plan for Bob's return on the 27th, when we will celebrate Christmas.

This year, the holidays were a bit crazy for us. We kind of already had Christmas with Trav before he left. On Dec. 25th, it won't feel much like Christmas here, but I'll be thinking of you all. Holidays are definitely what you make of them out here. No outside stimuli at all, only your own.

There is one thing I'm excited to tell you about that Bob and I discussed. We can still come visit in April. Bob said "Yes, this comes before anything else." YIPPEE! I can't wait, and I'm already planning.

December 27:

Bob got home, and we've been celebrating. For dinner, we had a turkey that the correspondence teacher left. I made pumpkin pie, and we opened a few gifts.

I'm really missing Traver, so I'm keeping busy. There's plenty to do. We also have a snow machine now, parked out front. I brought that back with me and T, crammed in the plane, with the pilot, 180 pounds of dog food, 75 pounds of traps, and some other gear and food. I had to cut way back on things I wanted to bring, but at least the important things made it. Bob says he feels like there's a Cadillac parked in his front yard when he walks out the door and sees it.

Trapping is going well. I'll be glad when Bob is back to living at B.C. full time; I feel the pressure of total responsibility when he's gone. Thank goodness the days are getting lighter instead of darker. Only three hours of light now.

Joe Mattie is flying past here tomorrow to deliver Heimo's Sno-Go. I'll have this letter ready, just in case. Love you!

216

Diaper Washing

Around this same time, I included a diaper washing description in one of the letters to my parents. Although I can't find the original letters, here is a good place to give readers a taste of diaper washing in the wilderness. Every modern parent should experience this – you'll never forget it!

First of all: no Pampers, no Huggies, no Luvs! And no diaper wipes either. No diaper washing services, no washer, and no dryer. Our supplies were limited to two dozen cloth diapers, two to three pairs of rubber pants (to go over diapers), diaper pins to hold diapers, and cut up rags for wipes. Oh, and occasionally moss was a good substitute if clean, dry rags were unavailable (for instance, on a trip in fall time).

Being that there was no washing machine, we had to fill a huge galvanized tub with river water. So, down to the river to fetch water. One can't forget all the tools needed for that job: axe, ice pick, pail, dipper, and in extreme cold, a chainsaw. If it was minus 50 or below, I'd have Bob chainsaw through the ice covering the water hole, which at that temperature would be too difficult to chop and a waste of energy for me. After the hole was opened up, I'd dip the pail into the water and haul it to the fire pit, where I'd get a fire going to heat the water in the galvanized tub. There would always be multiple trips for water, or if I cared to hook up dogs and go through that process, then one trip would do it with the toboggan.

The fire I built had to be hot – the water needed to boil in order to make a clean, disinfecting diaper wash; so, chopping wood was an addition to the process. When the water was finally boiling, I'd dump the detergent and diapers in, swish them around, plunge them with my homemade plunger (funnel and stick) and scrub them until they were relatively clean. Yippee – the hardest part is over!

Then, I'd drain the water and begin the process of collecting water again, this time for the rinse. The final step at the water hole and very important to remember was to insulate that water hole with cardboard and a blanket of snow to keep it from rapidly freezing up again. Sometimes,

I'd wash one day and rinse the next, due to time, energy, daylight, and temperatures. After the rinsing process, the diapers were wrung and hung on ropes strung across the cabin's rafters. After hanging for a day or so, depending on the temperatures, of course, the diapers were finally clean, dry, and also as hard as cardboard, but ready to wear.

Lucky Talicia. I would try to soften the diapers as you would a hide by rubbing and rubbing. Babies go through diapers quickly. I never did record the number of hours I spent diaper washing, but I'm exhausted just writing about it!

Chapter 7:

1984

Looking back to this time period on the trapline, I can still feel some of the emotions I felt back then. For instance, the joys of living out in the woods conflicting with the heavy responsibility of daily survival on my own with Talicia, but without Bob, for much of the time. My ideas of family and familial relationships were different than Bob's. Around this time, our differences began to bubble up. I am a mother first and a teacher by profession, second. Bob is a professional trapper first and a father second (placed in that order according to my own perception, of course). The conflicts mostly remained silent, wrapped up and tucked away, too scary for me to look at.

On the surface, we went about our daily lives of doing what had to be done and thinking about ways to improve our life and enjoy it more – always projects, plans, and ideas, all of which were nice to share with each other. But hiding just beneath the surface, even though in some ways Bob and I felt closer than ever, I felt an uneasiness churning around. When it was just the two of us, taking care of myself was easy, but adding an infant to the situation was a whole new level of responsibility. My ideas and feelings were not really acknowledged, not by me nor Bob. However, these internal feelings get highlighted with long, dark frigid evenings. The reality of 'something's missing here' nestled in.

I always pointed the finger at myself, thinking you made this choice. Yes, I loved it out on the trapline, in the woods, and I wanted to stay, but I felt disconnected from Bob in a way that is hard to explain. The trapline was Bob's home, and I was a part of it and loved it. But, sometimes it felt like I wasn't as much a part of it as I imagined. Sometimes I felt deflated – a bit squashed, honestly. At this point in time, 1984, I don't think I was able, or allowed myself, to fully express what I was feeling, except for an occasional explosion.

January 5th, 1984

You may not even get this letter until I hand deliver it in April, but I'm starting one anyway. Bob thinks the plane may come by in March. It's a very different feeling being out here alone (not counting T) when Bob goes on his trips. It's okay. My routine is different. I just feel I have to be very alert and responsible. I yap Bob's ear off for the first hour when he gets home. Bob and I have become even closer since I returned from town in December. We each can't imagine life without the other. Well, we can but don't want to. Bob's made some decisions for himself and that has brought me closer to him. He is an inspiration. Maybe, having a daughter out here has something to do with it.

While writing this story, I am very aware that the letters to my parents did not reveal all of what I was thinking about and going through. I did not get into some of the struggles Bob and I were facing, and I don't believe I ever mentioned Bob's drinking. Although from time to time I touched on our money differences, I don't believe I shared my concerns about our differences regarding the upbringing of Traver and Talicia.

Though I don't remember, the decisions Bob made (as mentioned above) were probably that he was going to stop drinking, and he was working on plans to make more money and/or educate himself. Furthermore, Bob was encouraged by the word of God and his relationship to the Spirit as he sought guidance to be a good father and a better husband. Of course, I appreciated all of these sentiments. From my perspective, though, our partnership was not improving. I was not part of Bob's decision making or planning because Bob was in charge and not open to my comments, suggestions, or feelings. I didn't know how to make this connection happen, and I was wearying of plans and efforts, that did not last long. Getting back to my letter of January 5th:

220

When Bob left to go south again, I sat down to try and determine what I wanted to accomplish while he's away. I decided to make more jewelry, try some beading projects, learn more on the dulcimer, and practice my patience! I've also been wanting to read the Bible for years now, and I'm finally doing it. Although my porcupine skin has about had it, I've been spending time pulling quills for jewelry. Talicia takes a lot of time, too. She's such a doll – she's eating solid foods sometimes and can almost crawl. I can't wait until spring, so I can dress her in light girly clothes instead of snow suits, hats, mittens, boots, and scarves. She loves going outside, but at 30 below zero it's difficult to put her in so many layers. She's like a stuffed turkey. How can anyone enjoy outside like that? Especially a baby. Arctic winter and kids... yuck!

I read somewhere that if you can't commit yourself to something big, then commit yourself to something little. I have a lot of little commitments but they all add up to my one big one – my family. Slowly, Bob and I have begun to talk about important things like kids, our lifestyle, and communication. It's been really good for us. Bob is very much looking forward to seeing you guys, as well as his folks too. We find ourselves talking a lot about our April trip 'outside.' Bob is going to talk to his dad about money stuff, taxes, budgets, etc. And he wants to talk to you, Dad, about plumbing among other things. He wants to get an idea of what to use, and how to use it for our house.

Trapping is going okay. This month is usually difficult. It snows and covers everything up. Then it blows and freezes things and makes life rough for us. Bob is plugging on. He's determined to do good this year.

January 31:

Yay, end of this dreadful month. It was a rough one. Too long. I realized how much I missed teaching Traver and preparing lessons. Doing something important. I'm not so excited about making jewelry anymore, so I've decided to do some more writing, or at least think more about what type of book to write. I need a challenge for my brain to work on.

Bob has been thinking a lot about getting back into education or independent work to develop a more efficient trapline. He's talking about something more professionally oriented for a future career. He's tired of reading novels when he could be doing something more challenging, like studying. I was surprised at that but excited too. If he can find the right people to talk to and not get discouraged, he has a lot of good ideas.
I got your Trapline Chatter message. Good, our reservations are made. Thanks!

We finally got our cold spell here. It was 50 below for about a week. Nasty, with wind. Now it's 30 below and not too bad. Trapping is blah, but Bob is hopeful for the next 2 months. The snow machine is helping him out, but to me, it seems more trouble than it's worth.

Talicia can pull up to a stand and is tickled pink about it. She has her two lower teeth popping up and she usually doesn't seem like a baby anymore. When I tell her, "No," she smiles and screams back at me. More like a yell, actually, telling me to cool it. Bob made a side ladder, similar to the side of a crib, to hook onto our bed, but it was too difficult to keep in place so we just put two rails up horizontally and Talicia can stand up with those. We have her tied from the waist to the back wall so she can't fall off the bed. It works okay. The floor is too cold for her and she dislikes being down so low anyway (she told me so).

Talicia, happily tied to the bed at our B.C. cabin.

February 15th:

I've been dreaming about food lately. It's about that time when we start running out of things like peanut butter, which I usually enjoy by the spoonful every day. We'll be out of butter by the end of February, and we have no goodies at all. When we come to visit in April, you'll have 3 guests that are easy to please. Just give us a peanut butter sandwich, a hunk of cheese, or a real egg, and we'll be happy!

Bob left yesterday for another trip south. Every time he leaves, I go through one hard day of switching gears. Then I'm into my new mode. It finally seems like spring is on the way – only 10 below today. When the sun is out, it feels so good. Everything seems to lighten up and awaken a bit. A little perk is in the air. I saw a mink slinking along the riverbank. Cute little guy. He didn't seem to mind that I was watching him, or maybe he just didn't see me. We also have a weasel that comes to visit about every other night. He climbs all over everything on the porch, eats whatever looks good to him. There's all kinds of goodies out there. Frozen meals for Bob, marten heads, moose meat, dead birds, rabbits. Late one night, I opened the door and just watched him scoot from one thing to the other. He almost came in the door. Bob said, "Let him in." So next time he comes around at a decent hour, I'll see if he'll come in for a visit.

I just started reading Northwest Passage and it's good. Historical novels are some of my favorite reading material. I'm also writing a piece called, "Cabin Fever."

When I think back to my time on the trapline, I don't really remember experiencing 'cabin fever,' nor do I remember writing this article; I recently found this story, and I definitely wrote it. Here it is:

Cabin Fever

It's 60 below, in the middle of January, the wind is howling, my six-year old is complaining of boredom, my husband is on a week-long trip down south on the frozen river, my six-month old is screaming, I have diapers to wash, meals to cook, and a cabin to clean. I am cool, calm, and collected. On the outside. For a few moments. Then, with no warning at all: It hits. I explode. The buildup of emotions; a collection of everyone's frustrations, mixing and churning inside my body. A desperation to release it becomes inevitable. It all rises like a wave and comes swelling out – a vicious, wide-mouthed loud yell: AHHHHHH!...What a release. The kids get quiet and the wind seems to die. No need to explain myself. I bet everyone else feels like shouting too. But, this is mom, who doesn't normally shout. Cabin fever can be a spooky thing and is definitely different for everyone. I just needed a bit of quiet space for myself, and I still find the best advice is to get out and take a long walk with Mother Nature, the best medicine given so freely and received so thankfully.

You won't find a good definition of cabin fever in any dictionary. You must define it for yourself. There are even classes, I have heard, offered on the Anchorage radio stations on how to deal with cabin fever. Of course, this is Alaska, and mostly you hear about cabin fever in northern country. But in Anchorage? I guess cabin fever is like any other illness – it can spread.

I first heard about cabin fever when I was teaching for the Yukon Flats School District, living in a tiny Athabascan village called Steven's Village. The population was anywhere from 30-80 people. Before arriving in the village late December, I was given this piece of advice: "If you start feeling crazy, get out and take a long walk in the woods."

I lived in a small cabin in Steven's village for over a year and remember being asked several times if I had experienced cabin fever. My reply was always, "No, not that I know of." I would take long walks almost every day, and being a teacher, I was also up in the school building for half of my day, which I'm sure helped.

However, now that I've spent four winters in Alaska, all of them in the bush, I feel I can recognize cabin fever in myself, my husband, and my children. We all get it at different times and deal with it in different ways. I believe for a great number of people, my children and my husband included, cabin fever sets in when winter is at its best. Long, dark, cold days in the Alaskan Bush make good conditions for cabin fever to invade. About mid-January, after the excitement of the holidays are over and there are not many festivities to look forward to, the daylight hours are minimal, giving only enough daylight to rush around completing outdoor chores. Temperatures drop to 50-60 below and the winds could subtract 10 more struggling degrees. In order to venture out on days that cold, it takes a good 15 minutes to dress properly. And, as mentioned, once you're out, there's not much daylight to stay out in, so that means you're in the cabin for about 22 out of the 24 hours in a day. I don't even like the sound of that.

For many people, these are excellent conditions for cabin fever to grab hold. My husband gets bored when he's not out trapping. He'll come in and pace or say a hundred times a day, "It's a rough life." Or, he'll bother me and the kids by teasing us. Or, he'll ask me to make a big batch of cookies, then sit around and eat cookies and be content until they're gone or he gets sick. Whichever comes first.

My six-year old son also gets bored from being cooped up inside. When he starts showing signs of cabin fever, such as boredom, complaining, restlessness, or meanness, my husband has "the cure" for him. He will tell Traver to go out and play with the dogs, to which Traver objects and complains but gets dressed and gets the kerosene lamp to light. I always feel sorry for him. Sometimes, it happens right before bedtime. But I'm always amazed that after a half hour to an hour and a half, Traver will come in and check in on us, smiling and yapping away excitedly about the happenings in the dog yard.

As for me… I observe all this; I am a part of it all. I feel Bob's antsiness. I feel Traver's lethargy. I feel the baby's need for the extra attention. But I have so many things to take care of that, for me, cabin fever is watching it happen all around me in the midst of just another busy day.

Both my letters and memories petered out from the end of that trapline season. Closing another winter on the trapline, Bob, Talicia and I flew into Fairbanks sometime in March of 1984. After settling in and beginning our town life, it was finally time for the long awaited spring trip back east to visit our families and show off Bob's and my little girl.

Our first stop was in Connecticut to visit my immediate family (Mom, Dad, Gail and Jeff), plus my grandma. Bob's older brother Vern, living in New Jersey, made the drive to Connecticut be with all of us as well. It was quite a get together with lots of delicious food and good laughs but, of course, ended way too quickly. My mom was an excellent planner whenever a group got together – she even thought of who would sit where at the dinner table to keep the flow of conversation moving. She had a chalk board where she would write the menu for the evening and place it like a sandwich board where we could all see it, like a real restaurant. And there was always cheesecake to devour, as our family was from New York and appreciated a good cheesecake. We would all take a piece of normal size cheesecake to begin with, eat it, Mmmmm and Ahhhhh to show our delight. Then, as the conversation at the table continued, that cheesecake would be passed around the table on its platter from one person to the next, each taking a tiny sliver…until the entire thing disappeared. Talicia was a lot of entertainment on this trip, since no one had met her yet. She did a fine job of entertaining the crowd, as children do at that young age. Just fun to watch.

Next, we flew into Florida, where Bob's parents were. Bob's other, younger brother, Jimmy, joined in on that reunion. All of us suffered in the heat – it was even too hot for Talicia to wear her Easter dress. However, despite the incredible heat, we did still manage to stuff ourselves with turkey on Easter. While we were there, Bob's mom, Eleanor, being the proud grandma that she was, strolled Talicia to the store each day to show her off. Talicia was delighted with all of the attention. Bob's father, Vern, is a bit of a stern guy and can be hard to get along with. He and Bob had the tendency to ruffle each other's feathers, and I could tell Bob was thinking of his home in Alaska. I tried to keep him busy with jogging on the beach, riding bikes, and eating ice cream. Bob and I thoroughly enjoyed the ocean, fresh seafood, and boating with his folks.

On the trip, I was wondering if this would be the time when Bob's parents would try to give him a set of front teeth to wear. Bob had told me that when he first came up to Alaska and lost his teeth, his parents tried to give him a set of front teeth several times. I don't think they could envision him without front teeth. Especially if he was out in public and smiling! (His dad even gave him a set when he came to visit Base Camp.) Bob told me he would always accept the teeth, wear them around his folks a little, and when he returned to B.C. in Alaska he placed the teeth on a makeshift driftwood boat, and sent them down the river! However, no teeth were gifted to Bob on this trip.

After about two weeks, Bob jumped on a plane heading for Fairbanks, while Talicia and I headed to Oregon for a visit with Traver and Tim. Talicia and my visit with the two of them was a very memorable time for all of us. The kids re-connected, playing together and sharing a special bond. Tim and I were able to have some heartwarming conversations regarding Traver and our shared memories. I also learned and saw that Trav was doing exceptionally well in school, and I finally began to feel good about the two very different lifestyles Traver was a participant in.

The week in Oregon went by very quickly, and then Talicia and I took off for Fairbanks to be reunited with Bob once again. I remember it took about a week to adjust – getting unspoiled from the convenience of living with others, running water, flush toilets, etc. However, soon enough we got back into our own lifestyle, feeling refreshed and content.

Now that we were back in Fairbanks with winter finally over, we began diligently working on the new cabin. We were waiting for Traver's arrival, and Bob was planning his boat trip to the woods. Talicia was into everything! And, of course, I was back to writing my letters.

Early May, 1984

Bob's been busy getting door jams and windows done. I'm supposed to be planning my kitchen space. Bob says hi. He's thinking about taking a ham radio course, starting next week. The neighborhood is going to have a huge yard sale next weekend, too. I picked up some good deals from one neighbor who's moving:

- *$2 wheelbarrow*
- *$2 sledgehammer*
- *$2 kerosene lamp*

Griz, our female Malamute, had two beautiful fat male pups. Talicia loves them, and I know Trav will also have a great time with them when he returns. They are just starting to roam away from their mom.

When I got back from our trip, I found most of my jewelry had sold at the store nearby, so I delivered what I had left to them. They have to take 30%, but it's still a source of income.

Looks like Bob did pretty good at the fur auction where he sends his furs. They sent the paper of what was sold and the average prices. Now we're just waiting for our check. Then we'll pay you what we owe.

I'm getting excited about moving into our big cabin. Talicia is into everything, and our cache is seeming quite inadequate. She'll be walking any day now. She's a go-getter, so look out! She understands a lot of words but hasn't spoken any yet. Besides us chasing after Talicia, the mosquitoes have started chasing us. We just put up our net over the front door. Well, time for me to get Talicia into the back of the pick-up for a picnic lunch. She's so much happier outside, and the truck serves as a great play-pen.

May 19:

Yes, to answer a question of yours, I am still collecting school stuff to take out to the woods for the kids. I am so convinced that a good home education does more for a child than public schools (from my experience), except for the socialization aspect. However, I also believe school is important for other things that a homeschool can't offer, like more of a variety. So we all make choices, and I'm going to do the best with what we have. It will be interesting to see what Trav says and thinks about homeschool as he grows up. Tim and I are discussing how to deal with Traver, his school education, and his travel back and forth from Alaska to Oregon. We're not sure if Trav will be going back out to the woods this fall with us. That will be difficult for me.

Hey, guess what? Talicia took her first two steps yesterday. It's so exciting for all of us. She will only try walking without our help. So we stay away, watch, and cheer.

The days here are beautiful. In the 70s, buds on the birch, and nature is bursting with spring in the air. Green, green, next the flowers will sing.

Bob is getting geared up for his boat trip up north. He's waiting for the river to break up* and he'll be gone for one to two weeks. We have plans for building a new cabin this fall (about 20 miles south of our B.C. cabin) and Bob has been clearing a spot. It will be 400 square feet, which will be the biggest yet out there. At last, a bedroom! The new cabin site is the area where he will take a load of our winter supplies and cache them for us when we come back up the river in August.

Early June:

Bob was gone for Talicia's birthday, but we had a good time. Talicia and I went to the neighbors for enchiladas, and Talicia loved it. I came home and gave her a little packaged instant pie with one candle – she loved the candle. I ate the pie! It wasn't very good, but I have no way to bake a cake and it's been busy around here.

Bob has already returned and his trip was good. He made good time and flew back unexpectedly a little early. So, we're all enjoying our time together. He's working on the door and window frames and will go to work for Bill in two days, laying block and getting paid; however, when the logs go up for Bill's place, Bob owes Bill one hundred hours of free labor. That will happen in about two weeks.

Talicia is changing and moving right along. She doesn't like napping anymore, but after a moment of protest, falls quickly

230

asleep. I finally gave her a taste of ice cream but she wasn't really impressed. She will beg for a banana or an orange, though. Three of her teeth are coming in at the top, and she's still taking a few steps now and then.

I'm looking into taking a correspondence course. I need 6 hours of credit to keep my teaching certificate updated. The three credit course on "Native Cultures of Alaska" is very attractive to me. Bob is already studying the ham radio. He enrolled in the class, and we'll be getting a radio before we go out. Well, it's 10:30 p.m., so I'm off for a jog – Talicia's in bed, I'll water the dogs and garden, bring in wood (we still have a small fire at night), make the bed up on the floor, and nighty-night.

June 11:

Bob and my day today – our first anniversary! What a beautiful day. And I got a gift from Bob! It's the second gift I've ever gotten from him – the first was when we met over three years ago. The gift I just received was something I admired in the store where my jewelry sells down the road. It's an etched-glass box with colored flowers and a humming bird on the cover, and it's a beauty. We actually celebrated yesterday and ate down the road at Two Rivers Lodge. It's a large log cabin with a view of a pond where ducks and geese hang out. We felt right at home. I had sautéed seafood and Bob had barbequed ribs. All so very delicious. Later, we had our friends, Nancy, Bill, and Joyce (from down the road), and the Bakkens (from across the road), over for our saved wedding cake top.

Trav finally comes back on Father's Day. Yippee! We have another soft ball picnic planned for that day. Talicia's up to six or seven steps but still likes crawling the best. She'll have on a nice clean outfit and then go out and play in the spruce pitch, dirt, sawdust, etc. Today she discovered the wind blowing while riding in the truck, and was giggling, playing, and laughing with *it for about half an hour. What a delightful discovery. We're definitely getting a ham radio to take out to the woods this year. Bob is studying the code now, and eventually, I will learn it too. I'm also signing up for that three credit course on Native cultures. I'll have one year to complete it.*

End of June:

My two kids really are great. Trav is out with the dogs now. Talicia is dragging clothes, toys, and papers outside, which she is sharing with the pups. Oh boy! We really enjoy watching Talicia and Traver interact with each other. I'm in the process of getting our road named "Skye-Lee Way" (for our kids' middle names, Talicia Skye and Traver Lee). I only need one more signature. The borough could still end up assigning us a name of their own choosing, but I wanted to try.

Beginning of July:

Well, we wish you could see the money you loaned us going to work! Today, Bob started nailing boards for the roof, and it's getting mighty exciting. Thanks so very much again. The roof should be mostly done in three days. Then Bob goes to work at Bill's, and then it's August. Tonight is my last night babysitting for Joyce's 8-month old. Joyce gives Bob a ride to the ham radio class while I babysit.

Since Tim and I have been discussing Traver's education, and Traver is starting the school year with Tim this year, I'm having a rough time knowing that Traver will be going back to his dad's soon. We're just getting adjusted to his being here again. This year I noticed Trav seems ready to go back, and he is too kind-hearted to say he'd rather be with his dad right now. This makes me sad, of course. But enough of that. Busy with town activities, church programs, berry picking – and, the first layer of the roof is up, which looks so beautiful!

August 4:

Any day now we'll have a radio. And guess what else we have set up? A telephone pole for electricity! Come springtime, when we return, we just have to call and get hooked up. We also have a real light in our cache now (12 volt battery-run). This year, we're going to take some lights out with us to the woods – going in style now.

We went fishing (in the rain) and had a lot of fun but no fish. Trav loves fishing, and he started talking about going into the woods again. But he's leaving soon, so I told him to think about it for next year.

This week we'll be very busy with getting things going for Bob's departure. Remember, Bob took the boat up to the trapline in May with the boat he built. The maiden voyage. A good first-trial run. The boat handled well, Bob was pleased, and this was a big added 'plus' for his trapping transportation. He left the boat in Fort Yukon and flew back to town. Now he plans to fly to Fort Yukon, pick up the boat, and motor to Circle where I'll meet him in the truck with our gear. We'll then load up that boat and head to the trapline.

Once again, Trav left, and this time way too soon, to begin the school year with his dad. This decision and experience was tough for me, but Tim and I agreed it was best for Trav at this time.

Talicia and I did meet Bob at Circle and with anticipating hearts took off for the trapline. All of us – Bob, Talicia, our dog team, and I on our first boating trip from Circle to B.C.

I thought the boat trip was miserable, but Bob liked it, of course. For me, there are memories of a nursing baby in diapers in a boat loaded with dogs. I remember, sometimes, when we hit a gravel bar and got stuck, we would have to unload all of the dogs, and even some of the gear, in order to lessen the weight and lift the boat until it was no longer stuck. At times, that also meant pushing the boat too – all of this while Talicia was needing attention and care. On top of all these struggles, while traveling upriver in the boat, the dogs could not always 'hold it' until the next stop, and would be left with no choice but to poop in the boat. How pleasant! Camping along the way was fine, as long as we could find a spot that wasn't too buggy with mosquitoes. Upon picking a spot, we set up our tents and made a campfire. I wouldn't call those nights a very relaxing time camping, as Bob was always eager to keep moving. However, we were able to eat some fresh geese, and that was a treat. Other than the geese, we brought and ate food that was easy to fix. Of course, we also had to feed the dogs each evening – and I remember being so keenly aware of where that dog food might end up the next day…

The trip was a bit chaotic, I'd say. I was, however, rather excited about arriving at our new cabin site after four long days on that river since our departure from Circle. As we got closer, along the way, we were given a few clues as to what we might find upon arriving at our new cabin site, where all of our gear was stashed. First clue: a piece of blue tarp on the bank of the river. Second clue: more tarp, and a large container that looked questionably familiar. Oh no, we thought. And, the third clue: up ahead of us, more scattered containers, a Christmas decoration, a small pile of clothes, some jars, and lots more blue tarp. What on earth? I wondered.

Yes, at our new cabin site, it was obvious that someone or something else decided they wanted to make home with all of our necessities and winter supplies, which were no longer cached, but smashed and totally demolished. Rice bags opened, and rice spread all over the ground, peanut butter jars with lids clawed into, peas, lentils, and oats spread across the earth, discarded bags from this and that, paper, books, school supplies, matches, etc. all spread about everywhere. The culprits had even munched on my winter books and the ruff of my coat – those rascals! Was it a bear? Or two? Even now, the memory is still too fresh in my mind to explain or contemplate without getting upset. Bob, Talicia, the dogs, and I all sat on the bank, deciding whether to go back to Fairbanks, get jobs in town, to stay in ANWR, or, what? Quite the discussion! There were so many questions about what to do, such as: Should I go back with Talicia, and Bob stays? Should we all go back and get jobs in town?

Ultimately, we decided our spirits said to keep going. We knew the Bakkens would be coming up soon – we could get a list of new supplies out with them and stay until at least December. At that point, I could go to town if needed. One major part of the plan would have to be changed: Bob would have to live in tents again during the second half of winter, and we'd have to wait until the next year to build the other cabin. I remember Bob saying, "Oh well, everything is a risk out here." So, we continued to head up to our Base Camp home, with no winter supplies, and check out what was left in our cache.

With roughly 20 miles to base camp, onward we continued. For the next few miles, gliding around the river bends, around gravel bars, listening to the continual murmuring of the boat motor, Bob and I were deep in our own private thoughts. As we were getting close to Base Camp, I saw a grin appear on Bob's face, which grabbed my attention. Then, he said, "There's our sign that we made the right decision! Look what's swimming across the river right in front of us – a caribou!"

That caribou would be our meat to hold us over for a while. Saved by the grace of nature, once again. This, of course, was a big blessing for us. At that point, I had a huge grin on my face. Thank you, thank you, thank you, I thought, we'll be okay.

Obviously, it was a rough start, that first boat trip to Base Camp. But there we were – home sweet home once again.

End of August, 1984

Bob and I are both taking correspondence courses. I'm really enjoying my Native Cultures of Alaska course. It fits right in with our present lifestyle, and is quite easy to relate to. I have reading and writing assignments which feels good because I get some different stimuli for my brain. It has also provided me with some new ideas to try in this lifestyle.

More discussions on getting different work. Trapping, and living on a trapline, is expensive due to a lot of transportation costs, equipment expenses, and various losses. And, we do need our cabin in town finished to live in. I'm going to look into job possibilities for this summer. Bob has signed up to work with Fish and Wildlife, and, if offered, he will take a job. That would be a seasonal summer job. As for me, until Talicia is a little older, I really want her with one of us. I feel at her age, the best care she can receive is from her parents.

Talicia has been another subject lately, and I've had to come to grips with myself and make some decisions about what I want for her, and us, and me; I think that this will become a new routine for us: all of us coming out in the fall time, then Talicia and I return to town in December (and also Traver when he is with us). Bob and I have differences of opinion about what kind of life we want for Talicia. We are trying to discuss this and it weighs heavily on me, but I think the fog is lifting with some decisions.

Right now, Bob's out fishing. I went too and came back with only nine. We usually go together and return with about 45 fish, but being as cold as it is today, I'm going to wash clothes, make soup, and get a tape done for Traver (we brought a tape recorder with batteries to verbally record messages to send to Trav).

I'm sure glad for the caribou that Bob got on the way here – we are eating pretty good. We're also eating some dry salmon strips that someone in Fort Yukon got us. Talicia loves the salmon.

Since Talicia's birth, I'd become aware of my wanting more stability for the kids. I was beginning to see that Bob's idea of 'family' was doing what he felt was best, and everyone else would just follow. That's how Bob was raised. However, that is not how I was raised, nor how I saw a healthy family functioning. I was more familiar with give and take, everyone sharing their opinions, and then, decisions are made. Frustration gripped me like a vice when I saw that Bob did not comprehend my way of family. I felt he did not listen to or even want to understand because he was so set that his way was the way. End of discussion. I often put things on hold to try and bring up at another time, because for me, the end of a discussion did not stop the discussions I was having with myself. I was thinking about Bob leaving again for tent camp at some point, Traver not being there, still with no way to contact someone in an emergency, and then, always, the lack of money. Bob had many great ideas, but they didn't seem to be working out. This weighed more heavily on me than when it was just Bob and I.

8:00pm:

Just gave Talicia a bath and myself a hair wash. Talicia's bath is relatively easy, just done in a large tub. My hair wash needs some preparation and consideration. I have to make sure there is enough water in our supply. This time of year is no problem, but in mid-winter, the ice covered water hole brings more effort. My hair, being long and thick, takes extra time to wash and dry. No faucet, no sink. A tub to wash in, and then possibly use that wash water for cleaning something else. Then, another bucket of water to rinse with. Also, my hair takes a day to dry, so I wear a warm hat to bed to keep off the chill. Ahhh, clean hair is worth all the work!

We had fresh caribou heart for dinner, because while Bob was out fishing he got another caribou. Yipee! Looks like a good year for caribou.

237

This evening, Bob is messing with his radio. He just informed me that he was picking up someone in France. What a toy that radio is going to be for him this year.

Other news: Since we weren't able to build that new cabin south of here, we are putting the bedroom addition (8x10) on the back of our cabin here at B.C. It's over halfway done now. I think I told you that we got a generator and have a couple 40 watt lights. Bob still has some work to do on the wiring, so I'm using kerosene lights on and off.

We'll be taking a short trip soon up to the upper cabin for a day or so. We'll fix it up a little and get it ready for some winter trips up there. After being unoccupied since last year, we never know what damage there might be that needs repair. It's that older cabin of Ed's and not quite as comfy as our base cabin, but definitely cozier than the yuck cabin. The windows and or stove may need repair. I'll be anxious to see Talicia's reaction to her first dog sled ride. All the dogs are very used to her now – they are all very gentle and let her crawl all over them.

September 5:

It's the first day of hunting season for moose. There will probably be a few hunters flying by us this weekend. Yesterday, Carl Bakken and his friend finally made it here. They're having a great time hunting and fishing with Bob. Carl's going to come back in a week or so with supplies we need, and with Sandy, too! So, now we're all set.

Last week, Bob got two big buck caribou, right across the creek. We didn't get to the upper cabin yet. Bob still needs to go down to our tent camp, the bear site, to pick up a few salvageable items plus the ratting canoe. Speaking of bears, we've been seeing lots of bear tracks, so I only go fishing with Bob now, not alone.

238

The weather is beautiful and our days very enjoyable. The fall colors are so magnificent, it is delightful to walk through the wonderland and be part of the gorgeous kaleidoscope of colors so strikingly clear and pure, untouched by any pollutants, or disruptions, other than nature itself.

Talicia is getting cuter by the day. She follows me to the creek and when I get water, she carries a little empty bucket. She also likes to play with the fish we catch. And she just loves meat—gobbles it right up. Even dry caribou. She likes to put hats and underwear on her head and imitates everything, like brushing her hair and teeth, when we laugh she laughs. No words yet, but I believe her first word might be 'hush' (the word we use to quiet the dogs). Other things she enjoys doing: stirring dog food, playing in her own food, climbing everywhere, and crawling into the dog houses. She also picks and eats berries. When she is cold and has mittens on her hands, she is unable to pick, so she just bends over, opens her mouth and zooms in to claim the berry. So adorable. Her diapers are always full of undigested cranberries and rose-hip seeds. More later, gotta go.

Talicia bending over, eating berries directly off the bush.

September 11:

We've had gorgeous weather, high 50s and sunny. Good fishing days and the bedroom addition to our cabin is almost complete. I'm chinking the logs with moss on the outside and Bob's doing final touches on the windows and the floor. It looks so nice. Carl and Sandy will be the first to use it. They sent a message they'd be here by the 14th. Bob's planning to make a bunk bed for it. Then we'll have the back corner of this original cabin open for a desk and a place to set the radio up in. We actually got a message from our neighbors Ron and Joyce in town, but didn't have enough juice that night to send a strong signal back. Bob says he needs a better antenna next year. I help practice Morse code at night and, therefore, I'm also learning it myself.

Photo of Bob at his desk in the corner of our B.C. cabin with the ham radio, sitting in one of the chairs he made.

Talicia is finally saying a few words. Bob says he has heard her say 'not' or 'hot' and 'hush.' But, she clearly says hi and waves at the same time. Of course, I have to watch her all the time, but she's a lot of fun. As I mentioned in the last letter, she's very content and happy playing around the cabin with the dogs, picking berries, or exploring this and that, but once in a while she takes off in any direction. Therefore, I have put bells on her shoes.

Well, for not having our food supplies here, we sure have been eating a wide variety lately. When Carl came with his friend on the 4th, he brought fresh eggs, fruit, and lettuce. Then we started eating some of his survival rations: dry goods, peanuts, shredded wheat, etc. Two days after Carl left another friend from Ft. Yukon stopped by and he had lunch here: soup and caribou backstrap steaks. He left us a loaf of whole wheat and honey bread, three pieces of Kentucky Fried Chicken, some pepperoni made from moose meat, and two cans of pudding.

September 15:

Nobody arrived yet. I started having food dreams. And, I'm keeping busy.

I cleaned out the cache today. It was a mess. Bob built the desk and put all of his radio stuff in that corner. It looks great and makes a terrific use of that corner. I love the added room. It is so nice to be able to walk in and out of two rooms!

Bob saw a big black bear right across the creek today. We knew something was around last night. The dogs barked and got all stirred up.

I finally learned how to bring a pike in without losing my lure and line. That's an accomplishment. I've lost many a lure to pike. Here's something for you to think about: when I have to go to the outhouse now, I take a pair of scissors with me. :) Can you guess why? (Answer on the back of envelope).

Answer: Because we are using old rags that must be cut up first... we're out of toilet paper and have no leftover paperback books!

September 22:

Carl and Sandy are finally here! And we're eating some new foods again! It's so nice having some company. We've been having a great time fishing together. And I got two wonderful letters from you. I didn't hear from Tim and Traver, so I really appreciate the news you shared about them – thanks.

Don't be surprised if Bob tries to talk you into getting a radio. We can hear people talking from all over the world, and very clearly from the east coast in the afternoon. We can only use code this year. In fact, right now Bob is talking with our neighbor Ron in Fairbanks. Sometimes there's a good connection and other times not so good. But it's coming along, and by next year we should be set up and maybe even able to do voice. We have a generator that juices up the lead acid car battery for the radio.

We're all feeling good and healthy and I'm very thankful for everything. My only confusing thoughts come from my thinking about staying in town later when December comes around. My concerns are around Talicia (like me and her alone at Base Camp while Bob goes to tent camp), money, and I'll talk with you more about it when I come out in December. Bob's okay if I stay in town longer, it's me that's torn with a decision.

Talicia calls Bob 'Dodin' and he loves it. She doesn't call me anything yet. She's great! A real joy. She also says 'gick' for stick and 'booboo' for caribou. Bye, Love you.

As I mentioned earlier, my pregnancy was kept secret until I got to Fairbanks – and there were other situations I did not write about in the letters to my parents. This was to keep my parents from worrying about us anymore than they were already. If one of us got hurt badly, I might not mention that, but I don't recall very many critical situations happening – except one. Because I didn't write about it at the time, the details are gone, but the memory is still very much alive. I'll just call it 'the critical situation.'

The Critical Situation

Through the years, I witnessed many incidents and accidents, like poor Bob's abscessed tooth, the bear that was between Bob, Traver, and me, our foster son Steve's deep knife wound, and Bob and/or Traver falling through the ice on the river. However, of all the accidents, injuries, close calls, and bad mistakes, one particular incident stays in my memory as the most worrisome.

To those that haven't experienced the kind of remoteness we lived, this situation might not seem like much; however, I am a mother, and if the reader is able to put themselves in my boots for just a few paragraphs, they might understand a touch of what it was like for me.

Talicia was a young infant, probably seven months old. One day, out of nowhere, she developed a very high fever and became listless. We could not figure out the cause. Something she ate? Beaver fever? I begged for an answer and searched through our go-to book, Where There Is No Doctor. If ever I had a prayer to be answered, it was now, I remember thinking. We could only do what we already knew to bring the fever down, trying to cool Talicia and nourish her if possible.

Talicia's condition did not get better as the day continued – she was barely moving for days. I believe it was three or four days of constant agony, both for Talicia and what was going on in my mind. Bob, I'm sure, was trying to get a message out on the radio, but, honestly, I don't remember. I only remember the fear, once again, of possibly losing our baby girl (the first time I experienced this fear was at her birth, when she was in the incubator for underdeveloped lungs). This time around, there was no other help though, and it was a very lonely, lost feeling. This was a time when fear took over for me: my mind driving itself crazy and me wondering, what am I doing out here?

Then, it broke. The fever came down, and, very slowly, there was life once again moving through Talicia's body. Never in my entire life had I been so thankful, grateful, and relieved. This little baby treasure was able once

244

again to join us in life together. I was filled with awe. It was probably this situation that, for me, made a working radio a mandatory priority.

Needless to say, the winter of 1984 Bob was getting more and more prepared for the radio, which would be a wonderful addition to our lives. We had a lot of the equipment and supplies that were needed, but the setup was not yet perfected. We were also still in the process of learning Morse code.

That December, when I returned to Fairbanks, I decided to stay in town the second half of winter and job hunt. If I thought tent camp was a rough life, I soon found out that town had its own version of rough. Tent life may have been rough, but it really was very serene, beautiful, and simple. However, the combination of town life, winter, job hunting, living in our cache, and caring for a baby on my own was rough. This lifestyle was my choice, so I couldn't complain, but that does not mean it was enjoyable.

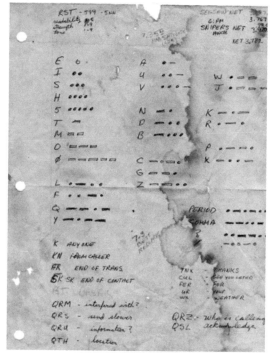

A page Nancy recently found at Bob's desk in the ANWR cabin from when we were learning Morse code.

Chapter 8:

1985

Although Talicia and I were living in our cache outside of Fairbanks and could more easily communicate with my family, we did live outside of town and did not have our own phone. Therefore, my letters continued.

January 14, 1985

I was waiting anxiously for a letter from you, and got one. Yes, I am quickly learning about job hunting, the public school screening process, insurance ins and outs, etc. What a rat race. Luckily I have friends here to help and support my efforts. I am borrowing cars and getting rides, using neighbors' telephones, and being thankful for it all. I am home now and it feels good inside our cache – cozy and warm. What a blessing to have the weather cooperate, staying in the teens and twenties. I have to snowshoe all over the property, dig out and chop wood, but at least there are no dogs to take care of. I won't let myself get into this position again. I feel alone with too much responsibility. Like I said, I am learning a lot about myself and the need to depend on myself more.

I got hired at a daycare center ($4.25/hour, but I had to pay ten dollars a day to have Talicia stay with me) which didn't last long. I worked nine hours with no break, taking care of twenty-five to thirty kids with only one other adult. The woman I worked with was great, but it was a bit much for both me and Talicia. I applied for a teacher's aide job for outdoor education in the public schools. I spoke directly to the one hiring and she gave it to me straight. There will be over sixty applicants, most from the natural resource department, along with some teachers. I also *will need clerical skills for the job, so I am practicing my typing. To me, it's funny sometimes, when I realize the rat race I got myself into. I'm still fired up for a job though, and I do have a greenhouse job at 4.50/hour if nothing else comes up. I'll give it my all, so root for me!*

Talicia's a real cutie. Even though some days I wonder what on earth I'm doing sitting in this cache wiping up oatmeal from floor to ceiling, when I hold her in my arms, I know. You know. I bought a plastic sled to tow her around in. She loves it, whether it is her and the groceries, or her and the firewood, or her and my backpack. I couldn't do without it.

Oh guess what? We got our road named. After all the paperwork then waiting... We got it! Skye-Lee Way. (Skye being Talicia's middle name and Lee being Traver's middle name.) I'm so pleased.

February 10:

I'm anxiously awaiting Bob's arrival. Charlie flew out to ANWR twice already. Once, he made it within two miles of Bob and had to turn back. Yesterday he only went to Fort Yukon. Bad weather. This is very frustrating. I then called Arctic Circle Air in Fort Yukon and sent out a charter for Bob. Now he is in Fort Yukon with the dogs, and Charlie's going up in the morning to get him.

I got the job! My first week of work was very trying as outdoor education aide, but by the end I was loving it. It's a good job. At this point, I'm looking at getting an economical car for myself. I'll wait on the selection for when Bob gets here, but I hope you can send that check now– and thanks so much.

March 3:

Bob finally got back home and started working today, shoveling roofs! What a business. He came home after five hours with aches and pains and seventy-five dollars. He's doing this business with another trapper friend of ours who is also a carpenter with no work at the moment. They'll do good. The snow on the roofs is four feet high, and three people called today. We're still looking at cars, too. Toyotas and Subarus now. I definitely want four-wheel drive – after two days and eight inches of snow here, we've had to use four wheel six times to get unstuck.

I register for my computer course this week. It's a five-week long Saturday course. After that, only two credits to go for my credentials to be updated. The other activity around here is Talicia! Her favorite thing to do around the house is to dress up in anything she finds lying around: hats, shirts, scarves, underwear, bags, bras, all draped all over her. What a ham! Then she gets a blanket and lays on the floor, collects all kinds of items and piles them on a chair and continues on and on. She's very active. Two days ago, the weather got warmer, almost thirty degrees, and she loved it. She didn't want to be carried or pulled but instead pulled her baby and bunny in the sled. We walked the neighborhoods for over an hour. It's great. Can't wait for all the mud next. Won't we all have fun?

March 17:

Bob remembered my birthday and got me a lovely necklace of ivory and silver. The necklace is a sculpted dog-sled team, made by a local artist.

Got our electricity in! Bob starts on the floor tomorrow. He might have a job building a carport addition to someone's house, too. That would mean full-time work for a while.

I'm going through a little bit of sadness missing Trav lately. It's been so long since I've seen him, but I did just get a great letter from him and Tim.

Otherwise, things are okay. I got my new car and love it – a four-wheel drive Subaru station wagon, 1980. Good condition. Feels good in my own vehicle, saves on gas, and thanks again for the loan.

May:

Weather's looking up, 45-50 degrees. I worked all week at 30 Mile Chena Hot Springs Road at a youth corps camp. The three of us outdoor education staff met the group of kids for these classes. After being outdoors all week, I look like a raccoon face (this is from wearing sunglasses during long sunny days). We still wear snow-pants. We teach temperature, wildlife habitat and tracks, tree aging, disease and ID, beaver ecology, language arts, compass and map, pond secession, etc. I worked with two excellent women this week. I'm learning a lot about stuff and about myself.

Bob's done with his job and watches T (our nickname for Talicia) now that I work. We're also working on our roof. The shakes go up soon. Then, we'll get a barrel stove, two doors (which Bob will make), and windows. In June, Bob goes to the woods to build another cabin and Traver arrives. Talicia is finally able to sit long enough to read through a short book before bed. But, one can't read every word, just a few quick words about each page and she's ready to move on. About two-thirds through, she starts saying "Bye-bye." That means we better wrap it up fast or T will close the book. She's something else. I'm making her a banana or apple cake for her birthday and trimming it with strawberries. Bob will be on the river, but we'll have fun.

June:

Yes – Trav will be here soon! Bob got back last week with a black bear. It's delicious and the hide is being tanned. Bob has decided not to go out and build that cabin after all. Instead, he's decided to look for work. For T's birthday, Bob made her a sandbox and swing. Now he's working on a window frame for our arched window.

Traver arrived in early June and we all settled into our activity-filled summer. I always looked forward to Trav's arrival, as for me, it made my family complete. The summer of 1985, Bob landed a job that would enhance our family for many years. Even though Bob and I were married and making compromises on lifestyle, money, and how to raise our family, I was struggling emotionally. There was a tug of war going on inside of me – I was struggling with the ideas of life on the trapline versus life in town, especially in regards to raising my children. On top of that, there was a struggle of understanding and dealing with the different perspectives Bob and I had regarding these monumental decisions. Of course, I was drawn to the woods, but raising kids made me consider their lives and needs as well. Bob was set on trapping. That was his way of life. However, I still believed maybe there could be some compromising. Some days, I felt sick to my stomach, thinking about this struggle, this tug of war, trying to know the best path to travel.

June 23rd, 1985:

I have one hour to myself. Trav's at a friend's, T is sleeping, and Bob is off trying to sell some beaver hides he tanned. It's been great having Trav with us again. He can change and dress T, then take her out to water the dogs. We're making up a list of jobs for Trav so he can earn an allowance. He already has a list of items he'd like to find at garage sales. Trav loves his skateboard, and now he's looking for a fishing pole and basketball hoop. He likes spending his own money on things that he wants and has already purchased some spoons for fishing, some bb's, and an arrow for the bow he made.

June 25th:

Bob did get a job at $12 something an hour. He's building a carport now, and then there will be more odd-jobs, like painting the house, etc. Just right for him. The people are very nice, too. It's the Binkley family who own Riverboat Discovery (the sternwheeler cruise you took when you were up here). Now we'll be able to put doors on and move things into our new home rapidly.

At this point in time, Bob and I were considering not going out to the trapline in the coming fall. Bob also decided not to build the cabin south of B.C., although I don't remember why. Moreover, we were trying to get our new cabin in town finished, but the task was difficult without much money coming in. However, Bob working for the Binkley's seemed to be an excellent opportunity for more future work with a great employer. That fall, there was also a good chance for me to obtain a decent paying job. These financial factors, of course, were weighing in on our decision of whether or not to head to the trapline. Additionally, Tim would be more into the idea of Trav staying with us if he was in town going to school. We could all be together. I liked that idea – all of us together.

August, 1985

It feels a little strange not packing up for the woods this year. We're still doing some fishing, but blueberry picking is over. Cranberries come next. Bob's mom is so excited that Talicia will be joining Bob at his brother's wedding. Currently, Bob is building a cabin for the Binkley's at Riverboat Discovery. The cabin will be viewed by all the tourists that ride on the sternwheeler boat. After that project he may be done, and hopefully by then, I'll be substitute teaching.

Mid-August:

We all went to the Tanana Valley Fair and had a great time. Trav just loved winning something at the booths. He always wins something at the dart throw, and this year he came out with three goldfish in a bag – two of which are already dead, but not his fault because he's VERY into caring for them. He named his fish Huey, Dewey, and Louie. We also went as a family on the Riverboat Discovery. It was very informative and I really enjoyed listening to the captain (Bob's boss). He even mentioned Bob in his work on the cabin, and said that Bob was aboard the ship that day. Several tourists looked around and asked where he was. That was funny. I was proud of Bob. Trav, T, and I were able to see the cabin Bob's been working on.

September:

Time is flying by with Traver in school while I'm substitute teaching and Bob is working for Binkleys. Each day, I go to bed later and later, with no time to fit everything in. It snowed for the last 3-4 days. Yuck! Trav is excited because he can't wait to start sledding. And then there's Talicia. She is a very busy body, a very social person, and always on the move.

Bob and I are also doing okay. I have to admit that I've been doing a lot of praying lately. For me, even to say that sounds very foreign, but I have no hesitation in saying that praying has helped me a lot. My uneasiness comes from wanting a deeper relationship, a closer relationship, but not knowing how to get it. Things I have tried seem to come to a dead end or get disregarded. Then, my feelings get shoved away and closed up.

This is an appropriate place to discuss something I wasn't writing about in the letters to my parents – one of the major problems I had regarding Bob and my relationship. We all have problems in our lives, and we all deal with them in different ways. Bob drank a lot, and I had a problem with that. It was difficult for me to watch Bob drink when there was confrontation or stress in our lives. To me, it seemed that drinking was Bob's way of solving annoyances in his life. Drinking with his buddies or a having a beer after work was different, and that kind of drinking never bothered me. However, when Bob turned to beer to avoid dealing with our struggles, that is when I got irritated.

Bob told me that he had been drinking since high school. He drank with his brothers and he drank with his buddies. He would try to stop, and actually would stop for short periods of time. I believe he even went without drinking for maybe a year in our early days together. But, eventually, he always went back to it. This not only made me sad, but I could feel the space between us expanding. I also was building up walls of annoyance and unacceptance.

In looking back at this period of my life, and re-rereading the letters I wrote, I am going through the process of dealing with the feelings I shoved away back then. I did not know how to face them then – I can feel my anxiety reading what I wrote. It was more than I would ever write or reveal to my parents. I kept the letter writing in a 'safe' arena, and I did the same with myself.

254

I can now clearly see that I was ignoring how I felt back then. Though I wanted my parents to know I was struggling a bit, I didn't want anybody to know how nervous I was about what I felt. Here is what I did feel: I didn't really believe that things were going to get better with Bob's and my relationship. I could see who he was. I could also see that he was fine with who he was, and that he felt we were progressing with our lives together. However, I was not feeling that way, and I didn't feel that he acknowledged my feelings. Period. That's just how it was between Bob and I.

October 1st, 1985

Our fall is almost over. The trees have been undressing their leaves, and there was snow in town today, but not out here. Talicia is doing well on potty-training, but only when it's her idea. Trav is off to a track meet at another school, and he's excited about that. Bob's folks called, and after that conversation, Bob said, "Well, we have windows." Sounds like a loan to be paid when we can. Bob is out window shopping tonight.

I'm in the process of figuring out some important things. Bob and I are okay, as long as I don't expect anything from him. I love him for who he is – he's basically a great guy, and I know he loves me and the kids. He's lived most of his life to himself, so that is how he is used to operating. Anything added to that way of his operation seems to be like an annoying mosquito. Bob told me to stop comparing him to my Dad, which is true. Most of my expectations come from being raised and used to a very responsible, attentive, and loving father that raised three daughters. Even Bob said, "Bruce is exceptional." Hmm... I try to remember that.

P.S. Traver will probably be leaving for Tim's December 27th. I spoke with Tim; he and his girlfriend Mindy set a wedding date for January 4th. We had a good talk and he sounded great.

October 19th: *The kids are in bed, Bob's at a party, and I'm babysitting one of T's friends. We had fun playing games and making popcorn. Trav was gloriously playing in the snow all day. I'm happy for him, but it is winter now. Going down to 5 below tonight. Bob's mom called and said it was 95 degrees in Florida and that they were swimming. Sickening!*

End of October:

The kids loved Halloween. Talicia was Big Bird and Trav was Dr. Jekyll! It was 30 below that night. "Trick or Freeze!" What a cute pair.

Traver and Talicia dressed up for Halloween in 1985.

November, 1985:

The note Bob got from Captain Jim and Mary Binkley (with a $150 bonus) said 'It was a pleasure to have a dependable, honest, skilled and pleasant person to work with. Keep in touch and we look forward to keeping you busy next spring and summer. Thanks again, Captain Jim and Mary Binkley.' Nice, huh?

Thanksgiving came and went. Living in town was very different than living on the trapline. The specialness of holidays in the woods is what we missed most. Because on the trapline there is no glitz, glitter, advertising, and no other people around, we depended on each other for the celebrations.

Town was very busy, especially around the holidays, which could be overwhelming and exhausting. Though we did enjoy a lot that town had to offer, I believe we all missed our homey closeness at B.C. and would tell each other stories of 'the good ol' days' when sometimes all we had to eat was bannock and rabbit.

December, 1985

I'm subbing a lot. Trav started cross-country skiing at his school, and since I sub there, I got to join him. It was fun.

Took the kids to a bazaar at our local general store to get their picture with Santa. Not a very good Santa or photographer, so I only got one photo for Bob's mom. Trav didn't want to get a picture taken with a fake Santa – only if he was the real one, Trav said. So I didn't dress him for the occasion, but at the last minute he decided he would.

When I get home from work, Talicia runs to me, hugs and kisses me, and then asks how my day was. She's great. She refuses to wear a bib, answers the phone and yaps on and on, likes to run in circles naked, likes Ring around the Rosie, says 2-4-6-8 (Traver taught her that), and says prayers before meals. Nobody knows what she says, except at the end – it's Amen, loud and clear.

This Sunday is our Christmas program at church. Talicia will place an angel at the manger scene. Trav will play "Jesus Loves Me" on the piano. I'll sing "Silent Night" with three other women, and Bob will read the scripture. By the way, we all participated in making our Christmas cards, even Bob! He's excited about everything too, although he doesn't show it outwardly. Today he went out and got a nice Christmas tree for the house: eleven feet high and reminds me of the ones at Grams when we were kids. It goes way up to the ceiling. When we decorate tomorrow, we'll need to climb the ladder up to the loft in order to decorate the top of the tree. Talicia loves all the Christmas lights. Traver is writing a letter to Santa tonight.

With the new year coming, we were all pretty much settled in our town life. I was glad we were all together. The kids were doing well in activities, we were establishing ourselves in a different church with new friends, and I was working a lot in the public schools providing some income while Bob stayed with Talicia. He was still very diligent about getting a boat business going, so we were planning a trip with all of us to go on the route that his future business would provide. Our trip would take us along the Porcupine River where the Hudson Bay Trading Company had established various fur trading posts, and the final destination would be the small settlement of Old Crow. We were all looking forward to that family excursion in August. There were also plans developing for both of our parents to visit us that coming summer, each at different times – another busy summer! As a family, we decided that all of us would join Bob on the trapline in the fall, then the kids and I would come back to town for the rest of winter. Come spring, Bob would join us in town, work for the Binkleys, and work on establishing his Porcupine River boating business. This felt like a good plan.

<u>Chapter 9:</u>

1986

January 5th, 1986

Hi! Well, we last spoke on Christmas, which seems so long ago. I started back subbing in schools. After one day in the schools, I really miss my outhouse at home. I can't wait to get back to the good old fresh-air bathroom. :) A simple pleasure, and a reminder of living out with nature.

The few days after Christmas were hard with Traver's departure again. We had several crying moments unexpectedly. Trav wanted Talicia by his side and broke down when he told her goodbye. It was tough but showed how close we'd all become. He had a good flight and is ready to go back to school. He says he'll be sure to write.

And one more major event...a car ran into Bob while he was driving the Subaru. Bob's okay, but they called the Subaru totaled. They gave us what the car was worth before the wreck. So now we're looking for another car.

Talicia is into clothes now and dresses herself. She was given five hand-me-down shirts by a friend. She liked them all. That night we went to dinner at a friend's and T dressed herself. When we got to our destination, I took off her coat and asked her, "Why don't you take off your sweatshirt too?" She did and we realized she had at least two other shirts on. By the end of the evening, we realized she had all five shirts on – and, planned well, from smallest to largest.

The Binkleys (of Riverboat Discovery) called Bob last week. They want him to work again this year as soon as the weather is good. Probably March until June. Then he'll have to stop work for that boat business (Porcupine River Voyages) he's been planning on. Bob will be going out trapping this coming fall and I believe we'll all be going too, then coming out in December. We'll just have to wait and see what happens. Bob's doing a great job at home with Talicia when I work, but I'm sure he's looking forward to getting back to work.

My letters from 1986 are fewer and farther apart, since we were in town and could call our families on the phone.

Once spring came, Bob was working full time, and I was subbing part time in the schools. In preparation for Bob's potential Porcupine River business, we started to look at boats and were collecting information needed for that type of business – insurance, chartered trips, loans, and overall planning. Bob was very positive and gung-ho about this project. He took a ten-day trip up river, so he missed Talicia's birthday. She loved the red wagon we got for her, and she carted around our little pup in that wagon. When Bob came back from the river trip, his parents visited for a week, and then Traver arrived on June 22nd.

July, 1986

All's going well. Trav's right back into his groove of testing Talicia, and forgetting to water the dogs – didn't take long.

When we picked Trav up at the airport, Talicia went crazy... she started showing off, telling everybody that her brother was here...watching Trav constantly and jumping up and down. It was something. They play together really well, and they get on each other's nerves quite well, too

Looks like we're going to be leaving early on our trip to Old Crow. Yikes! All of us are excited about the trip, but Bob gets a little frantic, leaving things to do last minute, even though he's always so anxious to get out. Today was his last day of work, and he sprained a wrist. That's one reason for us leaving early. It's basically the end of summer for us now. Not much more to yap about. I've enclosed a letter from Traver.

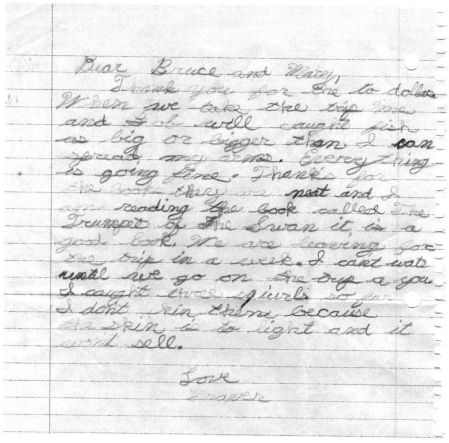

The letter from Traver to my parents.

August, 1986:

Last I wrote, we were leaving – now we're back, and oh, what a trip that was. This was an exploratory trip with our family, but checking it out as potential for Bob's boat business gave it dual purpose. First of all, it was LONG! We drove to Circle and began the voyage on the Yukon River, heading to Fort Yukon. In the late 1840s, the Hudson Bay Trading Company had established a post at Fort Yukon. They expanded to the Porcupine River, up into Old Crow. So, we were essentially following this route ourselves. It felt historical, as we stopped in these vacated places.

Passing Fort Yukon, we motored up the Porcupine River and explored the area around the Shuman House. Hospitality of that abandoned dwelling consisted of a note tacked to the wall stating visitors were welcome, but to please replace any supplies used, and only use what you need. There were a few rations of canned goods, some matches, firewood, and some other basic necessities. I appreciated the concern for other travelers.

The canyons we traveled through to our next destination of New Rampart were gorgeous. The river was winding and crystal clear. Canyon walls were craggy mysteries, where one might discover remnants of the past such as old bones or pieces of arrowheads. Blue skies with popcorn clouds told a story of their own above us. An untouched beauty. There we were, part of the left behind ghost towns.

New Rampart was treasure filled as we came upon old bibles, trading beads under the floorboards of the trading post, old dilapidated stoves, beds, and boat parts. It was also a gorgeous location in the rolling hills. Even the old cemetery held a certain intrigue and caused us to ponder the lives that were once lived here.

Being on the Canadian border at New Rampart, we all loved the idea of placing one foot in Canada and one in the USA. Getting a bit weary by this time, we pushed on into our final location of Old Crow before turning around and heading back down the river again. Old Crow was not much to talk about. A Native settlement in Yukon Territory with a population of around 200, this settlement reminded me of Fort Yukon. There were no roads leading to it. Bob was anxious to get a move on, so the trip back was much faster as it was a repeated route and we were eager to stop at our base camp off the Coleen River.

The kids have some rocks they collected from the Porcupine River trip. They are ready to show you so you can pick your favorite ones to take back with you.

A photograph of some of the New Rampart canyons.

An old, abandoned cache along the Porcupine River.

At the tail end of our Porcupine River voyage we stopped at B.C. briefly before booking it back to Fairbanks. Bob went right back up to B.C. and missed the visit with my mom and dad. My parents were visiting us and on a trip exploring NW Washington as a retirement home. They got re-acquainted with the kids and we got to show off the progress we'd made at our home outside of Fairbanks. They also met our friends, and we were so caught up in being together that we forgot to show them the rocks the kids had collected for them on our trip. I was so pleased when my family would travel all the way to Alaska to be with us.

That fall of 1986, I had decided to stay in town and diligently search for a teaching job, rather than heading back to the trapline. We were in need of more money for all of our needs, including finishing the house, raising two kids, and Bob's intentions for a boat business. After being turned down for a loan, we learned we would have to put the house up as collateral. Bob was frustrated, and I was nervous about that. But, Bob was going to trap. Period. He always said, 'do what you want,' which sounds nice, but was also somewhat of a catch 22. I really wanted to go to our base camp in ANWR as a family and continue that lifestyle with Bob, but it seemed like the trapline always came first and ate up all of our money. That left a financial decision up to me, and I decided town would be best. Talicia and Traver started happily into the school year while Bob and the dogs were on the trapline. We all adjusted.

November, 1986

Traver is really into birds now. He's checking out bird books and making bird reports for school. He's also reading Tom Sawyer and Jack London's White Fang.

We were in town today and bought Bob some books and magazines to send up there. I miss Bob. I just went through a tough week – no contact for so long. We're excited about putting a box together for him. He'll be getting it within two or three weeks, and at least we'll know then how he's doing.

Traver, Talicia and I are having Thanksgiving here – Traver's request. We were invited to three places, but I'm also glad to be home. Not much snow yet. Poor Trav. He watches the weather report and looks out longingly every morning. He loves the snow. And, last week he shot his first grouse! One morning when I was sleeping, he came in and woke me up to 'go get those birds' that were outside, so we did. He's been wanting to shoot the 22. He shot it. Shot again.

Missed twice – then got one. I got three. We cleaned them and he said he didn't feel too good. I talked to him about how I felt when I snared my first rabbit. We gave three grouse to a blind man at church (who got here to Alaska after 10 years of desire). The man loved them– and we ate one. They're delicious. As you know, Dad (you old bird hunter!). The next day we saw some more grouse, but after the initial excitement, we decided to let them go.

We just checked Trav's rabbit snares. It's 22° above! And I'm going to wrap this up! Love you lots and lots. Thanks for thinking of us and calling. We send hugs and kisses. Xxxooo Nancy, Trav, Talicia

December, 1986

Hi – well, I'll get this letter out to you, even though I think we'll probably call this weekend– to spread the good news and joy! No! I'm not pregnant! But, my husband is home! Surprise! Yup! My whole life has changed once again. And I like it! The news came over a week ago by ham radio that Bob wanted to come out. That's all. So I waited to get that confirmed, then sent out a plane – and here he is! Ahhhh. He didn't get much fur, but he did come home with some boo boo (caribou), as Talicia used to call them.

Eleanor (Bob's mom) called me Saturday. She's calling quite often and is waiting on a call from Bob. She said she knew he'd be in for Christmas.

Anyway, he's in to stay – for this year anyway. He's going to call his old employer to see if he can get work (after Christmas) and go full steam ahead this summer with the boat trip plans. I'm backing him and believing it will make a go. How can I resist when Bob is so positive?

The kids are thrilled to have him home. Talicia just stared at him all night Sunday when he got in, and since then, she must have said "daddy" one million times.

And Bob has come back with some changes too. First of all – he was wearing his teeth! Wow! He never wears his front teeth...

Secondly – Bob said he realized a lot of what he was missing out on and not doing with the kids. Within only two days, I see an effort in him to give and accept more from the kids. It's so nice. We are all talking and planning together. It's a real feeling of unity. I'm very happy.

So that's the big news. Now onto other things. It's warm here! 32°! Above! We borrowed skis from the school and Trav has been enjoying skiing a lot lately.

266

Hope all's well and healthy back your way – take care of each other! Love you both lots! Thanks for listening!

Nanc

P.S. Bob just gave me a letter to read – from him to me – I was supposed to get it before he decided to come in. Here's a paragraph quoted from there:

"I read the New Testament and am on the Old Testament and another book. Enlightening! I read three of Edwin Cole's books. Those really woke me up! I see and realize all my failings as a husband, father, and son of God. I have a lot of growing to do. Please forgive my immaturity! Will work on it when I'm around people again. Am praying and talking with God often now. It's a pretty easy habit when he's your only company."

Heading into a new year, I had hope for Bob's and my marriage working out better. Trav had left for his dad's to stay until summer, and I was working in the schools. I saw Bob trying to help more with Talicia and focus more on the family, but his efforts did not last long. He frustrated easily with others around him; he was used to being alone. Bob's boating business was clearly on his mind. Since I was not a big participant in that venture, I was thinking that a summer at Camp Daggett (a kid's summer camp where I previously worked) would be great for the kids and myself. I pursued that. As for the winter and spring, Bob continued working on our home, and I continued working in the schools, as we made separate plans for summer. Meanwhile, my parents were going to make their retirement move to the north west.

Chapter 10:

1987

January, 1987

Trav has gone back to Tim's. It's a lot more quiet.

I contacted Jerry Donnelly about my working at Camp Daggett this summer and found out training starts June 15! So, I'm working on plans to see my family either before or during camp time. The loan we wanted to get for Bob's boat tour business didn't go through, but we're building up credit. Bob is framing in the bathroom and utility room. Keeping busy until he goes back to work for the Binkleys in March.

Talicia is changing. Vocabulary and understanding are picking up...I'll give you a little chuckle:

When Trav was here he'd say "I want some i-c-e," (spelling out the beginning of ice cream) so that Talicia wouldn't know what he was saying (as this comes at T's bedtime). So, Trav is gone, but Bob last week said, "I'm going to have some i-c-e." Again, it was evening, and time for Talicia to be going to bed soon, but Bob was going to sneak some. Well, Talicia got up from her seat next to me, went over to Bob and said, "I want some i-c-e too!" She knows!

It's currently -60° with wind chill...that's cold! Especially since this whole winter thus far has been pretty mild.

I've been working with Outdoor Education and subbing in three schools. Bob's getting a little restless at home all the time with our little "yap." He says he can't get much done, listening to Talicia all day long...but she is also becoming a real pleasure to do things with. Every day, when I come home, Bob and Talicia open the door, Talicia says, "Here, let me help you," and she grabs my hand and helps me inside and takes my things. And neither one of us can leave in the morning without a hug and a kiss. That's nice.

February:

Happy Valentine's Day! Bob had candy for T and a red rose for me. That's a first – it was a nice surprise!

The weather has been a lovely 30-40° above, until now: it's back to -5° below. Spring IS coming though! Bob's taking some business courses and just completed CPR – all in preparation for his boating business this summer. Soon he'll be working for Binkley's again.

Talicia's doing fine but getting into a 'sassy' stage! She loves to go on dog sled rides with Bob. Bob's been training one of our dogs to pull weight. It's a hobby around here. The community has 'dog pulls' every Wednesday. He took his dog, Bandit, to one competition and won a 4th place ribbon and a bag of dog food. Bandit pulled 2,400 lbs. He weighs 90 lbs and pulled the load about 20 feet. Bob hasn't been this excited about anything in quite a while.

March:

Bob starts work on Monday. Yippee! But now this weekend we have to get a second car. And this month I'm on call for jury duty.

Bob just received notice that his marten were sold. He only sold 12, but the top price he got was $170 for one! That is fabulous. His average was $125, I believe. He is so excited – really fired up for next year now.

Talicia is excited about her plane ride coming up, "When the grass is green and we go on the airplane and I can wear my pretty dress to go see my grape grandma."

My contract for Camp Daggett is on the way. Jerry says I work my schedule around my family and have the old 'Snoopy Cabin' by the lake that I love.

Bob went to a dog pull all day and came back elated. He won a trophy, three ribbons, eight bags of dog food ($16-$20 a piece), and a $25 gift certificate for Pizza Pub. Pretty good!

Other news – Talicia cut her hair! I'm not too thrilled about that. I woke up one morning to find a clump of hair and her scissors at the foot of her potty chair. I almost died, almost cried, almost screamed – she had cut some of her bangs, some off the sides, and off the back. I decided to just let it grow out, such is life with our daughter!

April:

I'm so excited to hear all the news about your move to the northwest. Keep us posted.

All of our travel plans are in order. This summer at camp, I'll be getting three credits from doing an independent study – having fun and working toward my credentials that I need to continue teaching. Bob is working very hard. This might be his last year with the Binkley's at Riverboat Discovery, as he very much wants to get this boat business going. He's going to Circle when I leave at the end of May. He will try to do some trips out there. Lately, Bob has a lot on his mind: studying for code tests and his navigation license – planning, planning – he wakes up at 3am with ideas.

Talicia's getting ready for summer. She wants to go out barefoot and with no shirt. When we get ready to go to a friends, Talicia collects about ten different items which she says she needs. Then she gets a plastic shopping bag, crams it full, and calls it her purse. She dresses her babies like she dresses herself – about six layers of all her favorite clothes. When we go visiting, I usually am handed a collection of 'things' T has left from the last visit!

Well – three days of winter snow storms and now it's 50° and melting!

271

May:

Enclosed is our logo and advertisement for the riverboat business. Bob is going for it, as I said, and we believe it may take a while to get going, but that it will work!

The ad will go in the newspaper for tourists. I hope the original picture comes out better. The guy I worked with in Outdoor Education drew it, but it was Bob's idea for the design.

Bob's done with work this week for the Binkley's, and he got his new 115 Merc motor in, along with a bunch of other necessary equipment. He'll soon have all his information to send in to apply for the license he needs. We're shopping this week for the first 8-day river trip which is a test run with our neighbors that Bob will be guiding. He'll leave for Circle the second week of June. Advertising starts at the end of May. We'll have to wait and see what happens this year before making any further plans.

Traver gets in June 4th – Yippee! See you soon – love you lots!

Bob's boat for his Porcupine River Voyages – this is the same boat we took down the Porcupine River as a family.

That summer of 1987, the kids and I had tons of fun. Trav arrived in Fairbanks, and we quickly took off for Connecticut to visit my folks. As always, my mom and dad were very attentive. Dad enjoyed taking us on his sailboat. Then, onward to Camp Daggett in Petoskey, Michigan, where I had worked previously. While I earned a salary, the kids learned all kinds of new skills. Trav hung out frequently at the nature center, banding birds and feeding raccoons the fish he caught, and he also played a lot of basketball with other boys. Talicia was 'Miss Independent', all over camp participating in activities. She learned to swim and worked with me in the arts and crafts program. We lived in the little 'Snoopy Cabin' right on the lake, chased skunks away from our screen door, and sang camp songs at the evening campfires.

At this point in the story, my parents moved from the east coast to the west coast. I found no more letters of mine that they saved. To get back to where we left off, it was the summer of '87. The kids and I were at Camp Daggett. And Bob? He was off with his new business, Porcupine River Voyages. He was exploring, adventuring, and trying to share this great opportunity with others. It didn't take off like he had hoped, but that didn't stop his hopes and dreams. Next summer he would pursue this.

Bob flew out to the trapline alone on September 15, 1987 with our pilot friend, Charlie. I stayed in town with the kids that winter. Though I wasn't happy about Bob leaving, and I knew there would be struggles ahead, I was getting used to being apart from him and finding my own path. All I remember really wanting in life was a happy little family. Why was this so difficult to obtain, I often wondered?

I stayed in touch with Bob sending messages via Trapline Chatter. He could possibly get a message out by communication with his friend Ron on the ham radio. That all depended on many variables, including timing, weather, location, and desire. There was also the rare occasion that a plane might land at Bob's and Bob might have a letter for the pilot to mail or deliver to me. According to Bob's logbook, it was a very dry fall with lots of voles. Bob was using the snow machine but still ran the small team of six dogs he had. No moose. No caribou. But lots of rabbits!

Meanwhile, back at the cabin in town, I had landed a full-time teaching job for one year at North Pole Middle School as a special education teacher. The opportunity certainly perked up my life and stole a bunch of my time. I enjoyed teaching that year in many ways, but probably the best and most memorable aspect was one of my students, Steve Lilly. Steve was a fourteen-year old Inupiat that was having a difficult time with life. Being full of mischief and fun landed him in the Fairbanks Juvenile system. Steve had a kind heart and was very lovable, he just needed some attention and love.

With my recent employment as a teacher, there weren't as many money struggles and I found that using my teaching skills was very rewarding. However, there was still somewhat of a tug of war inside of me. The lifestyle on the trapline was so attractive – so addicting! I was constantly weighing the options, and the scale would tilt one way, then the other. Managing alone in town with the kids had its difficulties, but I was managing alone most of the time on the trapline too. Less money problems in town, but also less freedom and adventure. As for missing Bob, it was actually a nice break from all the hassle we had between us.

274

Chapter 11:

1988

Bob came out of the woods early that year, on February 8th, 1988 and because I felt Steve would get along well with our family, I checked into foster parenting, spoke with Bob, and one thing led to another. Steve was with us by springtime.

By spring of 1988 we were a family of five, plus our dogs. We had a great time adjusting to each other's quirks and character traits. After Steve joined us, Traver and Talicia bickered less, as he was a good buffer and got along great with both of them. There was a lot of neighborhood activities with campfires, picnics, and church programs. Summer was a big playground when we could stay up for all hours, as Alaska is the land of the midnight sun. We did just that at times – fishing, swimming at the gravel pit, camping, and joining wonderful softball picnics when all the trappers gathered at the park in town for a potluck. (To this day, in 2019, when end of May arrives, we gather for a potluck and play day. Now, our children are the age we were then, and they come with our grandkids!)

Summer does fly by in Alaska, and our family was rapidly preparing for fall and the trapline once again. At the end of August, 1988, before heading to B.C. to begin setting up and preparing for the rest of us to arrive, Bob and Steve (along with our seven dogs) did some exploring on the Porcupine River, all with Bob's future boat business in mind. Once Bob and Steve had camp set up on the trapline in late September, Traver, Talicia and I flew in with Charlie as our pilot. On October 14th, 1988, together again, our family of five began another season on the trapline!

That year, before the snow began, we had some good berry picking and time to explore. Talicia loved going out to explore. One day we came into a lovely little meadow, the sunbeams were highlighting the moss carpeted logs and the fall colors were showing off their splendor.

Bob fishing with Steve, Traver, and Talicia.

Talicia danced and twirled in the open spaces, throwing her arms wide open, exclaiming, "Oh mom– it's wonderland!" I will never forget that uninhibited display.

Hunting and trapping were good that fall. Bob's log book records two bull moose, two caribou, and, "Nanc shot Moose!" So – I'll tell you that story! And I'll just title it, "My Moose."

My Moose

We needed some meat. It was the fall of 1988 and all five of us were working hard and working up our appetites. There was the standby grayling, of course, and a few grouse, but we needed meat. Bob decided to take the boys out on the river for a hunting trip. That left five-year old Talicia, 7 dogs, and me on the home front to keep things running. The last thing Bob said was, "Keep your eye on the river," which meant, "We need meat, and if a moose or caribou comes by – shoot it." I said okay, not putting much thought into it.

Talicia and I had some time for individual school lessons, playing with the dogs, picking berries, and spreading out a bit in the cabin. We would take walks and check the river when we were out.

I believe it was the second morning after the guys had left, when Talicia and I were inside finishing up with some project, and I looked out the window to see more than normal activity in the dog yard. Seven black noses were up in the air and seven sets of ears 'on alert.' Something was up. I watched this behavior for a few more minutes and heard a few whines. And my thoughts began: "Oh, oh, and oh, no! A Moose!" Wasn't I excited and eager to grab my 30/30 and go get some meat for us? No! I was not! But my adrenaline was pumping rather quickly; I did grab my gun and instructed Talicia to stay put in the cabin while I went for a quick look.

Watching the dogs clued me in as to where I should head. Not to the river, but to the creek which was directly out front of the cabin, down a well-trodden path. I told the dogs to hush as I quickly, quietly, and on alert approached the creek. Staying hidden behind the trees, I peered around branches where I had a clear viewing of a lovely bull moose meandering along the creek. I gulped – I had never shot anything larger than a grouse or snowshoe hare. Grouse are easy with a .22. Snowshoe hares in winter are hard to spot, and even more difficult to claim; that took a little skill. But a moose? Bob, where are you?

I never had any desire to shoot a moose or caribou. I don't consider myself a 'hunter', but I am a good shot. I did not doubt that I could shoot and kill the moose. A big part of me just didn't want to – but we needed meat, and there it was. Right across the creek…

Okay, start hunting, I remember thinking. Followed by a series of thoughts: don't shoot while he is so close to the water – that will be difficult afterwards. Don't wait too long though, or he may get spooked and run up the bank and out of sight. Make it a good shot, so he is unable to move on. Okay, here it goes. Gun up in place, he's moving away from the water to the bank…aim…now! FIRE! And I whisper, "Thank you". I got him, but he was still standing and swaying a bit. I wanted to send one more shot, in case he decided to take off – BAM! Down he went. I looked and watched. The dogs were all very excited by this time, and I knew I needed to get back to the cabin to check on Talicia.

I went back to the cabin, past the jumping, barking dogs. Talicia greeted me excitedly at the front door, wondering. "I got a moose," I said, "We have some work to do, Talicia…"

Talicia got caught up in the excitement but had no idea what was in store for our day. Actually, neither did I! Shooting the moose? Piece of cake! Now I knew the work was going to begin, although I really didn't want to face the next chore. Bob! Where are you? I thought again. I stalled, and stalled some more…then I got my wits together and started collecting the tools I needed for the next step. My mind was racing again: Where is that knife? And where is the sharpener? Crap! Where is any knife? Did Bob take them all? Well, I'll take what I have, this old kitchen knife – better get going. Time is wasting.

Luckily, Bob had taken the boat, but our ratting canoe was waiting at the creek. Talicia and I climbed aboard with the few skinning tools we could find and we went to investigate this moose, which was lying quietly on the other side of the creek. It looked huge to me, and as large as some I'd seen Bob gut and skin. I made a sigh, wondering how much help Talicia was actually going to be through this process.

I tried to get Talicia to hold the hind leg back for me, but it was too much weight for her to handle, so I dug in and did the best I could. I knew the process was not going to be quick or easy. But boy, oh boy, did I learn a lot!

After gutting that monster, I looked at my blood covered clothes from head to foot and had to laugh. I remember when Bob came home once and I looked at the blood on his clothes – only from his knees down, and not nearly as much blood as my clothes had after gutting the moose. I asked if he could, "Please try to be more careful, because I was the one washing the clothes." After gutting a moose myself, I never said another word to Bob about bloody clothes.

After gutting, I was onto the chore of cutting up the moose and hauling it across the creek to hang up in camp. When I got the first ham severed off, I had to 'walk' it to the canoe as it was too heavy to lift. Then I lifted it into the canoe, loaded T and myself, and paddled across. On the other shore another problem appeared: how was I going to get the ham up the bank, and down the path, to where I would hang it from a pole between two trees?

Then – I spotted the old doll carriage we brought back from Ed's old cabin, long ago. I pulled it to the canoe, loaded the carriage with meat and off I went, slowly, to where I had to hoist the ham up with the rope I had attached. Then back down the trail to the creek, hop in the canoe, paddle across to the moose, saw, carve, or whatever I could to get another hunk of moose free – and repeat the same process with each piece, all day long! Of course, I had to take a few breaks as I had an active, lively, impatient 5 year old wanting to play, have a tea party, swing, anything but deal with the moose, all day. Talicia kept asking when we could do other things, and finally was so frustrated she said, "Why did you have to shoot that stupid thing?"

The whole process really did take all day long to complete. I don't think I was ever so tired in my life. I ached all over. But, I had to get it done because there was a good chance a bear would be around to discover whatever I left. Therefore, I didn't leave much: the head. I slept very well that night and felt great about what I had accomplished.

In the morning, I put the moose heart next to the trail on a stump where the boys would be sure to see it on their way to camp…

It was probably the third or fourth day they came back – empty handed – but with lots of stories. Bob said he was very delighted and happy to see that moose heart on the stump. I really don't remember much of what he said to me at the time, but in the years that followed, I loved to hear him tell others about 'the moose Nanc shot.' After all, he had reason to be proud. Everything I did that day, I learned by watching or helping Bob with other moose and caribou. It was a very good experience and I'm so thankful for that moose.

Even though Bob had built the 10'x8' addition to our Base Camp cabin a few years before, we added a bed in back for Steve. All of us certainly got a lot of interaction with each other in our little cabin. We all participated in the chores that needed to be done, such as firewood, water, cutting and hauling grass for dog beds, cooking dog food, and fishing. Bob usually left each day to work his traplines. The rest of us crowded around the kitchen table to complete our daily school lessons. Talicia, with kindergarten material, took quite a bit of my time and attention. Traver, being in 6th grade, had science experiments and was reading novels, which he could do independently, along with the regular math and language workbooks. Steve did his best in the junior high level studies, but he truly wasn't too interested at the time, unless it came easy.

There were a lot of distractions from school – and we were all thankful when lessons were complete, so we could go out and enjoy the winter-land of ice fishing, squirrel hunting, rabbit snaring, and simply being out in the elements. The boys would sometimes take a few dogs and go mushing – packing Talicia in the toboggan and giving her one heck of a ride. When the weather permitted, we hung ropes for the kids to swing on, built forts, and if all our work was caught up, we could all go for a hike to the 'throne' for a picnic and a good lookout – or we'd go down to Ed's old cabin to snoop around and see what treasures we could discover. Holidays were always an excuse for a day off chores, a day off school work, a day to celebrate, and to enjoy some different activities and food! The Halloween of 1988, Bob sat with the kids, drawing witches and spiders. I was surprised at the spiders. Bob disliked spiders. I would even say he was a bit afraid of them. Bob was known for teasing the kids, but if any of us spotted a spider, it could be a time to get back at Bob for all his teasing. All we had to do was dangle a spider in front of him, and Bob moved away rather quickly and gruffly saying, "Hey, get that thing outta here," acting like he was running the show, rather than running from it. Bob also challenged the boys to do a "trick" so they could earn a "treat." This trick was to go out in the dark evening alone, down the trail to our boat which was docked by the river, and bring something back from there to prove they had gone to the boat. Spooky! The boys loved it. They completed their challenge (the trick) and were rewarded with a treat, which was one of the dried strips of dried moose meat Bob had hanging over the stove.

As always, for Thanksgiving, ptarmigan were a sought after menu item – they were more difficult to spot and claim as a prize than grouse. But, luckily, we got a couple ptarmigan, prepared them with some herbs and rice, plopped them in the dutch oven, and then into the wood stove for several hours. There wasn't a pumpkin pie, but we always had a stash of cranberries, so I made deep fried cranberry tarts for dessert. The kids also talked Bob into making ice cream. We gathered all the snow, whipped it with powdered milk, sugar, and vanilla, then stashed it outside for a while – yum!

That year, with Steve, each of the kids got one Christmas gift brought from town (a real splurge). Other than that, we all made gifts for each other. I made hats and mittens for everyone, and Bob made some fry bread. Talicia got out the colored paper and crayons and made a drawing for everyone. The boys carved fishing lures for each other, for Bob, and me. Trav and Steve also attempted to carve little indescribable animals for Talicia. We made Christmas a very special time of year. All fun, no work, and lots of goodies to eat.

Steve loved to cook, and we gave him loose reigns after Bob taught him how to cook moose meat. The family would all sit at the table and have Steve serve chunks of cooked moose meat. When we had our fill, Steve would cook as much as he wanted for himself; he ate a lot of moose meat. Even when it was his turn to cook the dog food, we could see him picking out scraps of cooked moose meat we put in the pot for the dogs, and he would eat them.

Steve was a curious blend into our family. During fun times and family outings, he added joy and playfulness. But, the sad thing for me was that Steve did not really like being out in the woods, or on the river. He did everything with us, but without much enthusiasm during work time or outdoor activity time – Steve would have rather stayed in town. As time continued, Steve's behavior became more of a problem, most likely because of this fact. We had no idea he disliked the woods so much, nor did we understand the depths of some of the problems which were surfacing for Steve. For instance, he had Fetal Alcohol Syndrome and self-destructive patterns.

To help combat some of these struggles, we made the decision that I would go back to town a little earlier with the kids. For me, it was difficult to part from the woods and Bob again, but also a bit of a relief to know that the problems Steve was working through would not weigh as heavily on me. The kids and I left the trapline at the end of December, 1988, and Bob would plan to come out sometime in February. I would start the process of finding another foster home for Steve.

Part 3

Different Paths

"Things do not change, we change."
- Henry David Thoreau

Chapter 12:

1989 and Beyond - A Time of Change

O nce again, Bob and I were separated – he was on the trapline, and I was in town with the kids. Although I don't remember the details, I remember the feelings. I was worried about being alone in town and dealing with circumstances concerning Steve. The tug-of-war continued: the trapline vs. town, and Bob vs. no Bob. However, because of our physical separation – and our emotional distance, too – Bob and I could not talk about this. I was in town, and he was in the woods.

The following is taken from a letter I found in 2017 that Bob saved. I wrote this letter back in early January of 1989 when I had just gotten back to town with the three kids.

Start of New Year '89

Hi Honey,

I just had a nice shower and the kids are in bed. There's so much to tell you. And of course I've been blown away since I hit town, starting in Fort Yukon. What a trip! We at least got there okay. But no terminal, no phone, no place to warm up. We were taken to Larry's Air Service, and after much confusion, they said they might have room for us – but the plane was early, so Steve and I quickly ran the moose hams to some friends that we wanted to give meat to. We then rushed back to Traver and Talicia, who were watching the furs and they said, "The plane just left." That was 3:30. So here we are. What now?

I took Talicia and my frustrated self to knock on doors and ask for use of a phone. I ended up knocking on the Assembly of God door. Found out that Frontier Air Service had a flight out at

4:30. Down to the airstrip we went to wait. The kids were cold. Along came Joe Firman – he took the kids to warm up and gave them pop and cookies. The Frontier van came and loaded the gear. I told the driver I was frazzled and please don't leave – I have to go get the kids. I left and came back. No Frontier van in sight. Oh no! The FURS! But the Frontier driver showed up, drove us to the plane and off we went, flying to Fairbanks. My friend Cindy met us at the airport. Too much stimuli hitting me all at once: everyone is talking, the lights, and so much commotion. Yikes! Then Cindy's car trunk was frozen, so we had to pile everything – the gear, fur, three kids, and us, into the little car, and then stop by to check her house. Finally, the kids and I arrived at our place, which had been warmed by Tom and Cindy, and they had a hot meal waiting for us. It was wonderful! Jesse (T's best friend, Cindy and Tom's daughter) and T were absolutely going crazy, of course.

Then, there are the usual hectic town days ahead: arranging other flights, getting Steve to the doctor, and off to see his grandparents. I'm not sure about a plan for Steve yet. His counselor is out of town. All our friends are not happy to hear news about Steve, and since we got to town, his behavior has improved, which causes me to question the decision again.

But now, since he is at his grandparents, and Trav has gone to Tim's, I feel it's the right decision. Steve called from his grandparents and told me he had bought some corn meal and made cornbread just like 'Pa' (what he called Bob). It flopped, but he ate it anyway!

I went to Fish and Wildlife to give Roger some photos. He introduced us to a guy named Jagow who is going to trap on a river near our area. Then I got the lynx tagged. Fur was a hassle, as usual – I can never get it out easily and it cost $65 to register for their value. But, I was able to send it out today, and I met an old trapper buddy of yours that said to tell you hi and happy new year. He also said to tell you the reason you got so much good fur was because of the fire!

I'm sending out a package with the stollen (an excellent fruit bread) your mom sent and some tapes too.

We went to the Zielinski's for New Years. Besides Tom and Cindy, Carl, Sandy, and Barb were there. Good food, and I should have taped the conversation for you. We sat around the table laughing about farts, smelly feet, etc. I laughed so hard I was crying. Tom likes to tell stories. I told one too– all about what a sweet guy you are!

By the way, have you found any of the little notes I left for you? Here's one I wrote, but forgot to leave it in the beans: "Don't blame my cooking if you eat these!"

Okay, gotta go pack 'your stuff.' We love and miss you and will see you in March!

In January, Talicia and I went to my parents' new home in NW Washington State, Steve went to his grandparents in Anchorage, and Trav went to Oregon to be with his dad, where he would be staying at least until the school year began. After a visit with my parents, Talicia and I drove to Oregon to visit Trav for a few days. The kids were hugging and happy to be together again, with no fighting because they missed each other! When Talicia and I completed that trip, we returned to Fairbanks feeling refreshed.

As I mentioned earlier, at this point in time there are no saved letters to my parents; I'm instead relying on my memory, photo albums, and Bob's logbook. According to his log book, Bob caught a record amount of marten on the trapline that winter – 151 of them – and he returned to Fairbanks in early March to join Talicia and I in our town life. Talicia was enjoying school, I was working in the schools, and Bob continued work with the Binkleys. Together, we were getting ready for summer, family visits, and Bob's boat ventures. Otherwise, the spring of 1989 was uneventful.

However, what a wild and wonderful summer 1989 was. My mom, dad, and two sisters came up to visit, as did Bob's Dad. Bob and I were sharing our off-the-grid lives with our loved ones. Before we had electricity, I remember we dug holes in the permafrost behind our cache to make a homemade refrigerator, so during the summer months, we could still store our butter, cheese, milk, and things that needed to be kept cool outside. No ice cream, of course, but it worked. There was also the fact that we had no running water. Guests that came to stay overnight and were unfamiliar with the lack of conveniences would ask, "How do you brush your teeth?" This would make me smile! I would say, "Same as you do: getting the water and where you spit is different, but you can brush your teeth just the same!"

The summer of 1989, my dad and sister Jeff decided they would venture out with Bob on the Porcupine River Voyage – a 1,000 mile trip starting from Circle, AK. My mom, my sister Gail, Talicia and I waved goodbye as they took off on the Yukon River toward our home on the Coleen. They would be adventuring through Old Rampart and several ghost towns along the way, just as we did as a family in August of 1986, into Canada, to Ed's cabin site, our cabin sites, and then returning to Circle – a long trip. My dad and sister saw many miles of river and could imagine back when the fur traders did the same thing. The wildlife was abundant and my sister was able to capture a lot of footage on her video camera. (Some of that footage was recently used for stories Bob recorded for online listening – Seed Media did an excellent job in producing Bob's stories, now on a DVD called *Last Alaskan Bob*).

After completing that river voyage, Bob drove my dad and sister Jeff back to Fairbanks from Circle to reunite with me, Talicia, my mom, and my sister, Gail. It was difficult to say goodbye to my family that summer. However, it was time for me to prepare for the trapline once again. Although Steve continued to be a part of our lives over the years, he was now living with another family, so he would not be going back out to the trapline with us. Traver was also still with his dad to begin the school year in Oregon, so for the winter of 1989 to 1990, it would be Bob, Talicia, and I out at B.C. Eager to return, Bob boated back to B.C. in early September. Talicia and I flew out to join Bob in late September.

I have no recollection of the fall, other than that we missed the boys terribly – especially Talicia, who became quite lethargic and sucked her thumb a lot. Thinking back to the winter of 1989, I feel this was the beginning of the end of trapline days for me. Bob and I differed in how we saw ourselves in the role of parents, something which weighed heavily on me. That year, I was also concerned with Talicia's despondency. She missed the boys, of course, but she had also begun attending school – she missed her friends and loved being around other people. Bob thought she just needed to deal with it. I partially agreed, but also felt as a parent I needed to respond to her needs.

Talicia and I flew back to Fairbanks in December of 1989, as planned. Bob remained at B.C. and continued trapping. I recollect that during the fall of 1989 was when I let go of the rope from the internal tug of war with my thoughts. I had been feeling, at times, like a single parent. Also feeling like there was no decision making process for Bob and I to do together, other than, "You do what you want, and I'll do what I want." How can that happen when there are other family members to make decisions about? The following is a letter I wrote to Bob shortly after T and I got to town.

December '89, from town

Hi – I'm waiting to hear if my Trapline Chatter messages were sent. Hope you get them.

Yesterday's flight in seems like ages ago. It was a good, smooth flight – then to Dean's for a bid on the fur. Then Charlie took me to Joe's – Joe was happy we showed him the fur, although we ended up selling to Dean as even Joe said he would sell to Dean. Dean and Joe both said to keep the toes and claws on the wolves when you get them. Dean needs them skinned for a taxidermist. You get much more that way instead of cutting up for ruffs.

We have to tie the pups up now when we go to town because they can jump out of the pen. They did once and tried to follow the car. I chased them back, but when we got home, they were gone. We called Ron, who said their tracks were in his yard. So, we dressed and went out calling, following tracks – ending up at a house behind Ron's. The people living there said the pups had been there all day. It's -42°, so we let them in with us.

We're taking Steve to Royal Fork for dinner on Friday. Tomorrow, I start calling on job possibilities. The snow machine was $2,595, with no charge for the hitch. I tithed the fur and dividends. Paid Charlie $600 for the truck, $450 for the flight, $42 for gas, and $80 for a past flight. We still owe for this flight coming out.

Your folks sounded good, and all your brothers are fine, but they just don't communicate well. I want to end this and get the box ready for Charlie to bring to you.

Take care of yourself. See you in March.

In Bob's logbook he recorded several events from the beginning of 1990: 1) The month of January was extremely cold and he sat tight through most of it. 2) He waited 22 days for a plane to deliver his Elan snowmobile. 3) Our upper cabin was broken into –by humans, not critters – for the second time in two years. 4) This was the last year he would use dogs on the trapline.

After waiting six days for a plane due to inclement weather, Bob returned to town in March of 1990, when he began working for the Binkleys again. Bob was a huge part in developing Chena Village on the confluence of the Chena and Tanana Rivers, the site where the famous Riverboat

Discovery lands every summer. When Bob built the carport for Captain Jim Binkley back in the early 1980s, that was the beginning of a lifelong family-tied relationship with the Hartes and Binkleys, which continues today. I still live in one of the cabins that Bob built way back then. I love living here – it's as close as it gets to living the life I lived back in the early trapline days with Bob.

Here is a picture of the first cabin Bob built in the village. The furnishings are similar to our B. C. cabin, and there is now a plaque of Bob's Dedication hanging proudly above the window inside the cabin. Traver, Talicia, and I all ended up working with Riverboat Discovery at different times in our lives. Talicia and I still work there as I write this.

The first cabin Bob built for Riverboat Discovery on the Chena River.

While Bob worked that summer in 1990, Talicia and I went on a big road trip (I still love road trips!) down Highway 101, visited my parents, then headed to San Diego to visit my lifelong high school buddy, Lise. Meanwhile, back in Alaska, there was a huge forest fire where Bob recorded over 500,000 acres burned, very close to our trapline. Bob stayed in town with us that fall and winter, continuing to work for Binkley and other construction companies.

Nothing out of the ordinary was happening during the year of 1991 until the fall. We were living in town, going to work and school like most families. The kids were growing up and making new school friends. Traver and Talicia attended school where I was teaching, at The Lighthouse Christian Center.

That winter, Bob decided not to go out to the trapline, I believe mostly due to the big fire of 1990, but also because he had obtained good carpentry work in town. When school was out, we all played hard in the land of the midnight sun (with 24 hours of daylight), as everyone does in Fairbanks after being cooped up all winter. Bob and I were getting along on the surface, but, at least for me, it felt like there was more empty space between us – not much communication, and not a lot of bonding. During this time period, Bob and I did not agree on much. I was beginning to see that we were heading down different trails: Bob trying to find a way to be independent and still make money, and me trying to keep the family together and make money. Being so conditioned to living in the present moment, Bob could not relate to me bringing up past trials I didn't want to repeat, and trying to plan for the future. I was tired of the struggle and sad that we couldn't find the same path.

According to Bob's logbook, he and Traver boated out to the trapline on September 1, 1991. This was an unforgettable boating and hunting trip, as Trav got his first caribou. Trav had only really shot a .22 up to this point – he had been practicing shooting with my 30/30, but had never used the gun to hunt. Trav said even in practice he was a bit scared of the loud bang when he pulled the trigger. So, when Bob and he went out for a hunt, and a caribou stepped onto the river bank, Trav said his hesitation was in the expectancy of the loud bang, and when he primed and pulled the trigger, he was very shocked that he had actually shot and killed the caribou. Of course, he readily forgot the loud bang as his excitement took over.

On that same trip, Bob and Trav were returning to Circle to drop Trav off and Bob was picking up supplies for the winter. On their journey to Circle, it snowed. A September snow. Trav had on cotton gloves and was making snowballs taken from the snow on the bow of the boat, getting wet and cold. And, surprise, surprise! Out popped a moose from the brush – Trav had the 30/30 by his side and picked it up to aim. Bob was in the stern, watching, and thinking, as Trav was too, that the moose was 'a done deal.' As Trav tells the story, "I was so cold, I couldn't even pull the trigger." The moose got away, and although Trav was bummed, he had a story to remember forever. He learned that when he's out on the river, no matter what time of year, he knows he should dress to keep warm!
Traver and I both agree that Bob was 'tough as nails' and handled

Traver with his first caribou.

hardships without much thought. For instance, there were many days when I was in the boat with Bob, all bundled up, and Bob would be navigating all day with a light jean jacket, a baseball cap, and no gloves. With wind howling and water splashing up, Bob would be climbing in and out of the boat to get us off gravel bars. I always questioned how he could stand back there without shivering, complaining, or thinking about the uncomfortable circumstances. He just kept on, sturdy as the Rock of Gibraltar.

Speaking of uncomfortable circumstances, the up and coming next year of my life, 1992, was huge. Disastrous is a good word. Three life changing events to come were: I had cancer and a breast removed, my mom passed away, and Bob and I separated. None of these will be pleasant to write about. But they are part of what has made me today.

Here is part of another letter I found at the cabin recently. I had written it during the winter of 1991, before Christmas. As you may be able to tell from the letter, Bob and I had become more distant with one another, not just physically, but emotionally.

Hi Bob,

I have to whip out this box and letter to you quickly – Norm may or may not make it out – it's snowing like crazy here.

Talicia misses you a lot. Me too. At times I like to rag on you though, for the things I get stuck with…

You told me not to use dividends to go to WA. I said I wouldn't, but that I was going. End of conversation, because I know when not to push. I made plans, borrowed money, and am almost paid back now. If you got our Trapline Chatter, Talicia and I are leaving December 23rd.

The truck is almost okay now. No biggy to you, I know, but you know how that irks me. Trouble with that truck again and again. Charlie came to the rescue there.

The kids are fighting like crazy. Tomorrow we are going bowling and eating pizza with Steve.

Glad to hear trapping is looking good. And I'm glad to hear your feet are healing well (Bob had burnt the bottoms of his feet at tent camp). Your dividend came back and is in the bank.

I had a lump in my breast checked. It looks okay now, but I have to go back in 6 weeks.

I sent some pictures to your folks. Enclosed are some for you.

Okay, gotta go. Will try to talk with you some on the radio. You must be guzzling the coffee.

P.S. No time to cook this turkey I'm sending...sorry. But, put it in the dutch oven and cook like we used to. Should be good!

Love, Nanc

I can feel and sense my emotions in this letter – I was angry at being left with so many problems to deal with on my own, rather than with my partner. Bob did not consider my thoughts or input. It seemed to always be Bob's way or no way. However, I was lucky that my family was a place where I still felt heard and supported.

Talicia and I went to Washington to be with my entire family during December of 1991. Trav met us there and we had such a fun time. We made a video of us hamming it up, dancing around in diapers and wearing crazy googly-eyed glasses. Us Becker girls know we are having a good time if we are peeing our pants – that was definitely going on and I'm happy it was. Laughter is good medicine. That year ended up being the last Christmas with our mom. She passed away less than eight months later.

Sometime after returning from Washington, I had my six week check up with the doctor. I was delivered news I was not prepared to receive. Yes, I did have breast cancer and was advised to have a mastectomy. I felt like throwing up. I felt afraid. I didn't want to tell anybody. I also just felt alone. With this news, my mind started going down a dark hole. Telling Bob was just a matter of fact, as he didn't really know how to respond to my emotional needs. Honestly, I don't remember how I shared that news with him, or how he reacted. I worried constantly about death, the kids, and what might happen. But in sharing the news with my sisters, I got some comradery and relief with my burden. Because I didn't want my parents to worry, I asked my sisters to not spill the beans about this until it was very close to my operation date.

Bob came off the trapline during the first week of February, 1992. Even though by then I realized Bob didn't know how to be emotionally supportive for me, I was still saddened with disappointment upon his return. Instead, I sought out my church family and girlfriends to share my fears with.

When my parents finally heard the news about the cancer, and wrote to me, I broke down, cried, and secretly desired to crawl up in their laps to be rocked like a baby. Here is part of a letter my mom wrote to me on February 18, 1992 This is one I saved because it was special to me.

Dearest Nancy,

How can I express what I'm feeling at this moment? We just received the news from Gail and Jeff about your upcoming operation. Nancy, I'm overwhelmed – stunned – upset, and feeling downright unhappy about what's happened to you. The kids (Gail and Jeff) assure me that you're upbeat and positive and have great faith that all will be okay. You've got great support from Bob, Traver, Talicia, and the members of your church. How fortunate you are. Now, don't forget, we are also sending our own type of support your way (each of us very individually too, you understand). I'll be constantly praying for you. You know that, don't you, Nanc?

I'm crying right now, and praying in between. The kids advised me not to call until after the operation, and I'll abide by what you had told them. Nancy, I love you dearly, remember that. I'm so glad Bob is home. We'll call Friday and talk to him, even if you're not home yet.

You won't get this until next week, but it's doing me good to write to you now. I still can't believe you're going into the hospital. I remember we talked at Christmas and you were confident that your mammogram and your visit to the doctor were fine. Nancy, I'm so sorry this had to happen to you. You'll be in my thoughts constantly until we talk to you. Dad will be going through the same as I. We both love you dearly. Mom and Dad

During this time, when I was going through my cancer, I was unaware that my mom was dealing with blood transfusions and her own illness. At Christmas, we knew she was tired and a little 'off,' but didn't actually know the extent of what was happening. As her illness progressed, she did not share this information with me until I was done with my operation and almost through with chemotherapy. She didn't want me worrying.

My operation was over quickly. A mastectomy. I have to say, I was unearthed with my experience. When I was in the hospital, I intimately felt prayers that tamed my fears and swaddled me in peace. It was a revelation of the loving human spirit– life and love breathed into me. I did not want to leave this place of comfort. I remember opening my eyes one day to see my friend Sandy Mattie sitting by my bed reading her Bible. I was not alone. Thanks, Sandy.

The rounds of chemo lasted a bit longer, and I was distraught watching the poisonous fluid pump into my veins, which then made me feel sick. Going through chemo depressed me. I bore a port in my upper chest for easy access to my veins, causing me to feel mechanical and taste chemical. Sitting next to Bob in church one Sunday, the sadness leaked out of my eyes, rolling down my cheeks. All I could do was tip my head, rest it on Bob's shoulder which stiffened in discomfort.

When I really broke down was in the shower, when gobs of my hair would come out in my hands as I shampooed, which felt deathly spooky and like losing myself. I wore scarves, as it was still cold, and actually had fun with my students at the time, when I promised to 'unveil' my head – they waited with anticipation. The students were used to my long hair, and when I whipped off my scarf, their eyeballs popped out of their heads as their mouths dropped open! Kids being kids, it was amusing to observe their genuine curiosity unfold. What was left of my hair was a scary, scraggly mess – and a lot of baldness! I decided to get my head shaved. And – what a surprise when Trav and Bob accompanied me to the barber to have their heads shaved too, in support of me. I felt very loved and supported at that time. I was also very touched that Traver made the decision to stay with us for the entire school year.

The whole family, supporting me through chemotherapy.

During March of 1992, Bob had a few projects brewing. First, Joe Mattie came up with the idea of a trapper exchange with Russian trappers, and asked Bob if he was interested. Bob probably said something like, "Does a bear shit in the woods?" Of course, the ball got rolling on that one. Joe's plan involved communicating with the Russian government to arrange a time for Bob to travel to Siberia. Once in Siberia, Bob would live with trappers there, to experience their lifestyle and also share ideas with one another. Setting the plan in motion took some time and effort.

The second project included Traver. He and Bob were training some of our dogs for 'weight pulls.' It just so happened we had several lovely malamutes – strong, young, and full of energy – perfect for the annual weight pulling contests held in the Fairbanks area. Bob had started training his malamutes the year before, and continued into the current year. Traver was eagerly involved. The contests are just as the name suggests – a dog pulls a sled full of weight. The owner commands or coaxes the dogs to dig in, grab the snow, and pull like hell. They only have to pull a short distance; it's not a long race, only a short, intense pull. There are all weight classes, too. You want to try out your beagle or chow? Go for it– you'd probably win, as there are not many breeds like that in Fairbanks.

It was quite fascinating to observe how dog owners interacted with their dogs during the competition. An owner might give a command the dogs were familiar with (like Bob did), such as, "Let's go." Our dogs knew that command, as Bob took off with them each day on the trapline. For Traver, he only had to get out in front of the dogs and talk to them, because they were used to him playing and spending time with him. "Come on Snaggle, you can do it!"

Traver won a trophy that year and probably a big bag or two of dog food. He was so proud of the two dogs, Charlie and Snaggle, and Bob was so proud of Traver.

Traver with his trophy and one of his winning dogs from the weight pull.

During late spring, early summer of 1992, I found out about my mom's terminal illness. I was devastated. I had never experienced anybody dying, and this was my own mother. My friends and neighbors were very helpful during this time. I remember going over to Bruce and Barb's (our neighbors) and sitting around the table. I just broke down and Barb took me in her arms, held, and comforted me like I was her grieving child. Thank you, Barb.

The kids and I took off in July to go see my parents. After a while, Trav went back to his dad's and Talicia went to Fairbanks to be with Bob. I remained until my mom passed on into eternity on August 8, 1992. She was one of the greats. We had quite the memorial in her gardens that she loved. I am so very glad I was able to spend those last few weeks, days, and moments with my mom.

I returned to Fairbanks in late August, feeling very sad and somewhat lost. A huge chunk of me seemed to be missing. I had been grieving the loss of my Mom while with my family in Washington, and when I returned to my own home, it felt very empty to me. I did not know what to do with my feelings, so I hid them and tried to move on.

I felt like a ragdoll losing my stuffing. First my breast, then my hair, then my mom, and then my husband. Bob left for the trapline on September 12, 1992. Although I was dealing with so much emotionally, I wanted to stay composed. I actually felt some relief in the fact that I didn't have to deal with Bob's and my friction for a while. I could move ahead with my own life.

Additionally, since my mom's death, I was communicating regularly with my sisters. We needed each other's love and support, and we wanted to make sure Dad was doing okay.

Traver was with his dad and was unable to help me with the winter, my truck was having problems, and I had a job to get to daily. All of this was weighing me down, and again I felt alone in dealing with these issues, rather than in a partnership. When a house-sitting opportunity arose at a big potato farm only five miles from my work, I jumped on it, which made my life easier for a while. Talicia and I stayed on the potato farm until March of 1993.

The emotional separation with Bob and I had been draining me for quite awhile, but taking the step for a physical separation? I could feel the strength coming back like Popeye after eating a can of spinach. I was tired of dealing with the unsettled rumblings following a thunderstorm that my marriage had become. I was ready to take action, and the potato farm was my escape route. Although it did feel a bit like a guilty secret I was not sharing with Bob, I also felt the flutters of a bird being let out of a cage, knowing that I am leaving a place that had become a big headache for me. Including Bob. The physical separation I was hoping would be the means to bring some resolution for my marriage. If Bob and I could mend and design a new plan for our marriage, fine. If not, I was looking for an alternative plan for myself. At least, with a separation I felt I could breathe. I recently discovered some letters I wrote to my sister Gail around this time. Here are portions of two letters:

September, 1992

Hi Gail! I love and miss you. I am doing fine except for all the weather hassles. How are you doing? We have power outages and snow, snow, snow. But, I am smiling because I leave here the weekend of Oct. 10 to begin house sitting at a potato farm only 5 miles from work! Still on Chena Hot Springs Rd, in the country with lots of land, trees, and fields. The owners are grandparents of a family at church. It will be so good to get out of here! I went through a few heavy days after Bob left. I broke down and cried in school. Just too much pressure and stress on me. Then, it was the last straw when I thought my truck was having big problems. But, it's fixed and I am feeling better.

October, 1992

Hi, Gail! Time's a flyin'. Too much to do and too little time. When Bob goes out to the woods, my life changes, and when he returns, it changes again. Living in two different ways, and there is nobody to really share it with. My head partly wants to end the relationship, and not have to deal with it. Then, I think about what that would look like and it really doesn't change anything, does it? Oh, my! But, I don't feel like a closet case now. I'm telling people I'll be looking for a place in March (after the potato farm). Talicia also knows but doesn't say too much about it. I'll continue talking to her. I haven't told Traver yet.

I talked with Dad today and he seems to be doing good. He says he stays busy and also lets it out when he can't hold it in any longer. I, too, sometimes feel I am stuffing all my feelings about Mom lately. I miss her, and in a way it still all seems unreal. Does it to you?

We leave this Friday for the potato farm. Write to us at the school. I miss you. Love, Nanc

While I was teaching at Lighthouse Christian School, Talicia was a student there, where she got into writing wonderful stories and making new friends. During this winter, while Talicia and I were at the potato farm, Bob had finalized his trip and was off to Russia from February 1, 1993 through February 28, 1993. Here is the photo from a Fairbanks Newsminer Article written about that trip.

An American in Siberia
Alaskan trapper trades knowledge in Russian Far East

Bob Harte photo

DIFFERENT COUNTRY—Bob Harte, a professional Alaskan trapper, stands next to the snowmachine he used while on a trapper's line in Siberia. He spent five weeks in the country.

Article from the Daily News Miner in Fairbanks.

When Bob came back from Russia, Talicia and I were still at the potato farm. Obviously, over the past few years, Bob and I had spent a great deal of time apart from each other, especially during the year of 1992. To put it rather bluntly, from my perspective, absence did not make the heart grow fonder. I had settled into a church family and loved my teaching job. My sisters and I continued communication with each other and with our dad, as we were all still missing our mom. Bob's interests were in trapping and his own work. My life was taking a new direction as Bob and I became less involved with each other.

It was difficult to talk with Bob about my emotions or intimate issues for many reasons. For instance, when we tried to talk about separation or divorce, I was an emotional mess, whereas Bob presented himself almost as emotionally 'blank'. Talicia, too, appeared very emotionless when I tried to talk with her about what was going on between Bob and I – she has always been similar to her father in terms of emotion. At least, this is how it has appeared from my own perspective. However, Talicia also agrees with me on this matter: she is a lot like Bob as far as emotions are concerned. Like her father, Talicia was also in an incubator at birth, but only for a few days – not for two months, like her father. Whether or not this contributes to how they deal with emotions, no one can know. Although Bob and Talicia both may appear 'emotionless' to me at times, they both have an ability that I lack: getting through difficult times and situations for them almost seems effortless, while for me, it is agony.

Each time Bob left for the trapline, I would settle into my own comfortable routine. When he returned, after the initial 'glad to see you,' there was another transition for me to accommodate Bob back into my life. Our lives seemed like they were on two different paths. Trying to discuss this with Bob became a dead end. Bob wanted us together at our home on Chena Hot Springs Road. However, before that could happen again, I wanted for us to have more of a functional relationship. We did not see eye to eye. Instead, we gradually saw less of each other. Since Talicia and I were already living away from our home, at the potato farm, the physical distance made it easier for more emotional distance in the relationship. While Bob and I were trying to discuss how to get along better or the possibility of parting ways, I happened to fall into another living situation, which appealed to me at that time. There was a woman at church who had a small daycare, and she would occasionally watch Talicia for me. Betty was a grandmotherly type, and we both liked her. Betty's husband became terminally ill, and at the same time, Betty's health was deteriorating. She was having difficulties caring for her husband, as well as herself. Betty had an old farmhouse very close to the church (and school) which we both attended. We worked out a plan that would benefit all of us. Talicia and I would move into Betty's home for low rent in exchange for my help in caring for Betty and her husband. It worked well. Talicia and I stayed there through spring and summer. We made a lovely garden, Trav came up and hung out, and we also continued to see Bob occasionally. Betty's husband passed away while we were there. By the end of the summer, I felt the need for new scenery, but there was still much to be sorted out. Facing Bob during our separation was going nowhere due to the lack of communication. When Bob stopped by at Betty's place, in armored rigidity, I felt my shield go up. I was on guard. Bob got very irritated if I brought up something we needed to discuss.

For instance, one day I brought up some bills, "Bob, we need to discuss Talicia's medical bills."

"What about them?" Bob responded.

"How are we going to pay them?"

Bob replied only that he didn't know how.

My brain functioned differently. I needed more, so I responded, "Well, we need some sort of plan where the money will come from."

Bob once again replied that he didn't know, and then left. Again, our ways of dealing with money, emotions, and confrontation were just so very different from one another, which seemed to exacerbate the problems. His irritation attracted fear and anxiety within me. He would not open his armor, and I would not drop mine. He would leave, irritated. I would relax, tucking away my fears. Bob was actually the one to mention divorce. I remember his words, "I think it's time we went our own ways."

Before deciding on divorce, we tried one counseling session with our pastor. It melted some of the built up ice between Bob and I, but went no further. Bob refused to seek professional counseling. I suggested that each of us make a list of what we felt we needed to work on, and discuss it. We each took our paper and pen and went off to begin our list. I returned with a lengthy list and asked Bob about his list. His paper was empty.

I said, "What? Nothing?"

Bob replied, "We just need to love one another."

"And how do we do that?" I asked him.

No comment. Like I said, we were going nowhere – fast.

The desire to get away from this situation hung on me like a heavy back pack. I felt like I was sinking in quicksand with no way out – so all alone in my predicament. The title of a pamphlet I had seen recently at the Women's Clinic popped into my head: 'What if Your Happily Ever After Isn't?' That sure fit me. I was lost. It was happening again to me. I was back on my own, a single mom with no place to really call home. Coming apart at my seams. What should I do? Part of me was trying to hold onto the spider thread left of my marriage, another part teasing me for a clean get away and the risky unknown. Should I hang in there and keep trying? Should I go away for a while, get myself together, and then reassess? I constantly thought about how my decision also involved others. How would all of this affect Talicia and Traver? Questions, questions, questions, and no solid answers. I struggled with the tug of war day and night, until my prominent feeling won out.

I left. The month of May, 1993 brought the end of the school year. Also, the end of 14 years, living my Alaska Dream. And the end of a marriage.

After a huge yard sale at Betty's, Talicia and I packed our bags, loaded my car, and with a cloudy veil over us, left Alaska at the tail end of summer, 1993. I was sad. I was mad. I was glad. I didn't know what to feel – my heart was breaking. I did not want to let go of anything: our life, Alaska, the way things had been, but I felt that I would break if I didn't get away for at least a short while.

I can't say how Bob felt – I don't know. I'm guessing he felt a lot of the same things I experienced, but expressed it differently, or not at all. When I think of our differences in how we express and deal with emotion, I find comfort in a Shakespeare quote: "There is nothing either good or bad; only thought makes it so." Bob and I went our separate ways. He remained in the home we had built. Talicia and I left Alaska and headed for Washington state where my dad was living.

However, this is not the end of my story. Instead, it is a new beginning. Purposeful change!

Rather than a dead end, it was for the best that Bob and I went our own ways. Though we talked several times, briefly, about "getting back together," we never actually re-married. Despite our differences, we did remain family and got together for holidays, birthdays, trips, trapper get-togethers, etc. I lived on the same property with Bob and Talicia in several locations and at various times throughout the next twenty-five years. We did have a relationship. Just not your "normal" family type. We kept raising Talicia our own unique way, and Traver has also been with us throughout the years.

As I said, our divorce was not the end, just a time for an intermission. Time to freshen up your coffee or tea, take an 'outhouse break,' and I'll re-stoke the fire. We can then re-group once again. Get yourself comfy by the fire and I'll continue sharing with you, "The Rest of the Story."

The Rest of the Story

In my second book, *The Rest of the Story*, I'll be piecing together Bob's and my life from 1993 until Bob's death in 2017. Again, some of the information will be taken from letters of communication between Bob and me, Bob and Talicia and Traver, or between me and my sisters. There will be a few stories from Talicia and Traver, as well as memories from friends and family members. Some of the included stories will address questions I've been asked many times over the past few years from fans of Bob's from "The Last Alaskans" documentary TV show. Here is just some of what the book will cover:

- How did you remain 'family' with Bob, yet not live together?
- What traumatic event happened to Talicia in 2006 that changed all your lives forever?
- Was Bob always alone on the trapline after your marriage ended?
- What happened to Traver?
- What caused Bob's death?
- What will happen to Bob's cabin?
- Will you continue to go to the cabin?
- What is Talicia doing?

Happy Trails to you, until we meet again.

End

Family returning from a moose harvest

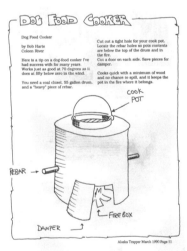

Above: Dog food cooker designed by Bob
Harte, Alaska Trapper magazine

Left: Traver and Talicia at Chena Hot
Spring Road outhouse, 1990

Living and trapping in the Bush

Story and photos by
Roger Kaye

As we traveled northward, upriver toward a promising wolf set, I was wondering how many trappers once dreamed of living the lifeway of Bob Hart, professional trapper.

Country exhilarating in its beauty, its wildness, its remoteness. Its cold slid past the handmade toboggan I was riding. Many have shared the dream of adventure, independence and self-reliance of such a wilderness trapline, but few have gone forward to test themselves against the challenge. And of those, fewer still found themselves up to the reality of the experience for more than a season or two in this country.

We stopped abruptly, and Bob began walking ahead, studying tracks that had intersected the trail.

"Wolverine—fresh. Probably this morning, the set is just ahead."

With that deep felt feeling of anticipation that every trapper knows, we continued on.

From a distance we could see that the set was disturbed. After arriving, we found the trap sprung, but in place. Without disturbing the scene, we stood there a few minutes trying to interpret the story in the windblown snow. The wolverine had

The Hart family at the main cabin. "Living in the bush involes a lot of work, says Nancy Hart," "but there is more time for the important things like sharing experiences as a family."

come from upriver. It had gotten into the bait. Perhaps too much snow had drifted over the trap. Perhaps the animal dug it up. We couldn't tell. Wondering how the animal perceived the set, speculating how it could have been made differently— it's part of the mystery and excitement of the art.

We returned to the main cabin early. Bob's wife Nancy was cooking ptarmigan for lunch. Steve, 15, Traver, 11, and five-year-old daughter Talecia had just finished their morning

school work. Sitting back in an easy chair crafted from spruce and moosehide, we continued the previous evenings discussion.

Bob talked about his families life in the bush, sharing some useful techniques and knowledge he had acquired over the years.

Bob runs slightly over 100 miles of trapline along the northern tributary of a river called Choonjek by the Athabascans. The main cabin lies 107 miles above the Arctic Circle, 40 miles

Article that appeared in "Alaska Trapper" magazine in 1986

311

Bob Harte and Joe Mattie in a playful moment, 1982

*Nancy's skin boots made in the early 1980s;
rediscovered at B.C. in 2017*

*Joe Mattie's plane landing
on the Coleen River, 1980s*

Nancy, pregnant at tent camp with dogs, 1983

Nancy in her cabin writing this book.

Epilogue

"Love isn't a state of perfect caring. It is an active noun-like struggle. To love someone is to strive to accept that person exactly the way he or she is, right here and now."

– Mr. Fred Rogers

Life and love. Since the day Bob and I met, we've been a part of each other's lives. For better or worse. Until death do us part. And beyond that. We shared a big adventure in ANWR together. Beyond that, we've struggled together through various life crises.

Looking back, and reliving this story, I have had to look at myself, acknowledge, accept and release past emotions I have held regarding Bob's and my relationship. I had heard that writing a memoir can be a cathartic process. I had no idea what that meant or what I was in for. I do now, and am so pleased I undertook that journey.

Bob and I did the best we could with the tools we had back then. I wanted Bob to continue being happy with his lifestyle, but I also wanted to be happy with mine. We made choices. After living together for many years, we needed to go our separate ways in order to continue living on our own paths. Family was important to us, so we remained our own sort of family throughout the years. Life taught us lessons about loving each other and loving ourselves. Our lives were the frontiers that we were exploring. As H. Boreland stated, "A frontier is never a place. It is a time and way of life."

We both loved living our lives together when we did. Period. I am so grateful for having the opportunity to live with Bob and the kids in the wilderness. I know he felt the same.

As for "happily ever after," well, this hyperbolic phrase ends many fairy tales. If there is a happily ever after, it is from a process and a journey which must contain the ups and downs of life and love.

Glossary

Base Camp (B.C.): Main cabin location.

Beaver Fever: A common name for giardia, a parasitic infection of the gut caused by drinking water contaminated by wildlife, usually beaver.

Break up: When the ice on rivers begins to break up and flow downstream.

Buhach: Powdered flower heads of pyrethrum used to kill bugs.

Cache: A stow away or hiding place. In Alaska, typically built on stilts to keep animals away from stored food and supplies.

Cheechako: A newcomer to Alaska.

Chinking: material used to fill the spaces between logs in a cabin.

Dividend checks: A state owned investment fund established using oil revenues. Permanent Fund Dividend checks are given every year to Alaska residents.

Dog salmon *(also known as chum salmon):* A less desirable salmon for eating, and instead usually fed to dogs.

Dry Cabin: A cabin without indoor plumbing, running water, or toilet.

Fish wheel: A device situated in rivers for catching fish, which looks and operates like a water mill. The fish wheel is outfitted with wire baskets designed to catch and carry fish from the water into a nearby drop-box.

Honeypot: In the age of outhouses, the pot one would urinate in if they didn't go outside to the outhouse.

Ice fog: A type of fog consisting of fine crystals suspended in the air (usually pollution particulates), which occurs only in cold areas of the world.

Lead (in a dog team): The front of the line sled dog.

Mukluks: Soft boots, usually made with seal skin, reindeer, moose, typically worn in the arctic.

Overflow: After a thaw or warming spell, the river flows and spills over the ice.

Pilot cracker: A dense, unleavened bread, usually unsalted; related to 'hard tack.'

Potlatch: A ceremonial feast at which possessions are given away.

Ptarmigan: A medium-sized game bird in the grouse family, chicken-like in stature, thick bodied. The bird is all white in the winter, and a mixture of browns in the summer. Alaska's state bird.

Ratting canoe: A simple, small, lightweight canoe with skin or canvas sides used for hunting muskrat.

Swede saw: A bow saw or finn saw, which is a metal framed cross cut saw in the shape of a bow with a coarse wide blade.

Toboggan: A simple, narrow sled which is a traditional form of transport used to carry people or gear.

Visqueen: The brand name of durable polyethylene plastic sheeting.

Yukon stove: A lightweight, portable stove consisting of a small metal box with legs, about two feet long, one foot wide, and one foot tall.

About the Author

Adventure comes naturally for Nancy. At the age of 12, she met the challenge to walk 100 miles in 2 days in the Adirondack Mts. of N. Y. State.

After exploring 48 more states, and volunteering in a few foreign countries, Nancy can presently be found at her HOME SWEET HOME in a dry cabin outside of Fairbanks, Alaska, which her husband Bob Harte built back in the 1980s.

During the harsh, but lovely winter days you might find Nancy skiing on the river or tracking in the woods.

Long summer days are packed with activities such as camping with her 3 grandchildren, working part time tending gardens, reindeer and cabins for Riverboat Discovery, and slowly, but surely completing the challenge of exploring all the dead end roads in Alaska.